Walking My Way

JOHN N. MERRILL

CHATTO & WINDUS · THE HOGARTH PRESS

LONDON

Published in 1984 by
Chatto & Windus · The Hogarth Press
40 William IV Street, London WC2N 4DF

British Library Cataloguing in Publication Data

Merrill, John
    Walking my way.
    1. Walking
    I. Title
    796.5'1   GV199.5
    ISBN 0-7011-2400-8   E

Copyright © John N. Merrill 1984

Maps by John Flower

Photoset by Rowland Phototypesetting Ltd
Bury St Edmunds, Suffolk

Printed in Great Britain by
Redwood Burn Ltd
Trowbridge, Wiltshire

Contents

List of illustrations and maps *page* vii
Acknowledgements viii
Introduction x
 1 Why walk? 1
 2 Clothing and equipment 8
 3 Planning the route 23
 4 Walking in England 30
      National Parks 32
      Long-distance footpaths 39
      Parkland Journey 58
 5 Walking in Wales 61
      National Parks 61
      Long-distance footpaths 63
 6 Walking in Scotland 72
      Long-distance footpaths 76
      Scottish Isles 79
      Marathon walks in Britain 83
 7 Walking in Ireland 86
      Northern Ireland 89
      Southern Ireland (Eire) 89
 8 Walking in Europe 93
      The Tour of Mont Blanc 94
      Across Austria 104
      European Trek 106
      Across Corsica 109
      Other walks in Europe 111
 9 Trekking in the Himalayas 117
      A walk to the Everest Base Camp 117
      Around Annapurna 121
      Helambu and Langtang 126

10 Walking in America 131
        The Appalachian Trail 131
        The Pacific Crest Trail 140
        American trails 145
11 Marathon walking 148
12 Merrill's Law 159

    APPENDICES
 1 The Countryside Commission 163
        Areas of Outstanding Natural Beauty 164
        Heritage Coasts 165
        Official long-distance footpaths 166
        Recreational Footpaths 166
 2 Unofficial long-distance footpaths in England and Wales 168
 3 Competitive and challenge walks in Britain 173
 4 Outdoor organisations in Britain and Eire 175
 5 Mountain Rescue 182
 6 Country Code 184

Bibliography 185
Index 189

Illustrations

PLATES *between pages 116–17*

1 *a* Self on an outward bound course, aged 16
 b after my first solo walk in Norway, 1961
 c ready for my first major walk, Hebridean Journey, 1970

2 *a* Walking near my home in Derbyshire
 b Camp at North Lees on the Peakland Way

3 On my Derbyshire boundary walk, 1976

4 *a* My favourite rocks, Cratcliffe Tor, close to where I live
 b Handa Stack, on Handa, my favourite island

5 *a* Suilven, my favourite mountain, in north-west Scotland
 b The French Alps, from Aiguille du Midi

6 In the Himalayas, bound for Everest, 1980

7 *a* On top of Mt Katahdin, the northern end of the Appalachian Trail,
 1979
 b Half-way along the Pacific Crest Trail, 1980

8 On the summit of Mt Whitney in California, 1980

MAPS

England and Wales *pages* 68–9
Scotland 70–71
Ireland 88
Europe 102–3
United States of America 132–3

ACKNOWLEDGEMENTS

Whilst this book was my own idea, I could not have included all the information it contains without the help of many people. I am grateful to my publishers, who gave me total freedom and graciously allowed me to overshoot my deadline; to the Ordnance Survey, who went to great pains to explain how their maps are made; to the many manufacturers of equipment; to the numerous societies, associations and government departments which willingly sent me material and answered all my questions; and finally to my wife, Sheila, who so ably typed the manuscript and understood my often illegible handwriting.

Thank you all.

'These men I have examined around the world who live in vigorous health to 100 or more years are great walkers. If you want to live a long, long time in sturdy health you can't go wrong in forming the habit of long vigorous walking every day . . . until it becomes a habit as important to you as eating and sleeping.'

Dr Leaf, *Executive Health*, California 1977

Introduction

For a long time I have felt that walking is a greatly underrated activity. It is practised in Great Britain by millions of people in varying forms; yet, while it is accepted as a satisfying outdoor recreation, it is not regarded as a 'sport'. For me, it is both. True, it may not have the same glamour as, for example, climbing, nor as much danger and excitement; and it can often take longer to accomplish. Nevertheless, walking over long distances demands a high level of fitness, technique and dedication, and needs considerable athletic ability. As I know very well from personal experience, it can tax one to the limit both physically and mentally. I also know that it offers plenty of adventure and variety.

This book is primarily for those who have already begun to discover, or have a mind to experience, the enjoyment and the challenge of long-distance walking. It will, I hope, contain information and advice that is of use even to the motorist who parks his car and sets off on a short walk for an hour or two. If it were to encourage such a motorist to become a regular weekend walker, and then, with due preparation, to start exploring the long-distance footpaths which are such a glorious feature of our countryside, I would be extremely pleased, for I would have found a way of sharing the pleasure and fulfilment that I derive from walking myself. That is why in the early chapters, and in the appendices, I have concentrated on the kind of walking that is within the reach of anyone who has the time and the inclination to practise it.

But just as my own experience of walking has grown from short distances locally to marathons of 2,000 miles or more (over 3,000 km), so in this book I hope to carry the reader with me from modest beginnings on my own doorstep in Derbyshire to the major walks I have accomplished in Britain, Europe and the United States – with three treks to the Himalayas thrown in for good measure. It is at this level that walking becomes a 'sport', in the sense that I intended earlier.

When I am on a major walk, I average at least 25 miles (40 km) a day, carry more than 50 lb (23 kg) on my back, camp out as much as possible, stock up with food every two weeks, and never take a day off. This kind of walking demands everything you have. Your body has to keep going day after day in all kinds of weather for months on end, often in remote country where you may not see another human being for a week or even two weeks at a time. Walking like this requires strength and stamina, and can, I believe, be looked upon as a considerable human achievement.

I do not set out to break records but, because I know that I operate best when I am fully extended, I always walk a given route in the fastest time I can. In this way I set my own standards. There are in fact no 'rules' to long-distance walking, and people set about it in different ways. A good example is David Brett's splendid high-level walk across the Alps in 1981: whereas he chose to use buses or lifts to cross the valleys, I would always make these crossings on foot. Some 1,000 mile (1,600 km) walkers will average around 15 miles (24 km) a day and have two or three days off every couple of weeks. Others average nearer 20 miles (32 km) a day and have one day off a week. Some cover 400–500 miles (600–800 km) and then have a week or more off. All these approaches are perfectly valid, and they require both skill and determination to be successful. But for me they are not 'pure' walking: they are a relatively easy way of reaching one's destination without much discomfort. And I believe they constitute a principal reason why marathon walks are not generally recognised as a major achievement. Time is a critical factor; time and the weight that one carries. Naturally, a person who completes a walk carrying a heavy load has accomplished far more than a person who finishes in the same time carrying a lighter load.

In this connection, an interesting comparison can be made with the remarkable and much-publicised performance of Richard and Adrian Crane, the brothers from Cumbria who ran 2,029 miles (3,265 km) across the Himalayas in 101 days during the summer of 1983, carrying clothing and equipment weighing 12–13 lb (5–6 kg) and ascending a total of 329,000 ft (100,279 m) in the course of their journey. In 1982, on my walk across Europe, the Alps and the Pyrenees (see pp. 106–9), much of which was at an equivalent altitude, I covered a distance of 2,800 miles (4,500 km) in 107 days with 45 lb (20 kg) on my back. Whereas they ran a marathon every day, I walked one every day for three and a half months without a break, on my own, carrying nearly four times as much weight and ascending over 500,000 ft (152,000 m).

For me there is a competitive element to walking: that is part of its challenge and never-ending appeal. For me it *is* a sport that compares with climbing or other such physically demanding activities. But I am aware that there are few people who regard it in this light, and I have not written this book for them. They have no need of it. My aim in writing it is to present the beginner and the more experienced walker alike with the benefit of my experience. I started out as a novice with an idea. I developed my art and have been lucky enough to make it my profession. My hope is that, with this book, I will help to start other newcomers off in the right direction and give the experienced walker the urge to venture further afield into other, less familiar parts of the world.

CHAPTER I

Why walk?

Walking, for me, has become a way of life. It has been so for the past ten years or more, and I cannot imagine myself ever wanting to stop. Indeed I hope to walk the Pennine Way when I am a hundred!

My love of the countryside and the outdoor life goes back almost as far as I can remember. I was only six and a half when, on a school outing from Sheffield, my form was taken to some nearby rocks known as Bell Hagg, on the edge of the Peak District National Park. Suddenly being free, running along the cliffs and scrambling up the rocks, produced a feeling of exhilaration that I shall never forget. There is a deep satisfaction in the sense of reward for one's own efforts; and the joy that I experience today from reaching the top of a mountain is no different from the elation I felt that afternoon at climbing the dizzy heights of a small boulder.

At school, I was never one to succeed in the classroom. In fact I was hopeless at lessons and, at the age of twelve, failed all my exams. But in the gym and in the playing field it was a different story: I was in all the first teams, and regularly (embarrassingly) swept the board on sports days. Then, for my secondary education, I was lucky enough to go to a co-educational boarding school, which I enjoyed immensely; I am sure it played a decisive role in shaping my future life. I took a long time to settle down to being a member of a close community which was largely self-contained and self-run. Apart from all the school work, we washed the dishes, peeled potatoes, worked in the gardens, built tennis courts and sewerage schemes. In many ways it was like an outward bound course; and we even had our own 100 acre wood.

My love of the countryside did not diminish, and, with the Yorkshire Dales on our doorstep, I often went there. Sundays were free, and I would make up some sandwiches in the kitchen and disappear for the day on my bicycle. Fifteen miles (24 km) away was Armscliff crag, a splendid gritstone climbing area. There I began tentative moves up the rock, soloing, and learning by trial and error. During the summer we were allowed to camp out, and I did this every year, becoming the camp warden in time. Also during the summer we had weekends away on a camp, usually in the Dales. One year I led my school on a week's hostelling trip to the Lake District.

By now I was totally preoccupied with the outdoor life. During class I paid little attention: instead, I would be reading a book on the Himalayas beneath the desk. At the age of fifteen I had more than 300 books on mountaineering and was writing a history of it. I was still active in sport and excelled in everything, breaking numerous school records. At the age of sixteen I was running the mile regularly in 4½ minutes, but there was never anyone to push me hard or to encourage me to go further.

The headmaster knew where my heart lay and, after watching me scale the 90 ft-high building solo, he managed to get me on an outward bound course to be trained properly. I went to Eskdale, although I was not really old enough, and spent a month on the course. To me it was the realisation of a dream. The object of the course is supposed to be character training through adventure, but for me it was a marvellous holiday spent walking, climbing, running, doing rope courses, and canoeing. I returned to school more than ever determined to devote myself to mountains, and somehow to earn a living in the process.

Shortly after the outward bound course, my father put my name forward for a place on a three-week expedition to Norway. More than 350 people applied, and by sheer good fortune I was one of the twelve people to go. Most of the trip was spent at Finse and the Hardanger glacier. I revelled in glacier work and enjoyed a week's walk through the mountains. I made friends with the organiser and asked if he could train me to be a guide. He agreed, and I went back the following year for a month. For a week I did extensive advanced training on the glaciers, before going off with two others on a major trip through the Jotunheimen, Norway's highest mountain area. I spent three weeks there, crossing more than thirty glaciers and ascending the highest mountains.

The following summer I left school, having failed all my exams except G.C.E. Pottery. I wanted to go back to Norway and to take my guide's certificate, but my father said 'no'. He had two factories and, as I was the only son, it was my duty to work there. I started on the shop floor, first making tea then operating lathes, working on the fitting bench, then taking over the running of the stores. I continued and eventually became Commercial Manager. By the summer of 1969 I had had enough; after eight years, I felt highly frustrated. From the age of twelve I had conceived the idea that my life would be linked with mountains, and that to earn my living I would have to write and lecture. I told my father in the summer of 1969 that I must try what I believed in. Understandably, he disapproved.

In the evenings I began writing a book on walking in Derbyshire and, much to my amazement, it was accepted for publication. I was then invited to run adult education courses on walking and I accepted, realising that this was the beginning of my new way of life. I was still working for my father, and it was not until May 1972 that he finally let me go. In between times he allowed me three months off during the summer. In 1970 I undertook my first major walk, a walk of 1,003 miles (1,614 km) through all the islands of the Inner and Outer Hebrides (see p. 79). In 1971 I walked through all the islands of the Orkneys and Shetlands (see p. 81), a walk of about 900 miles (1,450 km). Both are described in my book, *From Arran to Orkney*.

I had never attempted a big walk before, but my approach and planning came naturally, and I have set about all my major walks in the same way ever since (see Chapter 11). I started giving lectures on my walks and went round all the Women's Institutes and Townswomen's Guilds, charging just £3 a time. Whilst I had very little money coming in, I managed to survive and to continue on my chosen course. To help my teaching, I went to evening classes and took a teaching certificate. I also went to elocution lessons, which I thoroughly enjoyed, but when I had reached Grade 7 I had to give up through lack of time. I also took G.C.E. English and passed with flying colours.

In 1974 I walked 1,500 miles (2,400 km) up the whole of the west coast of Ireland (see p. 90) and en route conceived the idea of walking the entire British coastline. By now, I was writing at least six books a year and dozens of articles. I joined a lecture agency, but after two years I felt I could do better on my own; rightly, because in the first year I arranged five times as many bookings. All the time now I was building up for the coast walk, although I kept it secret. That walk, which I have described in my book *Turn Right at Land's End*, established me in my unique way of life.

Over the last ten years I have walked more than 40,000 miles (over 64,000 km) on major walks, and have averaged annually about 4,000 miles (say, 6,500 km). Apart from the walks I have already mentioned, I completed a heritage walk from Norwich Cathedral to Durham Cathedral of 420 miles (676 km); a 2,100 mile (3,380 km) walk linking all the National Parks and highest summits of England and Wales; a 300 mile (483 km) walk round the Derbyshire boundary; a 1,600 mile (2,575 km) Land's End to John o'Groats training walk for my 7,000 mile (11,000 km) walk around the entire coastline of Britain; a 2,200 mile (3,540 km) walk up the Appalachian Trail in America, from Georgia to Maine via fourteen states; a trek to the Everest base camp; a walk of 2,700 miles (4,345 km) up the Pacific Crest Trail, from Mexico to Canada; around Annapurna and to its base camp in the Himalayas; and a 700 mile (1,125 km) walk across the mountains of Austria. In 1982 I was again in the Himalayas, in the Helambu and Langtang region, before walking 2,800 miles (4,500 km) across Europe, the Alps and the Pyrenees. To this list I should add walks along the many long-distance footpaths such as the Peakland Way (fourteen times), the Pennine Way (four times) and the Pembrokeshire Coast Path (three times).

The way of life I have chosen is not a simple one. Marathon walking makes great physical and mental demands, takes a long time in preparation, and is by no means lucrative. Also, I prefer walking by myself, and can imagine people finding my approach too unsociable for their liking. But I do not walk for companionship. I know that I am lucky because my wife, Sheila, is there to share my life with me when I am at home, yet she appreciates and understands my need to go off, sometimes for months on end, in order to accomplish a walk. Unselfishly, she does not stand in my way, perhaps because she too is an independent person who enjoys both the sharing and the being alone.

We met while I was on my British coast walk. After 3,300 miles (5,310 km), I suffered a stress fracture in my right foot not far from where she lived in Drymen, close to Loch Lomond. As she was the organising secretary for the Scottish section of the Royal Commonwealth Society for the Blind, the charity that was benefiting from the walk, she suggested that I should recuperate at her home. We had met only briefly before, but there was instant rapport between us. Before I continued the walk, five weeks later, I had proposed.

In many ways our parting was a good thing, for we both had time to reflect on whether we really wanted to commit ourselves. We also had a better understanding of what it would mean to be separated while I was on major walks. In the following year, before we married, I spent four months in America and a month in the Alps.

Parting is always a deep emotional experience for us both, because when I am not away we are together constantly, running a shop and business. Once the walk is underway, I concentrate solely on it, and Sheila is fully occupied with the day-to-day affairs of the business. We have communication points along the route where she sends letters

I write frequently. Occasionally I telephone, but we both find this a 'tough' experience. The return home is problematical, for we both have to adjust to sharing our lives, and I need time to unwind from the mental and physical pressures of the walk. But we trust each other explicitly, and the return always bring a renewal of our love.

I hope these autobiographical notes provide some background information to a question which people often ask me: why do I walk? The truth is, I walk for many reasons. I like to be in the countryside at dawn to hear and see a new day emerge. I like to wander down a footpath alone and see what lies ahead, or to watch, fascinated, as a fox or deer goes about its business unaware that a human is looking on. I like to make my way up a high mountain and enjoy the thrill of reaching the summit and admiring a well-earned view. I like to stretch myself with a full pack of equipment on my back and walk 30 miles (48 km) or more in a day, for several weeks.

Walking is not just exercise but, for me, *the* method of seeing and coming to terms with the countryside and learning its secrets. In Britain we are fortunate to have within a relatively small area such a remarkably diverse countryside.

One joy of walking is discovery. You do not have to walk far to discover a completely different world. One of my most memorable moments was on the Pembrokeshire Coast Path, near Manorbier. I had just reached the top of a small rise and begun the descent when I saw a stoat running towards me along the path. I stopped instantly and watched. The stoat came running along quite unaware of me. I stood perfectly still as he came right up to me. Suddenly he registered something unfamiliar and stretched to sniff my boot. Catching my scent, he jumped into the air, like a Walt Disney creature, and dived off into the undergrowth. It is moments like these that make walking so enjoyable: to stand on a path and feel the wind brush against one's cheeks, or admire the breathtaking clarity of a June day in the mountains of Scotland. You return home glowing with pleasure at having seen and experienced something unforgettable.

As I walk I am doing several things, which not only make the walk enjoyable but give me a sense of purpose. Whether the terrain is in open moorland or along the hedgerows, I am constantly looking for wild flowers. Through the year I witness all the seasons: winter's silent mantle; the spring flowers, such as celandines, anemones and violets; the glow of summer; and the golden autumn colours ablaze with glory. I usually carry a guidebook to the flowers so that I can identify them. I always carry a camera, and any new flower I come across I photograph, first with a general view of it in its setting and then a close-up of the flower head. In this way I learn the flower names, and can identify plants more easily when I project colour slides during lectures.

I am also looking at the birds; again watching the seasons. I usually carry a pair of binoculars (10 mm x 50 mm) which help me to recognise the birds. Their songs are a joy too: few things give me more pleasure than walking in midsummer on a hot sunny day, when a skylark takes to the air and sings it melody. The binoculars are also useful for checking out the footpath ahead, as well as observing animals such as squirrels, red deer and badgers.

When reaching a village I always look at the buildings, for many of them have a story to tell. The date stones on the lintels or dates on the guttering heads all give an indication of age. The market square, stocks, or manor house are also worth exploring. If the hall is open to the public, I like to go in. But my favourite place to visit is the church. It is more than likely the oldest building; its inside walls tell the village story down the centuries; and the stained-glass windows, font, chancel and tombs all provide added interest. I also keep a look out for signs of industrial archaeology; for example, ruins of an old mill or a disused mine. Again it adds interest to the walk.

But perhaps most intriguing of all are the place names that I come to. I am a great lover of legends and folklore, and I am always seeking the story behind the names on the map. Gibbet Moor, for example, conjures up stories of horror from yesteryear. I discovered after my walk over the moors that it was named after the last live gibbet in Derbyshire. The victim's crime was murder, and he had killed a woman by pouring hot fat down her throat! To give another example, after coming across two hills in the Peak District, Lose Hill and Win Hill, I learnt that the losers had camped on the one and the winners on the other before a battle which had taken place in the eleventh century.

Walking in Britain is extensive and varied, and personally I find none of it dull or uninteresting. Every region has its own character. Walking across the fields in rural countryside below 1,000 ft (300 m) is enjoyable, as I stride along over the wooden stiles, through copses and woods, surprising the wildlife on the way. Equally attractive and not nearly as demanding are walks along the canal towpaths. While watching the boats pass there are numerous birds, flowers, and examples of a bygone age to be seen. More recently, a new form of walking has emerged as the old disused railway lines have been converted to footpaths and bridle-ways.

Whilst this kind of walking exists in and around our major cities and towns, there are many other excellent walking areas throughout Britain, such as the National Parks, long-distance footpaths, Areas of Outstanding National Beauty, Heritage Coasts, islands and mountains. One of the simple luxuries of life is to drive to a National Park and camp for the weekend. In the morning I awake to the glow of a new day with towering peaks above. To me there is nothing finer than to break away completely from my normal routine and walk up a mountain. At the end of the day I am mentally and physically refreshed.

I walk because I enjoy it and because I want to learn more about the surrounding countryside and how it works. The following chapters describe, in detail, my approach to walking, how to walk, where to walk, what to carry, as well as my walking experiences in various parts of the world. Walking is a pleasure, and I hope that some of the following information will add to your enjoyment of it and give you the urge to lace up your boots and be on your way.

CHAPTER 2

Clothing and equipment

Anyone who wants to purchase the equipment necessary for serious walking is today met with a bewildering range of excellent items, an indication of how popular walking has become in Britain. It is hard to recommend specific items as being the best, for what suits one person may well not please or suit another. But the following are my thoughts and comments on the principal items of equipment, starting at the feet and working upwards.

Boots

The quality of boots that you need depends on the amount of walking you do. Someone who only goes out occasionally during the year will find a pair of boots with a moulded sole quite sufficient. Someone walking the Pennine Way or other long-distance paths needs a sturdy pair with a vibram sole. For sustained use, such as my major walks, I use the best available boots, which will last me for about four months.

You need to analyse just how much walking you are going to do. There is little point in purchasing an expensive pair of boots if for the next two years you will be breaking them in on occasional walks. Basically a pair of boots should cushion your feet, provide a grip on slippery terrain, and support your ankle against twists and turns on rough ground.

For the last few years I have chosen boots made in Italy. They are made from one piece of leather, have a leather through sole, several mid-soles, the welt double-stitched, bellow tongue, 'D' rings at the bottom and hooks at the top, and the top of the boot, above the ankle, is well padded. The thickness on the sole is important. I prefer three or four layers to act as a shock absorber against the rough ground underneath.

When wearing the boots I lace them reasonably tight but not so tight as to restrict foot movement. To cushion the sole of my feet even more, I always place a thick foam insole inside. On a major walk there is little time to clean and waterproof them, although before I set off they have been frequently waxed. I do not usually have the soles renewed as I find the inside of the boot, especially around the heel, goes first, wearing away the inner leather, then the padding and finally the outer leather. This is a problem, for there is no satisfactory alternative to putting in a soft, and therefore thin, inner leather to make boots more comfortable and to minimise blisters.

Where possible it is advisable to clean and waterproof your boots regularly after a walk. Two of the best waxes available today are Nikwax and Mars oil, which have been made specially for leather. Both help to keep the boots soft and supple as well as waterproof. After several applications the leather builds up a layer of wax that is thick enough to dispel water. It is important to ensure that the stitching is well waxed. When the boots are wet, fill them with newspapers and place them in a room well away from a fire and let them dry out slowly, otherwise the leather will crack.

A pair of good walking boots weighs about 4½ lb (2 kg). Recently there has been a movement towards lighter boots with an 'environmental' sole, as people begin to calculate the foot poundage required to walk certain distances. Personally, I feel that lighter walking boots are a hazard to the serious walker. Whatever type of boot is used, you must have good ankle support and thick soles. To lighten a boot is to do away with these two fundamentals of boot design.

For the last year I have been trying 'light' boots. This is a slight misnomer, for on average all the boots I have used weigh around 3½ lb (1.5 kg). Their cost is relatively high, and for not much more money you can purchase a top-quality all-leather boot. As with Gore-Tex (see p. 13) and other 'breathable' fabrics, the general public is brainwashed by massive advertising extolling the virtues and 'breakthroughs' of lightweight boots. Most have been tested in the laboratory under false conditions producing spectacular results. 'Experts' are asked to test them, and magazine editors go out on one-day product-testing programmes. All produce inaccurate statements. To get to know your footwear or your clothing well you have to use it constantly over a few months. Only then can you evaluate its characteristics. All too often the public are 'conned' into purchasing an item which is not fully tested. From the consumers' comments the item is then modified and improved. Much of this should have been found out *before* it was marketed. My comments on lightweight boots are as follows.

Early in 1982 I tried boots with canvas, suede, nylon and cordura uppers. I found that all types, when wet, remained wet, and my feet felt uncomfortable. The new Klets 'environmental' sole became more clogged with mud and peat than the normal vibram sole, although the heel arrangement made descending steep grass much easier. I carried very little weight – about 15 lb (7 kg) on my back – yet all the time I was very conscious of how vulnerable my ankle was to the uneven ground. At other times I found the protection around the foot inadequate, and often stubbed my toes, which in full walking boots I would never have done.

Whilst on my 2,800 mile (4,500 km) European walk my boots after 2,000 miles (3,200 km) had split across the sole and the metal stiffener had split in half. Never before has this happened to me, and at Nice I bought a new pair of boots. While I was breaking these in, I often changed to trainers when the boots hurt too much. I found the trainers just like lightweight boots – quite lethal with a heavy load of about 50 lb (23 kg). They provided insufficient ankle support, and the foam cushioning on the sole just would not absorb the rugged terrain like normal boots. I also found that at the end of the day I was far more tired, with puffed-up feet, than if I had been wearing my normal type of boot. I am convinced that for the serious walker there is no satisfactory alternative to a proper leather walking boot with vibram sole.

In recent years ski boots have been successfully made from plastic. Plastic readily lends itself to ski-boot design, where rigidity is necessary. It is also possible to produce a good plastic climbing boot where rigidity is again a necessity. However, for a walking boot there are other considerations, including flexibility and porosity. Introduced in America in 1980 were boots partially made from Gore-Tex. The boots were much lighter than conventional ones with the uppers made of Gore-Tex. In 1983 I used a pair and found they did not breathe (so the boots stank) and I also found they did not support my ankles; in fact, the heels moved to one side on both boots.

Clothing

Socks

I strongly recommend wearing two pairs, 80 or 100 per cent woollen. I wear a short pair of loop-stitch socks inside a thick pair of long knee-length Norwegian ragg socks. The loop-stitch sock acts as a cushion and protects your feet; and the long ragg sock gives body to your feet and again helps to cushion them from the rubbing of the boot. The elasticated top to the ragg sock serves two purposes. When the weather is warm, the sock is pushed down to the top of the boot and helps to stop stones from finding their way into the boot. When it is cold, the long sock is pulled up to just below the knee under the walking breeches. Wearing two pairs of socks is very important, for they *do* minimise blisters. With only one pair, blisters and sore spots on the foot soon appear.

When on a long-distance footpath walk, it is important to change your socks every two or three days. This again helps to minimise blisters. It takes many days – about three weeks – before your feet really settle down to their new way of life, and you can then wear your socks for a week or more at a time. I rarely wash my socks, and prefer instead to wear them for about three weeks and then throw them away. I find that after about three weeks' use they are wearing too thin at the heel.

Breeches

Despite the accidents and the constant publicity about what to wear in the mountains, I still see the majority of people wearing jeans. Wherever I go I carry a pair of breeches. During the summer I wear shorts, but in my rucksack is a pair of breeches, in case there is a change in the weather.

During the last five years there has been a revolution in the style of walking clothes. Instead of the old baggy needlecord, breeches are now styled with a closer cut. Breeches give you the freedom of movement that trousers never can. One of the great innovators in clothing design and material has been Rohan. Their 'Super-Striders' have revolutionised the design of breeches. Instead of cord, 'helanca' (a stretch material) has been introduced, which not only gives greater freedom of movement but dries much more quickly than corduroy. Other stretch materials are coming on the market.

Breeches also allow you to regulate your heat. In the summer you can wear thinner pairs, and, with your calves bare, you can feel comfortable and not too hot. When it turns colder you simply pull up your socks. For winter you can have the breeches made from tweed and needlecord as well as stretch materials.

Gaiters

On walks in wet country, through heather or long grass, across boggy terrain or through snow, gaiters are a help in keeping you dry. They simply clip onto your bootlaces near the toe with a hook, and a zip at the back of the heel fastens the material to just below the knee. A cord at the top tightens them, and a strap or cord secures them under the instep. Only about half the boot, the lower half, is now visible. The gaiters are made from four types of material – proofed nylon, canvas, cordura and

Gore-Tex. I very rarely wear gaiters, because they are a struggle to put on and because they make my legs hot and clammy. When I do wear them I prefer canvas, because of its robustness and porosity to air. Also available are zipped anklets that fit around your sock above the boot and slip over the boot upper. They are tied under the boot instep. Again they help to keep your feet and socks dry, and prevent small stones from finding their way into your boot.

A new concept in gaiter design has come from Berghaus, who have produced 'Yeti gaiters'. They have a thick rubber rand which fits into the welt of the boot, thereby totally enclosing the boot, with the remainder of the gaiter stretching to the knee. They are secured to the boot by the rubber rand which incorporates a wide rubber instep. They are difficult to fit onto the boot, which is an advantage, for the rand is unlikely to ride up the boot during use. Once they are fitted to the boot it is best to keep them on for a few days; unlike a normal gaiter, which you put on when conditions dictate. These Yeti gaiters turn the boots into 'wellingtons' and keep you dry when crossing a river, provided the water does not go over the top. They are also excellent in snow, and the ultimate gaiter is the double version – which has a layer of 'thinsulate' in its construction that is not only warm but light.

Shirts

During the summer, on a major walk, I wear a pure cotton shirt with two breast pockets. The pockets are useful for holding money, pedometer (see p. 28) and pen. I usually carry two of these shirts; one that I wear all the time, the other in reserve should I need to appear tidy. Many people wear just a T-shirt, but when you carry cameras a collar is useful; it stops the strap from rubbing and also shields your neck from sunburn.

In winter I still prefer a cotton shirt, but many people choose the heavier type of shirt made from wool or a wool mixture. Personally I find the wool irritates my skin and I do not wear them, although there are now woollen shirts which have a cotton material stitched inside the collar and cuffs.

Pullovers

There are two main styles: either crew-neck or V-neck. Personally I prefer the V-neck, as this gives greater freedom and allows ventilation. During the summer I use a V-necked sweater and always carry a spare in my rucksack. In the winter I wear a fibre-pile jacket, with a high collar and full-length zip. Again this allows an air flow and regulation of heat.

Windjackets

Recent developments such as Gore-Tex have produced a jacket that is not only waterproof but windproof. Because of the high cost of Gore-Tex clothing, many people who have Gore-Tex do not bother with having a separate windjacket and waterproof cagoule. Although I use Gore-Tex, I still prefer in many ways to use a double-layered windjacket made from cotton. When it rains, I slip on a nylon cagoule. I can well remember the days, for almost ten years, when I wore a windjacket made from ventile (100 per cent cotton), and only when it became really frayed did I stop using it.

Ten years ago windjackets were of the smock design with a large map pocket in the centre. Now they have a full-length zip, several pockets and a hood either in the collar or fixed permanently. Many of these jackets are also shower-proofed with silicone. The full-length zip again allows air flow and regulation of heat. The cuffs can annoy me, and elastic cuffs I find unbearable. I much prefer the knitted type of cuff, which feels kinder to the skin.

As a basic rule I prefer to wear several thin layers of clothing, thereby trapping the air which forms pockets of warm air, rather than have one thick heavy garment which does not keep me very warm.

Waterproof clothing

When it rains, the vast majority of people don their waterproof cagoule and overtrousers. These are made from 3 oz (85 g) or 5 oz (141 g) proofed nylon, or 4 oz (113 g) or 8 oz (227 g) neoprene-coated nylon. All keep you dry but, as they cannot breathe, condensation forms inside and one soon becomes as wet inside as outside. The cagoules usually come down to just above the knee and have two large pockets and a hood. Some have a wired hood, which helps to make vision better by keeping the hood away from the face. The overtrousers usually have a 24 inch (610 mm) or longer zip on the legs, which allows reasonable access for putting them on over a pair of boots. More expensive trousers have a large gusset behind the zip to ensure better weather protection.

During the last five years there has appeared on the market a possible 'ultimate' in waterproof fabric – Gore-Tex – which is reputed to be both waterproof and porous. The principle of Gore-Tex is simple. A microporous film, which has 9 billion pores per square inch, is trapped between two layers of material. The pores are small enough to allow perspiration molecules to pass through, but not the bigger molecules of rain water. Now, this may sound good in theory, but in the field there are conflicting reports, and it has still not been conclusively proved that it works. There are other materials coming on the market with similar properties, such as 'Entrant' (see below).

The methods of production have been greatly improved, for the seams are now specially heat-welded. At first they were found to be brittle and liable to leak. Sealant was used, but this does not last long, and the seams have to be re-doped. Another problem was that the early Gore-Tex had to be washed frequently to unclog the pores. Now it has been chemically treated, and you do not need to wash the garment as often.

I have been using Gore-Tex extensively for the last four years, and have come to the following conclusions. As a waterproof breathable jacket it is by no means the 'ultimate' material. On all my walks I have found that it leaks and does not breathe. During the first two wearings it usually keeps the water out, but from then on the rain comes in. I find the material very delicate and it soon chafes. After a few weeks the lamination begins to separate and bubbles appear all over. I may generate heat more than others, perhaps because I ascend hills more quickly. Whatever the reason, I become drenched inside from sweat; the material just does not breathe. In my shop I have sold Gore-Tex jackets and trousers in the past, and more than half of them have had to be returned to the manufacturers because of complaints from the users. Because of my own and others' experiences, I do not stock Gore-Tex clothing any more in my shop.

Gore-Tex as a tent material is another matter. On my last four major walks I have used a Gore-Tex hooped-shape tent. In all manner of conditions the tents have been stable and waterproof. Very little condensation has gathered inside. However, the major problem is sealing the seams; all have leaked so far, despite very careful and frequent doping. One reason why the tent is waterproof must be because, unlike a jacket, there is a very good air space between me and the fabric.

Gore-Tex is extremely expensive, and personally I would far rather wear a cotton jacket and get wet but feel comfortable. Late 1982 saw the emergence of another breathable material called 'Entrant'. During my European walk I wore a jacket made from this material which is 'MPC' – moisture porous coated. Whilst the design and workmanship of the jacket was excellent, it just did not work. I would walk along in the rain and have a stream of water running down my arms inside.

Hat

You lose 30 per cent of your heat through your head. Personally I find it hard to wear anything on my head, even when it is raining. However, in winter a woollen hat does help to retain the heat and keep the ears warm. The most useful garment is a balaclava. This can be worn as a hat with a small peak, and, when it gets cold, it can be pulled down to cover the ears and neck, leaving just your eyes and nose open to the elements.

Winter clothing

Waistcoat

Popular in the United States and in Britain are waistcoats filled with down or manmade fibre such as Hollofill, polyester and Thinsulate. This item of walking dress, which can be worn under an anorak or cagoule, allows your body to keep warm while your arms remain reasonably free. Although it took me a while to get used to waistcoats, I have now grown to like them and find them very comfortable. As emergency clothing they are ideal, being light and compact.

Duvet

For a long time a down-filled jacket with a hood was considered the ultimate in winter clothing. Although bulky, these jackets give considerable warmth in freezing conditions. In recent years down has become very expensive, and man-made fibres, which give warmth without bulkiness, have started 'taking over'. Hollofill, a synthetic which is as warm as down, has become popular and has the advantage of being warm even when wet. Another material, Thinsulate, is becoming increasingly popular; it is light, dries quickly and has exceptional thermal capacity. Jackets made from this material are not bulky and are much warmer in use than one would suppose from their appearance.

Thermal underwear

For a long while thermal underwear was mentioned only in private, but it has now emerged as a thoroughly sensible and useful type of clothing. The vest and longjohn are worn next to the skin and, being made of polypropylene, they soak away the moisture, leaving your skin feeling dry and warm. They are light and take up little room in the rucksack, and are ideal for an emergency. Even in the coldest weather I feel warm wearing my thermal underwear under a shirt, pullover and windjacket.

Once I went skiing with only thermal underwear and windproof clothing. The temperature was minus 32°C (−26°F), but I remained warm and dry.

Gloves

For normal walking in winter I wear a pair of woollen gloves or mitts, such as the Dachstein mitt. Another favourite is a mitten-type glove, with a fleecy lining and nylon outer. They are not waterproof but they keep my hands warm. In wet weather I often put on a pair of waterproof outer gloves made from proofed nylon.

All the above equipment can be found on display at your local outdoor shop. The outdoor magazines carry test reports on various items of equipment, which help you to select what to purchase.

The cost of kitting yourself out can be frightening: a good pair of boots costs about £50–£60, a Gore-Tex jacket £60 or more. Select with care, and don't rush in and buy something which is not quite suited to your needs.

Rucksacks

Day sacks

For a day's outing you only require a small sack without a frame and hip belt. A sack with a capacity of 15–20 litres (915–1,220 cubic inches) is ample (I use 'litres' here as rucksacks are sized by litre capacity) and allows room for spare clothing, waterproof clothing and food etc. Usually such sacks are made from 5 oz (142 g) proofed nylon in a variety of colours.

For carrying more equipment during the day, a sack with a capacity of 50–60 litres is quite adequate. The advantage of a sack of this size is that it will usually have a frame and a waist strap, as well as attachments for carrying an ice-axe and crampons. It may also have room where pockets can be added, thereby increasing the capacity. This is the type I use for day walking, and it is suitable for both summer and winter. They are made from cordura, proofed nylon or canvas.

Multiple day sacks

On my first major walk ten years ago, I carried 45 lb (20 kg) of equipment in a Bergans canvas rucksack with a heavy metal frame. It was comfortable and lasted well. However, the 1970s saw a major change in rucksack design in Britain, brought about by Berghaus of Newcastle. Until then anyone walking the Pennine Way or on an extended trip carried his equipment in a pack-frame rucksack. Today such rucksacks are little used, for they have many disadvantages, being remote from your body movement, and the hip belt is never completely satisfactory. They are still popular in America, but, as I soon discovered on the Appalachian Trail, they just did not last, with frames breaking and hip belts collapsing after three weeks' use.

Berghaus introduced the Cyclops system, the first 'anatomic' range in Britain. The Cyclops was a new approach to rucksack design, and enables the rucksack to go with, rather than against, the body's movements. Whilst being a snug fit, the thin flat frame allows it to be bent to the shape of your back and enables you to spread the load on your back between your shoulders and hips. A well-padded hip belt integral to the sack allows you to secure the sack firmly to your body, making the whole rucksack very stable. The thick padded shoulder-straps ensure a comfortable carry. The sack can be adjusted to fit the different shapes and sizes of back. With the adjusting straps on the sack it is possible to get a perfect fit.

There is one major disadvantage with an anatomic sack. Being snug-fitting, it does not allow air through, and you soon sweat at the back. I have carried the anatomic sack system for thousands of miles and certainly found it a comfortable method of carrying 50–60 lb (23–27 kg) for days on end. I generally prefer a sack that has a capacity of around 90 litres, with a good hip belt, pocket on the top of the sack and two side pockets. They are made from proofed nylon or cordura.

Since 1982 I have been using a Lowe rucksack. These rucksacks have been made in America for the last twenty years and are now being manufactured in Ireland. They are very well made to an exacting design which the majority of manufacturers have now copied. As far as I am concerned, they are by far the best rucksacks in the world and the most comfortable. The workmanship is to a very high standard, and I can say from my own experience that after 3,000 miles (say, 5,000 km) or five months' use the sack was still in very good order; better than any other I have had after such use. At the moment they are not as well known as Karrimor or Berghaus but for the serious walker there is none finer.

The following is a basic checklist of the minimum amount of equipment* needed:

A day hike – carrying a small pack

Map	Food for lunch	Windproof anorak
Guidebook	Food for emergency,	Waterproof cagoule and
Compass	such as Kendal Mint	overtrousers
Whistle	Cake	Space blanket
Flashlight	Mug	Watch
Knife	Spare pullover	Toilet tissue
Matches	Spare socks	Notebook
Candle	Woollen hat	Coins – for telephone
First-aid kit	Gloves (in winter)	calls etc.

There are additional items which are more of a personal requirement, such as thermos flask, camera and film, binoculars and a walking stick.

A week's walk – such as the Peak District High-Level Route (90 miles, 145 km)

Tent – flysheet, poles	Towel	scissors and tweezers
and pegs (with a few	Stove	Water purification
spare)	Spare gas cylinders/fuel	tablets
Sleeping bag	Cooking pans	Sewing kit
Insulation mat	Cutlery	Candle
Spare socks	Can opener	Whistle
Underwear	Matches	Torch, with spare bulb
Shirts	Food (2 days' supply)	and batteries
Windproof jacket	Tea towel and	Notebook
Pullovers (two)	washing-up liquid;	Maps
Waterproof cagoule	pan scourer	Guides
Waterproof overtrousers	Spare boot laces and	Pen
Gaiters	waterproofing wax	Camera and film
Spare trousers	First-aid kit – bandages,	Spare blanket
Toilet bag – tooth brush	safety pins, moleskin,	Money and credit cards
and paste, soap and	Elastoplast, antiseptic	Handkerchief and
toilet paper	cream, aspirins,	Kleenex

You will be carrying these items in a rucksack with more than 60 litres capacity. Added to this list are the clothes you will be wearing and a pair of boots. Exactly what you take will depend on the season. In winter you will need a warmer sleeping bag and clothes, such as a duvet and thermal

*See also equipment lists on pp. 104, 121, 139–40, 144–5.

underwear, and you will perhaps carry an ice-axe (see equipment list on p. 104).

How you pack your rucksacks is very important: you should have all your light and little-needed equipment down in the bottom of the sack. Carry the heaviest items at the top, such as the tent. Use the side pockets to hold the things you need handy, such as further maps, day food and rain gear.

Backpacking equipment

For weekend or longer trips when you plan to camp out en route, you will need several major items of equipment – tent, sleeping bag, stove and food.

Tent

For all my solo walking I prefer to use a two-person tent, rather than feel cramped and restricted in a single-person tent. Another important feature of a two-person tent is that the additional room allows you to store your equipment inside it. I have never supported the practice of storing the equipment outside the tent. You need it close at hand and to keep it dry.

As a basic rule, if you plan to carry a tent, you should select one that is light but sturdy enough to endure rough use. There are trends to make tents ultra-lightweight, but really this is a false economy, because making them light means losing some of the important features of a tent. Instead of having a groundsheet that is tough and water-repellent, it is made from thin nylon which soon tears and does not keep the water out, forcing you to use an insulation mat. When choosing a tent I look for a strong groundsheet, 'A' poles or hooped-shape at the front to allow easy access, a single pole at the rear, a flysheet which is kept a minimum of 4 in (102 mm) away from the inner tent, so that they don't rub together and leak, and the flysheet should have an extension or bell-end around the front to allow for cooking or to act as a windbreak in bad weather. A ridge pole makes the the tent more stable and more suitable for all-year-round use.

The majority of tents are made from rip-stop nylon, both inner and outer. As a result, many people experience condensation problems. Personally, I very rarely have any problem, largely because I always allow ample ventilation. In the past the inner has been made of cotton, which breathes, but to make them cheaper and more competitive, nylon has been used. However, a growing number of manufacturers are reverting back to cotton. A good lightweight backpackers' two-person tent will weigh about 5–6 lb (2–3 kg).

The 1980s saw the introduction into Britain of hoop-shaped tents, which have been used very successfully in America for several years. A fibreglass or aluminium tube is fitted into a sleeve of the tent and, when the ends are interlocked together, makes a dome shape, which is not only very stable but allows greater room in the tent. These thin poles are usually about 18 in (457 mm) long and, when slotted into place, measure 12 ft (366 cm) long. With a flysheet, these tents have large storage areas, and together weigh about 6 lb (3 kg) or more.

Gore-Tex is now being used in tent manufacture, and although it is expensive, it does obviate the use of a flysheet. From my experience of walking long distances in the U.S.A. with a Gore-Tex tent, I am convinced that it is the best tent material. It breathes and is water-repellent, although the seams and stitching have to be carefully sealed with sealant. A tent of this material, although more expensive than a nylon tent, weighs about 5½ lb (2.5 kg).

Sleeping bag

Today there is a large choice of bags made from down and man-made fibres, for two or more seasons' use. Down used to be the main filling material, but the escalating cost of down has allowed man-made fibres, such as Hollofil, to become more popular. Down has the advantage of being lighter and less bulky, but requires careful washing. Hollofil, on the other hand, can go into the washing machine.

Unless you have ample funds, it is sensible to purchase a sleeping bag that is suitable for three or four seasons rather than two separate bags. I personally select a good quality three-season bag made from 12 oz (340 g) of Hollofil or 2 lb (nearly 1 kg) of down with a full-length zip, which is well baffled. The zip is important: in winter the bag can be zipped all the way up, and in the summer, with the zip down, it can be used as a duvet. To reduce cost, manufacturers put in a nylon inner, but for a better feeling of warmth a cotton inner is by far the best. The majority of bags are mummy-shaped, with a hood that can be pulled tight around your head by means of a drawcord. You can also purchase cotton sheet-linings for your bag, but personally I have found these a nuisance and I never use one. If camping in winter I put on thermal underwear which, with a three-season bag, keeps me very warm in cold conditions.

Insulation mat

To cushion you off the ground, and as a protective layer against cold from the ground, a foam mat about ½ in thick x 5 ft long (1.3 x 152 cm) is indispensable. They weigh very little. If you want added luxury you can get self-inflating mattresses, which are only slightly heavier.

Stove

For general backpacking, I prefer to use a gas stove. They are light, efficient and clean. The spare cylinders weigh very little and, if used carefully, can last a week. For solo backpacking, some of these stoves come complete with pans, making a neat small item that is ample for one person's use.

While gas stoves are the most popular, many people still prefer the primus stove, burning either paraffin or petrol. It was one of these that I used on my first trip. They are efficient and boil quickly, but they are messy. You have to carry spare fuel, and this, together with the heavy metal stove, takes up a lot of space in the sack.

I have, on several occasions, used a Trangia stove, made in Sweden, which burns methylated spirits. Again, these are very efficient stoves and, as the stove incorporates pans, they are light to carry.

The MSR stove, which is the lightest stove on the market at 15½ oz (say, 440 g), is produced in America but can also be bought in the U.K. I used one all the way up the Appalachian Trail and was greatly impressed by its performance. The pump for the stove fits into a Sigg bottle (aluminium, screw-top) which also acts as the fuel bottle. Its great advantage is that it will take any type of liquid fuel. I used unleaded petrol, paraffin, methylated spirits, charcoal starter fuel and normal petrol. It worked faultlessly on all.

Ice-axe

Ice-axes and crampons should be more widely used when walking in winter on hills. The winter months see a great change in the approach to hill and mountain walking in areas such as the Lake District, North Wales and especially Scotland. An ice-axe is a very necessary and useful tool and one that I carry often, even on Kinder Scout in the Peak District. The axe acts as a third arm or leg, and gives added security when you are crossing a snow slope or ascending an icy gully. In case of a fall, by throwing your weight over the axe and digging the pick end in, your fall is soon arrested.

When choosing an axe, there are various climbers' axes, which tend to have shorter shafts, and special walkers' axes which are not so refined but quite adequate for walkers. Ideally, they have a pick and adaze at the top, a metal shaft, and a spike on the bottom. They are made in a variety of lengths to suit a person's height. When selecting your size, the pick should be just above the ground when the shaft is held in the hand.

Walkers' crampons have ten points and climbers' twelve points.

Food

I have an unusual diet on a walk and pay no attention to the calorific value or protein content of what I eat. For breakfast I like a bowl of muesli and a mug of tea or coffee. I do not drink during the day and just eat chocolate, as many as nine 2 oz (56 g) bars. In the evening I have a packet of soup, a dehydrated main meal, dessert, and a mug of coffee or tea and some biscuits. It may sound spartan, but often I have to walk ten or more days without seeing a shop and, therefore, have to carry the lightest foods. I find that dehydrated food is very palatable and there are several good makes on the market. But when I reach a shop or restaurant I eat as much as I can.

On my European Trek (see p. 106) I changed my usual diet. For breakfast I would have a roll, butter and honey. During the day I ate very little, and never more than three chocolate bars. My evening meal was rarely a cooked one. Instead, I would have a soup, followed by a salad of tomatoes, cucumber, lettuce, cheese, with tuna, ham or sardines; and a couple of yoghurts for dessert. This diet was a great contrast to what I had been eating in the past, but I found it did not hinder or alter my daily performance. After 2,800 miles (4,500 km) I returned home much fitter and healthier than before. From being 12½ stone (80 kg) – which at 6 ft (1.8 m) tall is quite acceptable – I had lost 2 stone (13 kg), and my weight remained the same when I returned to home life.

Some further notes on clothing, equipment and food that I have taken with me on my marathon walks may be found in Chapter 11.

CHAPTER 3

Planning the route

Ordnance Survey Maps

The Ordnance Survey is a British institution of the highest order, and its maps are second to none. For a walker they are indispensable and utterly dependable. Opening a map out on a given area is like looking at a 3-D picture: one can see the layout of the land, amenities, footpaths, historical buildings, and much else besides. They are essential in planning a walk, and essential to its execution.

In 1980 I was a guest of the Ordnance Survey at its headquarters in Southampton. I spent a day exploring and seeing how maps are made, from outdoor surveying activities, aerial photography, conventional and digital mapping techniques, to compiling and printing a 1:50,000 series map. This scale means that 1 unit on the map represents 50,000 units on the ground, or 1 cm equals 0.5 km. I was most impressed by the dedication and thoroughness in every department: all map users should be thankful that such an establishment exists.

The traditional founder of the Ordnance Survey was General William Roy, who, after the rebellion of 1745, made a map of the Scottish Highlands. Later he conducted the first scientific survey in this country, the measurement of the Hounslow Heath Base. He had exceptional foresight and suggested that a national survey and mapping organisation be set up. Regrettably he died in 1790, a year before the Ordnance Survey was officially founded.

At first the Ordnance Survey was based in the Tower of London but, following a fire in 1841, it moved to a barracks in Southampton. During the Second World War the barracks was bombed and many valuable records were lost. Part of the organisation was housed temporarily at Chessington near London. In 1968 the Ordnance Survey (now a civilian organisation) moved to its purpose-built site at Maybush, Southampton.

1 inch to 1 mile (1:63,360 or 1 cm to 0.63 km) Ordnance Survey (O.S.) maps
These were the first maps to be produced by the Ordnance Survey, starting with Kent in 1801 and Essex in 1805. The mapping of England

and Wales at this scale was completed in 1873 with the Isle of Man map. Scottish maps first came out in 1856. Before the National Series of 1 inch maps was discontinued in 1976, there were 189 sheets covering the whole of England, Wales and Scotland. Each map represented an area of 40 x 45 km, or approximately 700 square miles. The maps have now been superseded by the metric 1:50,000 scale Landranger series, and what was once a walker's best friend is now usually found on a bookshelf at home, with the tell-tale red and cream cover.

Some special 1 inch to 1 mile maps still remain: the Tourist Maps. These cover areas of principal interest to the tourist. The first to be published (in 1920) was Snowdonia. Today, there are ten maps available: Exmoor, Dartmoor, New Forest, Peak District, Lake District, North York Moors, Loch Lomond and The Trossachs, Ben Nevis and Glencoe, and the Cotswolds, while the Snowdonia National Park is at ½ inch scale in order to cover the entire area on one sheet.

1¼ inches to 1 mile (1:50,000 or 2 cm to 1 km) Landranger Series
Metric maps had frequently been suggested even in the nineteenth century. By the 1950s the 1 inch maps were beginning to look rather full, especially with the rapid growth of motorways and building development. Map users were also pressing for more information to be contained on the map. Following extensive market study, it was found that the best size of map for users would be at a scale of 1:50,000 – approximately 1¼ inches to a mile. As this is an internationally accepted scale, it would also offer other advantages when Britain became fully metric.

To have redrawn the 1 inch map to the new scale would have been a mammoth task and beyond the means of the Ordnance Survey. It was decided that the 1 inch maps would be enlarged to fit the new scale. To keep them manageable in size, the area covered was reduced to 40 km square. Instead of 189 sheets (1 inch maps), the number was increased to 204 sheets (1¼ inch maps).

By enlarging the 1 inch maps it was possible to publish the new maps within two years, 1974–76. The country was divided into two halves, with a line running through Yorkshire and Lancashire. The southern half was published in 1974 and the northern half in 1976. A second series of maps is now underway, with the maps being totally redrawn and redesigned. It will be about twenty years before the second series is complete.

The maps are printed on a four-colour press, using black and combinations of cyan, yellow and magenta to make the different colours. Except where new metric contouring surveys were available, the contour lines had to remain the same as on the 1 inch map – 50 ft apart – but they were labelled to the nearest metre. It will be the mid-1980s before the whole of the country is metrically surveyed.

Information supplied by the Tourist Boards and Countryside Commission is put on the maps where possible.

Perhaps the most important aspect of the maps for a walker is that the public rights of way in England and Wales are shown, whether or not topographical evidence exists. The information is taken from the definitive maps compiled by the local authorities. The maps are constantly being revised and, as a map comes up for reprinting, any major changes (such as roads and building development) are detailed. Where appropriate, maps also show the proposed lines of motorways and those under construction. In 1979 the series was given the name 'Landranger', which will appear on the map covers as they are reprinted.

2½ inches to 1 mile (1:25,000 or 4 cm to 1 km) Outdoor Leisure Maps (of popular recreational areas only)
Based on the national series of 1:25,000 maps, these maps were introduced in 1972 to meet a growing demand for accurate and detailed maps to cover principal walking and leisure areas. Most sheets cover an area 21 x 26 km, about 200 square miles, with contours at 25 ft intervals, or at 10 m intervals in the Second Series. Each map details access land in a National Park, National Trust property, long-distance and other footpaths, mountain rescue posts and youth hostels, camp and caravan sites and places of interest. The first map was 'The Dark Peak' – the moorland areas of the Peak District National Park, Kinder and Bleaklow. The next to come out, in 1973, was 'The Three Peaks', covering the three mountains – Pen-y-ghent, Whernside and Ingleborough Hill – a popular day's walk in the Yorkshire Dales. Several more maps have since been published, and others are planned. In April 1980 'The White Peak' was published, a two-sided map covering the whole of the limestone country of the Peak District National Park.

Outdoor Leisure Maps available

1 The Dark Peak	5 The English Lakes NE
2 The Three Peaks	6 The English Lakes SW
3 Aviemore and the Cairngorms	7 The English Lakes SE
4 The English Lakes NW	8 The Cuillin and Torridon Hills

9   Brighton and Sussex Vale
10 Malham and Upper Wharfedale
11 Brecon Beacons (Central)
12 Brecon Beacons (Western)
13 Brecon Beacons (Eastern)
14 Wye Valley and Forest of Dean
15 Purbeck
16 Snowdonia National Park (Conwy Valley)
17 Snowdonia National Park (Snowdon)
18 Snowdonia National Park (Bala)
19 Snowdonia National Park (Harlech)
20 South Devon
21 South Pennines
22 New Forest
23 Snowdonia National Park (Cader Idris/Dovey Forest)
24 The White Peak
25 Isles of Scilly
26 North York Moors (West)
27 North York Moors (East)

2½ inches to 1 mile (1:25,000) Pathfinder Series

Unlike the Outdoor Leisure Maps, this series covers the whole of Great Britain. The Pathfinder Series (or Second Series), with green covers, is gradually replacing the First Series (blue covers) and will be complete in 1990. Most sheets are 20 km x 10 km (approx. 13 miles x 6½ miles) whereas the First Series were 10 x 10 km. Fields and public rights of way are clearly shown.

Triangulation pillars

The concrete white posts that sit on the summits of many of Britain's mountains are one of the walker's most useful aids when walking in thick mist by compass. There are about 5,000 of them, and they and some 20,000 other points (such as church spires, bolts in church towers and in buried concrete blocks, as well as lightning conductors on factory chimneys) together form the precise framework to position all the topographical features that appear on O.S. maps. In mountainous areas these horizontal control points may be about 6–10 miles (10–16 km) apart, in most rural areas about 3 miles (5 km) apart, and in urban areas about 1 mile (2 km) apart.

The triangulation pillar is usually 4 ft (1.2 m) high, 2 ft (60 cm) square at its base, tapering to 1 ft 2 in (35 cm) at the top. The brass plate on the top is for the feet on the tribrach of a theodolite – an instrument used for measuring horizontal and vertical angles. Today, precise *distance* measuring may be carried out using a laser beam instrument. Just as much of the pillar is below the ground as above it, to ensure that the location of the pillar is preserved, even if the top is damaged or knocked over.

The next few years will see great changes in mapping techniques, with the increasing use of computers. Digital mapping will be the norm, and plastic maps, rather than paper, will become the walker's best friend. Looking towards the year 2000, one can envisage walking along with a pocket television-like map, which would give us an instant picture of where we are in any area of Britain.

Compass and map-reading

I am often asked whether I lose my way on my walks. The answer is, hardly ever. The principal reason why I don't is that, while I am walking, I hold the map open in my hand, folded to show the area I am passing through. I keep checking my position and mentally ticking off the features on the map as I go by. It is a question of practice: first, to learn the symbols on the map and what contour lines mean; and secondly, to observe the area you are walking through and to compare it constantly with what the map shows. If you check regularly, there should be no difficulty in following your chosen route. You can buy clear plastic map cases which help to protect the map from rain and to prolong its life. Personally I don't use one, as I am often opening it all out at a viewpoint to observe and locate the distant places. The cases can be carried around the neck or shoulder, and usually have a velcro opening down one side. A more refined version includes a zipped pouch to store your compass, pencil and notebook.

Today there is no mystery about using a compass. The best models have a circular dial on a perspex base and are made by Suunto or Silva. As soon as the weather deteriorates, or when you have to cross a featureless area, take a compass bearing. It is particularly important to take a bearing before you become enshrouded in cloud or mist. Place the compass on the map, using the long edge of the perspex base, and draw an imaginary straight line from the point where you are to the next principal feature on the map, such as a barn or trig point. You then dial the compass so that the north sign is pointing due north and parallel to the grid lines. The compass is usually liquid-filled, to steady the needle, and the base of it is marked with parallel lines. The top of all Ordnance Survey maps is north. Take the compass off the map and add on the magnetic variation, as detailed on the map. Hold the compass in your hand, and when the needle and north sign are together, your direction of travel is along the arrow line marked on the perspex base.

Before you leave, you should estimate what time you think you will reach the next point. Don't worry if you are a few minutes out at first; in time you will learn your speed of travel. If, after walking for your estimated time, you have not found your barn or trig point, keep looking, for if you have worked out your bearing correctly you should walk into it! In time you will learn to be totally dependent on your bearings, and you will quite confidently cross miles of bogland on bearings going from point to point, and be within a minute or two of your estimated time. Indeed, crossing remote country on bearings and, after several hours, arriving at your destination, is one of the most satisfying parts of walking.

Measuring distance and pace

In planning my walks I use a map measurer (see p. 150), as distances on a map work out slightly longer on the ground. You place the measurer on the map, move it over the course of your route, and read off the miles/kilometres against the map scale shown on the dial.

I sometimes use a pedometer, which records the actual mileage you have walked. I find that 25 miles (40 km) on the map is 27 miles (43 km) on the ground, using a pedometer.

As you learn the secrets of map reading, you will also subconsciously be learning about yourself and what your average pace is. This is most useful, for with experience you will come to learn how long it will take to ascend that mountain, cross that valley or walk that stretch of coast. This will help in guiding you along in normal conditions, but will be especially useful when you are going by compass across a desolate area in thick mist.

I reckon on walking at an average pace of 3 miles (5 km) an hour on level ground if I am carrying no more than an ordinary day pack. This is probably a fair guide for others to follow, given straightforward conditions. For mountain walking W. Naismith worked out a formula which is generally regarded as the rule: allow 1 hour for every 3 miles (5 km) and half an hour for every 1,000 ft (300 m) of uphill climbing.

This assumes that the walker is in reasonable physical condition and not carrying a load. Obviously a person carrying 40 lb (18 kg) or more will walk more slowly. I find that on a major walk my pace at first is very steady, about 2½ miles (4 km) per hour with 60 lb (27 kg) on my back. After about six weeks my pace becomes noticeably quicker as I become adjusted to the task and the pack weight. I start doing 3 miles (5 km) per hour, and am capable of 4 miles (6 km) per hour.

I don't think I walk fast; rather, I keep up a steady pace throughout the day, with the result that when I camp I am tired but still have enough energy to continue for long distances (see p. 157). I don't stop for lunch, preferring to eat a bar of chocolate while I carry on walking. Stopping spoils the rhythm of the walk, and I always find it hard to get going again after a stop of, say, three-quarters of an hour.

Finally, a word of advice about ascending hills: the secret is to keep going, no matter how slowly. Don't stop. If you do, you will lose your rhythm and your mental concentration. Invariably, when you rest you look down and up the hill, and this begins to affect you mentally: you start wondering when you will get to the top. If you just keep going you will be surprised how quickly you get there.

Maps – some specialist sources
Cook, Hammond & Kell Ltd, 22 Caxton Street, London, SW1H 0QU
Cordee, 249 Knighton Church Road, Leicester LE2 3JQ (by mail order)
McCarta Ltd, 122 King's Cross Road, London, WC1X 9DS
Edward Stanford Ltd, 12 Long Acre, London, WC2P 9LP
The Map Shop, Upton-upon-Severn, near Malvern, Worcestershire
John Merrill Trail-Blazer, King Street, Bakewell, Derbyshire.
The Youth Hostels' Association runs several 'YHA Adventure Shops'
    for maps and publications:
14 Southampton Street, Covent Garden, London, WC2E 7HY
90–98 Corporation Street, Birmingham, B4 6XS
6–7 Bridge Street, Cambridge, CB2 1UA
131 Woodville Road, Cardiff, CF2 4DZ
166 Deansgate, Manchester, M3 3FE

CHAPTER 4

Walking in England

England has hundreds of walks, both short and long, all of them easily accessible. The scope is limitless, and the walking as varied as the scenery – from the magnificent coastal walking of the south-west peninsula and the gentle ridge-walking of the Downs to the more demanding walks in the National Parks and along the Pennine Way. In this chapter, and in the chapters that follow, I shall concentrate mainly on the National Parks and the principal long-distance footpaths, for these are where I do most of my own walking. I shall also touch briefly on three of my major walks in Britain – one that linked all the National Parks and the highest mountains, another from Land's End to John o'Groats, and finally my 7,000 mile (11,000 km) walk all the way round the coastline of England, Wales and Scotland. In this way I shall hope to convey some of the possibilities and pleasures of walking in these islands, even though I know I cannot hope to do more than skim the surface. Further information is given in the appendices, with lists of heritage coasts, areas of outstanding natural beauty, recreational paths, unofficial long-distance footpaths, and competitive and challenge walks.

England is endowed with a quite astonishing number of rights of way:* for example, public footpaths, coaching roads, drove roads, ancient military roads, bridleways, forest rides and tracks. You have only to look at a map to see how much ground they cover. My county, Derbyshire, for example, has some 9,000 miles (14,500 km) to explore.

Once, as part of a training programme, I decided to walk around the county boundary – and in the process, incidentally, to raise money for the National Trust's Derbyshire and Peak District Appeal Fund. Before I started I worked out a ten-day schedule which allowed me to use public footpaths and bridleways on or very close to the border for almost the whole distance of 280 miles (450 km).

The route I took on this occasion began at Sudbury Hall, a National Trust property in the south of the county, and led across the flat countryside to the River Dove. At Ilam Hall I entered the Peak District

*The Ramblers' Association leaflet, 'Right of Way', is a brief but useful guide to the law on walking in the countryside of England and Wales.

National Park, and walked up Dovedale following the river to its source on Axe Edge. A rough moorland crossing brought me to Buxton, a 3 mile (5 km) deviation from the border which I was asked to make in connection with the fund-raising activities, before continuing across the moorland to the Goyts valley and Lyme Park. The next day I headed for the remotest section of the walk, Black Hill and Bleaklow, through which the Pennine Way passes. Here I was not following paths but going on compass bearings, keeping as close to the boundary as possible. Through the oozing peat for which this moorland is renowned, I squelched my way to the Holme Moss transmitter station in time to make one of my regular local radio broadcasts, and camped that night in solitude on the wet ground.

Further moorland brought me across Bleaklow to the source of the Derwent, which I followed for a while before the boundary left the valley to the gritstone edges of Stanage and Burbage. After an overnight stop at Longshaw on the city of Sheffield and South Yorkshire border, I covered the final stretch of heather moorland to Chesterfield for a lunchtime celebration and then returned to the boundary proper at Dronfield.

I had now left the National Park and entered a cluster of small industrial towns. The walking was still good along footpaths across fields and between the houses. On the eastern boundary with Nottinghamshire, I entered Cresswell Crags country park, whose caves have yielded remains of prehistoric man, and that night I slept beside a graveyard. After a visit to the National Trust's Hardwick Hall in the morning, and a fast stretch alongside the Erewash Canal to make up for lost time, I was approaching the final stages of the walk round the southern tip of the county. Here it was quiet, with little-used paths across the fields and rural countryside.

My final night was in Burton-upon-Trent. I only had another 12 miles (19 km) to go to reach Sudbury Hall and complete the circuit, but by the time the celebrations were over, the champagne drunk and the speeches made, and having just spent ten days averaging 28 miles (45 km) per day with 40 lb (18 kg) on my back and the pressure of many public functions into the bargain, I felt mentally and physically drained. And I had just four days to recover before setting off on my 1,600 mile (2,575 km) walk from Land's End to John o'Groats!

Another unusual sponsorship walk that I undertook was at the invitation of the York Department of Tourism, which had created the East of England Heritage Route linking the six mediaeval cathedral cities of Norwich, Ely, Peterborough, Lincoln, York and Durham. Apart from being glad to help raise money for cathedral restoration, I was attracted to the idea because the area was new to me, not being traversed by long-distance footpaths. I covered the 420 miles (676 km) in seventeen days, passing through an area of England that is seldom walked. And yet, as on my Derbyshire boundary walk, for most of the time I was on rights of way through lovely countryside studded with places that are rich in history.

One of the glories of walking in England is that you don't have to go far to find beautiful scenery and somewhere to camp or stay. No matter whether you follow an established route or create one of your own, you can never exhaust all that there is to see and enjoy.

NATIONAL PARKS

The National Parks in England and Wales are: Peak District, Lake District, Yorkshire Dales, North York Moors, Northumberland, Exmoor, Dartmoor, Pembrokeshire Coast, Snowdonia and Brecon Beacons.

One of the most rewarding routes I have taken, which I describe more fully on pp. 58–60, was the 2,100 mile (3,380 km) walk I completed in the summer of 1976, linking together the National Parks of England and Wales. I was lucky with the weather (only four days of rain in the eighty-four days, otherwise just hot sun), and I camped out much of the time, using youth hostels occasionally, as I made my way via Dartmoor, Exmoor, the Cotswold Way, the Malvern Hills, Pembrokeshire, Snowdonia, the Peak District, the Pennine Way, the Lakeland fells, the North York Moors and the Cleveland Way.

The National Parks now cover an area of 9,066 sq miles (13,600 sq km), but they are relatively new in this country. Whereas the Yellowstone National Park in the u.s.a. was created by Act of Congress over a hundred years ago in 1872, and Yosemite twenty years later in 1892, the National Parks in Britain have come into being only since 1950. It was over a century ago when William Wordsworth, in his *Guide through the District of the Lakes*, suggested that the area should be 'a sort of national property, in which every man has an interest who has an eye to perceive and a heart to enjoy'; and in the late nineteenth century several societies were formed by people who wished to explore their countryside or share their interest in natural history. The Commons, Open Spaces and

Footpaths Preservation Society was the first, in 1865, and others followed, such as The Royal Society for the Protection of Birds (1891) and The National Trust for England and Wales (1895). But little attention was paid to the idea of National Parks in Parliament until the mass trespass on Kinder in the Peak District in 1932, which was the culmination of many acts of trespass designed to gain access to some of the bleak moorland of the Pennines. Even then, although various Acts of Parliament were passed over the next fifteen years, it was not until 1949 that the National Parks and Access to the Countryside Act came into force.

The man who did more than anyone else to bring this about was John Dower, an architect, who had been asked by the newly formed Ministry of Town and Country Planning in 1943 to look into the question of National Parks. Dower defined a National Park as 'an extensive area of beauty and relatively wild country in which, for the nation's benefit and by appropriate national decision and action, (a) the characteristic landscape beauty is strictly preserved; (b) access and facilities for public open-air enjoyment are amply provided; (c) wildlife and buildings and places of architectural and historic interest are suitably protected; (d) established farming area is effectively maintained.'

In 1945 a committee was set up, under the chairmanship of Arthur Hobhouse, to consider Dower's proposals, and it recommended that the following twelve areas should be National Parks: Brecon Beacons, Dartmoor, Exmoor, Lake District, North York Moors, Norfolk Broads, Northumberland, Peak District, Pembrokeshire Coast, Snowdonia, South Downs, and Yorkshire Dales. With the exceptions of the Norfolk Broads and the South Downs, all of them are now National Parks. The land they occupy is for the most part privately owned, although some areas are managed by the Forestry Commission (p. 176), leased by the Crown for defence purposes, controlled by the Nature Conservancy Council (p. 179), or maintained under the guardianship of the National Trust (p. 178).

In 1968 the National Parks became the responsibility of the Countryside Commission (see p. 163). Through the individual Park offices, whose addresses appear after each description below, the Commission is able to provide information about the particular area and how to make the most of it, with due regard to the local countryside, its problems, and natural history, as well as to the general guidelines set out in the Country Code (see p. 184). Much of the information available at these offices is free: the cost is largely borne by the National Park authorities.

Peak District

O.S. MAPS 1:25,000 OUTDOOR LEISURE SERIES
sheet 24 (The White Peak)
Designated in 1950, this was the first National Park in Britain, and it is also where I live and train. I hope I may be forgiven, therefore, for describing it first.

It is an area of 542 sq miles (1,404 sq km) which lies at the southern end of the Pennine chain, and, surrounded as it is by several major cities, it is extremely popular among walkers. Its landscape has helped to create and develop some of today's most cherished countryside activities: I have already mentioned the mass trespass in 1932 which opened up the moorland country on Kinder; and the gritstone edges have enabled men like Joe Brown and Don Whillans to achieve world renown for British rock-climbing.

The character of the walking reflects the varied nature of the landscape. To the north, where the Pennine Way meanders (see p. 39), are the gritstone moorlands of Kinder and Bleaklow. The central area is all limestone, with a cluster of dales through which my Limey Way wanders (see p. 47). And there is high-level walking along the outer edges of gritstone, which constitute the third scenic attribute.

Circling the Park is my 100 mile (161 km) Peakland Way and my new high-level route (see pp. 45–6 for both). For tough and competent walkers there is the Derwent Watershed Walk of 40 miles (64 km), or the famous annual Marston-to-Edale walk. Gentler walks can be enjoyed along the Tissington, Monsal, and High Peak trails.

The National Park office address is Baslow Road, Bakewell, Derbyshire.

GUIDEBOOKS
Steve Burton, Max Maughan, and Ian Quarrington, *The Derbyshire Gritstone Way* (Thornhill Press, 1980)
Geoffrey Carr, *The Cal-der-Went Walk* (Dalesman, 1979)
Cheshire County Council, *The Gritstone Trail* (1980)
– *The Sandstone Trail* (1980)
W. A. Poucher, *Peak and Pennines* (Constable, 4th edition, 1983)
G. Sellers, *Walks on the West Pennine Moors* (Cicerone Press, 1978)
C. Thompson, *Walking in the South Pennines* (Dalesman, 1979)

Books by John Merrill
Published by Dalesman:
Walking in Derbyshire (1969), *Peak District Walks No. 1, Short Walks for the*

Motorist (1973), *Peak District Walks No. 2, Long Walks for the Rambler* (1974), *The Peakland Way* (1975), *Walking in South Derbyshire* (1977), *Derbyshire Trails* (1977), *The Limey Way* (1979), *Walks in the White Peak* (1981), *Walks in the Dark Peak* (1982)

Published by JNM Publications:
Peak District Marathons (1982), *The Trail-Blazer Challenge Walk* (1983), *Peak District: Short Circular Walks* (1983), *Peak District: Long Circular Walks* (1983), *The Rivers' Way* (1983), *The High Level Route* (1983).

Lake District

O.S. MAPS 1:25,000 OUTDOOR LEISURE SERIES
sheets 4–7 (The English Lakes)
This, the largest of the National Parks, occupies an area of 866 sq miles (2,243 sq km) and contains England's highest mountain, Scafell Pike (3,210 ft, 978 m). With numerous extensive lakes and 2,000 ft (600 m) mountains, it is a walker's paradise. Places like Buttermere, Great Gable, Wast Water, the Langdale Pikes, Grasmere, Helvellyn and Windermere conjure up countless ideas for walking.

For challenge walks, there is an ascent of all the 3,000 ft (900 m) mountains – Scafell, Scafell Pike, Helvellyn and Skiddaw – to be accomplished in one day. Alternatively you could train for, or attempt to join, the club named after Bob Graham who traversed forty-two peaks within twenty-four hours some fifty years ago (see p. 174): this circuit is still the country's toughest mountain race.

A route that passes through an area of exceptional quality is Wainwright's Coast to Coast walk, which crosses from St Bee's Head on the west coast to Robin Hood's Bay in the east.

The changing seasons on the mountains provide a backcloth to countless walks, the richness of the colours in early summer and autumn contrasting with the starker shades of winter, when the fells take on a more challenging aspect.

The National Park offices are in Busher Walk, Kendal.

GUIDEBOOKS
A. Wainwright, *The Eastern Fells* (Westmorland Gazette)
– *The Far-Eastern Fells* (Westmorland Gazette)
– *The Central Fells* (Westmorland Gazette)
– *The Southern Fells* (Westmorland Gazette)
– *The Northern Fells* (Westmorland Gazette)

- *The North-Western Fells* (Westmorland Gazette)
- *The Western Fells* (Westmorland Gazette)
W. A. Poucher, *The Lakeland Peaks* (Constable, 1982)
Elizabeth Cull, *Walks in the Lake District* (Spurbooks, 1979)
R. B. Evans, *Scrambles in the Lake District* (Cicerone Press, 1982)

Yorkshire Dales

O.S. MAPS 1:25,000 OUTDOOR LEISURE SERIES
sheets 2 and 10 (The Three Peaks, and Malham and Upper Wharfe-dale)
Linked to the Lake District by Wainwright's Coast to Coast path and to the Peak District by the Pennine Way is this lovely park of 680 sq miles (1,761 sq km). It is an area of gentle rolling countryside, whose highest mountain, Whernside, stands at 2,419 ft (738 m). Running through this grassy upland are several long and wide limestone dales – Swaledale, Wensleydale, Littondale, and Dentdale.

There are numerous long walks in the area. The Dales Way runs across from Ilkley to Lake Windermere, and the Pennine Way (see p. 39) passes through many of the choicest places which have become loved by walkers – Malham Cove, Pen-y-ghent, Hawes, and Great Shunner Fell. Then there is the Centurion Way, a 100 mile (161 km) circular route from Horton-in-Ribblesdale, which is also the starting point for the classic Three Peaks of Yorkshire challenge walk. For other excellent routes see pp. 170–74.

The National Park Office is at 'Colvend', Hebden Road, Grassington, North Yorkshire.

GUIDEBOOKS
P. Abbott, *Abbott's Hike* (P. Abbott, 1981)
J. Ginesi, *The Centurion Walk* (J. Siddall, 1980)
Ramblers' Association, *Rambles in the Dales* (F. Warne, 1979)
C. Speakman, *The Dales Way* (Dalesman, 1979)
B. Spencer, *A Visitor's Guide to the Yorkshire Dales, Teesdale and Weardale* (Moorland Publishing, 1982)
H. O. Wade, *Afoot in the Yorkshire Dales* (Spurbooks, 1981)
A. Wainwright, *Walks in the Limestone Country* (Westmorland Gazette, 1970)
– *Walks on the Howgill Fells* (Westmorland Gazette, 1972)
K. Watson, *Walking in Teesdale* (Dalesman, 1978)

North York Moors

O.S. MAPS 1:25,000 OUTDOOR LEISURE SERIES
sheets 26 and 27 (North York Moors)

An area of 553 sq miles (1,430 sq km), this is the only National Park that includes high rugged moorlands with a delightful coastline. Here you can sample both on one long walk, the Cleveland Way (p. 42), a 100 mile (161 km) route from Helmsley to Filey which runs around much of the park boundary. The moorland lies on the eastern side, interspersed with valleys and views across the Yorkshire plain. The coast has a continuous footpath, which descends to several picturesque fishing villages – Staithes, Runswick, and Robin Hood's Bay, to name but three.

Crossing the moorlands is the ever-popular twenty-four hour walk, the Lyke Wake Walk, from Osmotherley to Ravenscar. Other long walks include the White Rose Walk from Newton-under-Roseberry to Kilburn White Horse; and weaving its way in and out of the park is the Cleveland Way 'Missing Link', from Scarborough to Helmsley.

While places like Hasty Bank and Urra Moor have their devotees, Goatland is of gentler beauty and is deservedly popular. Rosedale and Farndale (with its daffodils) are two more excellent walking areas.

The National Park Offices are at The Old Vicarage, Bondgate, Helmsley.

GUIDEBOOKS

For books on the Cleveland Way, see p. 44, and on the Wolds Way, see p. 45. Books on other long walks in the area include:

Malcolm Boyes, *The Crosses Walk* (Dalesman, 1979)
Bill Cowley, *Lyke Wake Walk* (Dalesman, 1979)
Richard C. Kenchington, *The Derwent Way* (Dalesman, 1978)
A. Wainwright, *A Coast to Coast Walk* (Westmorland Gazette, 1975)
Geoffrey White, *The White Rose Walk* (Dalesman, 1973)

Northumberland

O.S. MAP 1:50,000 LANDRANGER SERIES
sheets 75 (Berwick-upon-Tweed), 80 (Cheviot Hills), and 81 (Alnwick and Rothbury)

The Pennine Way (p. 39) runs from south to north through this high moorland park, an area of 398 sq miles (1,031 sq km) which stretches to the borders of Scotland. Along the southern border runs the best section of Hadrian's Wall, around Housesteads Fort, and from the park's highest point, the Cheviot (2,674 ft, 815 m), there are fine views of the dramatic Northumberland coast.

Regarded not so long ago as one of the remotest areas of Britain, this park has now been 'discovered' and is deservedly appreciated for its marvellous walking. Apart from the Pennine Way, there is extensive moorland which is little frequented; indeed it is one of the few places in England where you can walk all day and not see another human being.

The National Park Offices are at Eastburn, South Park, Hexham.

Exmoor

O.S. MAP I INCH TO I MILE TOURIST SERIES sheet 5
O.S. MAPS 1:50,000 LANDRANGER SERIES
sheet 180 (Barnstaple and Ilfracombe), and 181 (Minehead and Brendon Hills)

An area of 265 sq miles (686 sq km) mostly in Somerset, this park combines a rugged coastline with extensive moorland, which reaches a height of 1,704 ft (519 m) at Dunkery Beacon.

The coastline forms part of the South-West Peninsula Coast Path (p. 54), and there is a sequence of fascinating places to walk, such as the cliffs east of Combe Martin, around Heddon Mouth, the Valley of the Rocks near Lynmouth, and Porlock and Selworthy Beacon. Lynmouth is the terminus of the Two Moors Way, which starts just over 100 miles away at Ivybridge on the southernmost point of Dartmoor.

Inland is a haven where red deer may be seen, and of course, the famous ponies. Here there is heathland to explore, the gentle Brendon Hills to ascent, the Tarr Steps to cross, and the river valleys of the Exe and the Barle and Badgworthy Water to wander through. And the Oare Valley and surrounding countryside are famous as the setting for Richard Blackmore's novel, *Lorna Doone*.

The National Park Office is at Exmoor House, Dulverton, Somerset.

Dartmoor

O.S. MAP I INCH TO I MILE TOURIST SERIES sheet I
O.S. MAP 1:50,000 LANDRANGER SERIES
sheet 191 (Okehampton and North Dartmoor)

Situated in central Devon, this is an area of 365 sq miles (945 sq km) which contains the highest heath-clad moorland in southern England.

The many granite tors scattered throughout the park are one of its special features. Footpaths and bridleways abound, and there are numerous ancient monuments to be seen, dating back some 4,000 years.

There are many exceptional walks in the area, from Widecombe-in-the-Moor, for example, or around Sheepstor or Fingle Bridge. Crossing the park is the Two Moors Way, from Ivymouth to Lynmouth in Exmoor. And in April there is an annual team walk for parties of four or more: known as the Oats Cross Dartmoor Walk, it starts from Cornwood and ends at Okehampton, a distance of 27 miles (43 km).

The address of the National Park Office is 'Parke', Haytor Road, Bovey Tracey, Newton Abbot, Devon.

LONG-DISTANCE FOOTPATHS

Among the many functions of the Countryside Commission is the creation of official long-distance footpaths (see p. 166). Several of these have been referred to in the section on National Parks, and I shall now describe those that are to be found in England, as well as some other walks which I have helped to develop and can warmly recommend. Further ideas for long-distance walking may be found in the appendices.

The Pennine Way

271 miles (433 km) from Edale, in the Peak District National Park, to Kirk Yetholm, just inside the Scottish border.

O.S. MAPS 1:50,000 LANDRANGER SERIES
sheets 74 (Kelso), 80 (The Cheviot Hills), 86 (Haltwhistle and Bewcastle), 91 (Appleby), 92 (Barnard Castle and Richmond), 98 (Wensleydale and Wharfedale), 103 (Blackburn and Burnley), 109 (Manchester), 110 (Sheffield and Huddersfield)

The idea of a route along the Pennine chain was conceived by the first secretary of the Ramblers' Association (see p. 179), Tom Stephenson. His tenacity and dedication brought about the formation of this magnificent walk, which was opened in 1965. I did not walk it until 1976, but then, having thoroughly enjoyed it, I walked it three more times in the next twelve months. It is a walk of great character, and because of its length it is a challenge. Yet I think it is a pity that it receives quite so much attention: other walks are more scenic and more demanding.

In 1977 it was estimated that approximately 25,000 people set off from Edale with the intention of walking all the way to Scotland. Out of that number only about 5,000 covered the full distance. Because the route has gained such notoriety, it is generally regarded as the prime long walk to accomplish. The reverse should be the case, for if everyone who set off had already done a shorter long walk, such as the Cleveland Way (p. 42), they would have been better prepared.

There were two main reasons why so many people failed. First, they had not selected the right equipment for the rigours of a long walk. Boots were a classic example. They were either very cheap and leaked profusely, or they were new, and not broken in. After a couple of days their owners had bad blisters. Secondly, because they had not done a long walk before, people had no idea of the mental problems. After three days on the route and hardly seeing a soul in remote wild country, they felt insecure and fled.

I usually start from Edale and walk northwards, although I have once walked south, with the sun in my eyes. It has been calculated that the difference in the amount of ascent and descent you have to do, whether starting from the north or south end, is only a couple of feet. On average the route is completed in seventeen days. Some take twenty-one days and others will complete it in ten days. You can stop at youth hostels along the route, but personally I prefer not to. I feel that if you are going to tackle this walk you should be self-contained, with stove, tent, sleeping bag, spare clothes, etc. Then you have the freedom to take the route in your stride whatever the weather. You also know that in an emergency you have food and shelter.

Being a high-level route along the mountain backbone of England, and along much of its watershed, you should expect bad weather and persistent rain. It is rare to walk the Way without rain; usually you can count on a good five days of rain on the trip. Only once have I had a rain-free time and that was one Easter – the sun shone every day.

I have evolved a schedule for the walk which I stick to on each crossing. I generally aim at a ten-day timetable, although this sometimes stretches to eleven because of bad weather. Leaving Edale the first day, I plan to cross Kinder and Bleaklow and camp within reach of Black Hill. This moorland crossing through acres of wet bog is acknowledged to be the hardest part of the Way. The next day I cross more moorland and usually camp near Stoodley Pike. I then know that on the following day I will reach my first shop and the limestone country of the Yorkshire Dales. Malham is usually my goal.

Depending on how I feel and how much daylight there is left, I decide on my objective for the day. After Malham Cove, Fountains Fell and the beautifully shaped Pen-y-ghent, I head for Hawes. If I still feel full of energy I press on over Great Shunner Fell to Thwaite. Now back in moorland and bog I press on next day past Tan Hill Inn, England's highest inn, and cross the moorland to the river Tees at Middleton in Teesdale. The walk from here is particularly attractive beside the river, past Little and High Force to Cauldron Snout, before heading away and over High Cup Nick to Dufton.

Dufton, which has a hostel, is a logical overnight stop before you ascend England's highest hill outside a National Park, Cross Fell. In bad weather it can be quite tricky, and a compass is essential, as it is on all the route. On the northern side of Cross Fell is a bothy, which makes a welcome haven if you have been struggling against lashing rain. I usually try to reach Garrigill and camp on the playing field there. On one occasion I ate a whole block of dextrosol tablets and I simply flew down the path and stopped at Alston four miles further on. From Alston you follow part of the Maiden's Way before gaining the line of Hadrian's Wall. I have on two occasions stopped at Thirwell Castle and camped there, close to the line of Hadrian's Wall. Normally I try to get well along the wall towards Housesteads before stopping. I then know that Scotland is no more than four days away.

Near Housesteads you leave the wall and walk through Wark Forest, and you are now in the third National Park of the route – Northumberland (p. 37). Bellingham is what I aim for, as this is the last principal place where you can stock up with food before Scotland. From Bellingham I plan to reach Kirk Yetholm in two days. First I head for Bryness and, after purchasing a few bars of chocolate, I press on into the Cheviot Hills and camp near Lamb Hill, where there is a shelter. At Bryness, depending on my fitness and condition, I either plan to cross the Cheviots in a day, covering 27 miles (43 km), or, by walking 7 or so miles (11 km) to Lamb Hill, I shall reach Kirk Yetholm for lunch.

The final day across the Cheviots is a fitting end to the route. It is hard, remote and high, although the views are not extensive or really attractive. A slight detour can be made to the summit of the Cheviots, but personally I prefer to press on and ascend the Schill and begin the descent to Kirk Yetholm. There I can relax in a hot bath and reflect on the joys of the walk. It is a hard walk, requiring determination and good preparation. There is no short cut. Treat it with respect, and enjoy one of the finest walks England has to offer.

GUIDEBOOKS

K. Oldham, *The Pennine Way* (Dalesman, 1968)

Tom Stephenson, *The Pennine Way* (H.M.S.O., 1980)

A. Wainwright, *The Pennine Way Companion* (Westmorland Gazette)

C. J. Wright, *The Pennine Way* (Constable, 1982)

The Cleveland Way

100 miles (161 km) from Helmsley to Filey around much of the boundary of the North York Moors National Park.

O.S. MAPS 1:50,000 LANDRANGER SERIES

sheets 93 (Teesside and Darlington), 94 (Whitby), 100 (Malton and Pickering), 101 (Scarborough)

In the Spring of 1974 the Cleveland Way became the first official long-distance footpath that I walked. Since then it has become a firm favourite of mine, and I have walked it four more times. What appeals to me about the route is the contrasting scenery. First you cross the hills and moorland to reach the sea at Saltburn-by-the-Sea, concluding half the walk. The other half is along the cliffs and beaches to Filey. The walk can be done comfortably in a week, or alternatively as a challenge in four days.

I generally can't reach the market town of Helmsley from my home until mid-afternoon. Instead of staying there, I usually set off and walk the first 8 miles (13 km) to Sutton Bank, where I camp beside the path. On the way the route goes close to Rievaulx Abbey, a magnificent Cistercian abbey, and well worth the slight detour to explore. The route from Sutton Bank, with its views over the Yorkshire plain and to Lake Gormire below, is delightful as you walk through the Hambleton Hills to Osmotherley. It is all gentle walking across rolling hills and moorland. The descent from Black Hambleton to Osmotherley is gradual, and goes past two small reservoirs.

Osmotherley is the fabled rendezvous point for the start of the Lyke Wake Walk – 40 miles (64 km) across the North York Moors to Ravenscar above Robin Hood's Bay. Near Osmotherley is Mount Grace Priory which, although not on the official route, is also worth seeing. I generally press on from Osmotherley and ascend the many hills, such as Hasty Bank, before descending to Kildale to camp. It does make it a very long day, but on this 27 mile (43 km) stretch you pass through the finest hill scenery of the route; I also know that the sea is within striking distance the next day.

The route from Kildale ascends out of the valley to Captain Cook's monument and on across more moorland to near Roseberry Topping. This intriguingly named hill lies just off the route but is a worthwhile diversion. Soon afterwards, the route begins to descend through forests, first to Skelton then Saltburn-by-the-Sea. I usually stay at the youth hostel here. There are five hostels on or close to the route.

Saltburn has a beautiful stretch of beach, and the sea is very tempting to swim in after a hard day's walk. I usually indulge in a few ice-creams before embarking upon the 'coast path' of the Way. It is 20 miles (32 km) from here to Whitby via the Boulby Cliffs, which at 660 ft (200 m) are the highest cliffs on the English coast. This is rather a misnomer, for the cliffs do not have a solid vertical face, but are of a shaly nature, and they have been mined extensively for alum. From the cliffs you descend to the attractive smuggler village of Staithes. Before the cliffs you will have walked through the old steel town of Skinningrove. To reach Whitby you pass through another attractive village, Runswick, before descending to the beach at Sandsend. Whether you walk along the sands or the cliff tops and the road to Whitby will depend on the state of the tide.

Whitby comes as rather a shock after the solitude of the hills, for it is a bustling coastal town full of fish-and-chip shops and bingo. I don't linger, and after crossing the harbour via the swing-bridge I ascend the 199 steps to the church, abbey, youth hostel and camp ground. There are now 30 miles (48 km) left of the route – 22 miles (35 km) to Scarborough and 8 miles (13 km) to Filey. Whether I stop at Scarborough or press on in a 'do or die' finish to Filey depends on how I feel. The coastal walking is excellent, with pleasing cliffs all the way to the sweep of Robin Hood's Bay. You descend to this fascinating village and can walk along the beach, if the tide is out, to Boggle Hole Youth Hostel. From here you climb steadily to Ravenscar and continue along the cliff top, passing the nature reserve at Hayburn Wyke. Three more miles (5 km) and you leave the undisturbed scenery behind and descend to Scarborough. I generally walk around the beaches and beneath the castle to join the coast path at the end of the south beach.

The final stretch is at first rather a disappointment as you pass beside several large caravan sites. In time you leave these behind and reach the rocky spur of Filey Brigg, the walk's end. It is an apt end, being a wild place with waves crashing over the rocks in rough weather. A short walk brings you into Filey itself. Filey is the starting point for two other walks – the Wolds Way and the 'Missing Link' back to Helmsley.

GUIDEBOOKS
Malcolm Boyes, *The Cleveland Way and Missing Link* (Constable, 1977)
Bill Cowley, *The Cleveland Way* (Dalesman, 3rd edn. 1975)
Alan Falconer, *The Cleveland Way* (H.M.S.O., 1972)

The Wolds Way

67 miles (115 km) from Filey Brigg to North Ferriby, on the River Humber.

O.S. MAPS 1:50,000 LANDRANGER SERIES
sheets 100 (Malton and Pickering), 101 (Scarborough), 106 (Market Weighton)

A walk through the Yorkshire Wolds was first suggested by the East Riding Area of the Ramblers' Association in 1968. By 1971 it was approved in principle by the East Riding County Council and the Countryside Commission. Since then it has grown in popularity and was officially opened in September 1982. The walk is conveniently located at the end of the Cleveland Way and can be walked either as part of a long walk combining both or in its own right.

I first walked the route over Easter in 1972, taking three days. I camped each night although I did plan to stay at Thixendale Youth Hostel en route, but this was full and I therefore camped on the lawn of a house nearby. I chose to walk north to south, for it seemed to me that the North Ferriby end appeared on paper a more attractive end than Filey. Instead of a popular seaside resort it would be a quiet settlement. The only snag was that I had to wait five hours for a train in North Ferriby.

The route is not mountainous; instead it passes through rolling farmland and gentle downs, and very rarely do you go above the 600 ft (183 m) contour line. Among the route's greatest attractions are the many unspoilt villages you pass through. Each has an attractive church and building of architectural interest. I made first for Sherburn before descending through the forest to the attractive village of Wintringham. The view down to this village is, in my opinion, the loveliest on the whole walk.

Where possible the route uses existing rights of way, and in 1972 I had to do a lot of road walking to link it all together. Since I walked it new footpaths have been negotiated and in time the route will be on paths for almost all its length. April proved a good time to walk it, although walking across wet ploughed fields became a gruelling task. The farms were a hive of activity with new lambs in the fields and clusters of daffodils swaying in the breeze.

The churches were always fascinating, many with Norman workmanship and fonts. Welton Church, close to North Ferriby, has a gravestone to Jeremiah Simpson who died in 1719 aged eighty-four. The inscription recalls that he married eight times. In between the villages and churches the Way passes through delightful dales, and it is these I will remember most. The Wolds Way is a very pleasant walk for those wanting an introduction to backpacking or for those wanting a relatively easy walk while they study the local scene, at a leisurely pace.

GUIDEBOOKS
Roger Ratcliffe, *The Wolds Way* (H.M.S.O., 1982)
David Rubinstein, *The Wolds Way* (Dalesman, 1972)

The Peakland Way

100 miles (161 km) circular walk around the Peak District National Park.
O.S. MAPS 1 INCH TO 1 MILE TOURIST SERIES (The Peak District);
1:50,000 LANDRANGER SERIES
sheets 110 (Sheffield and Huddersfield) and 119 (Buxton, Matlock and Dovedale)
1:25,000 OUTDOOR LEISURE SERIES
sheets 1 (The Dark Peak) and 24 (The White Peak)
The Peak District, my home ground, has the Pennine Way (p. 39) in the northern half and several classic walks, such as the Derwent Watershed Walk, but it seemed to me to lack a long-distance route, the kind that would suit the average walker who wants an interesting, but not too demanding, walk through varied terrain. The Peak District is unique in the fact that it has three distinct types of scenery – limestone dales, gritstone edges and gritstone moorland. The area is also uncommonly rich in historical buildings and customs. With these thoughts in mind, I devised a circular walk linking the best scenery together with as much interest as possible. Wherever I could, I chose paths that are not often used, but in some areas, such as Kinder, there was no alternative but to use popular paths. Here in one fell swoop you can appreciate much of the character and beauty of the area. I walked the route first in 1974 and have now completed it fourteen times. (In late summer 1983 I devised a new 90 mile (145 km) circular walk of the Peak District, known as the

High-Level Route. Starting from Matlock, the route keeps to the highest and most rugged areas of the Peak District. As in the case of my Limey Way (p. 47), successful walkers can get a badge.)

My book on the walk came out in 1975, and in it I broke the route down into eight stages of about 12 miles (19 km) each. This was to enable people to complete the walk comfortably in a week. If you are so minded, you can do the walk in four days. At the end of each stage of the route there is a campsite and, in many cases, a youth hostel or 'bed and breakfast' close by. As it is circular, you can begin the walk where it suits you. In the book, I start at Ashbourne, close to the southern boundary of the National Park; the route then goes clockwise.

The first stage of the walk is through limestone scenery to the impressive Manifold Valley with Beeston Tor and Thor's Cave. From here you begin crossing further limestone scenery to reach Blackwell. It's about 15 miles (24 km), and many find this a hard day, especially because of the long rocky walk through Deep Dale. The third stage is easier as you leave the limestone country and ascend Mam Tor and descend to Barber Booth, near Edale in the gritstone country. Ahead towers the Kinder plateau, a moorland mass approximately 2,000 ft (600 m) above sea level. To cross it you follow the alternative route of the Pennine Way as you ascend Jacob's Ladder to the plateau and onto the impressive Kinder downfall. Shortly afterwards you leave the Pennine Way and descend Ashop Clough to the Snake Pass. The final few miles are along the line of a Roman road before you reach Hagg Farm, and hostel and campground.

The fifth stage is short after the previous hard section. You ascend Win Hill, which is a marvellous viewpoint towards Kinder, Bleaklow, Hope Valley and ahead to the gritstone edges. You descend to Hathersage by walking beside the river Derwent. Hathersage makes a good stocking-up point, and has a hostel and a campsite a mile away close to the route near North Lees. The sixth day is beautiful walking as you ascend to the Stanage Edge and proceed along the top of the gritstone edges to near Baslow. The following day you continue through gritstone country and past Chatsworth House. The final day takes you back into limestone country as you walk through Gratton Dale and on to Tissington village. The final 4 miles (6 km) are along the Tissington Trail, a converted railway line, back to Ashbourne.

GUIDEBOOKS

John N. Merrill, *The Peakland Way* (Dalesman, 1975)
- *Peak District Marathons* (JNM Publications, 1982)
- *The High Level Route* (JNM Publications, 1983)

The Limey Way

40 miles (64 km) through the limestone dales of the Peak District National Park.

O.S. MAPS I INCH TO I MILE TOURIST SERIES (The Peak District); 1:50,000 LANDRANGER SERIES

sheets 110 (Sheffield and Huddersfield) and 119 (Buxton, Matlock and Dove Dale)

1:25,000 OUTDOOR LEISURE SERIES

sheets 1 (The Dark Peak) and 24 (The White Peak)

It was in 1969, while looking over the 1 inch Tourist Map of the Peak District, that I suddenly realised you could walk from north to south through the limestone area of the National Park. By linking various limestone dale systems together, about sixteen dales could be walked through. I set off one early summer day from Castleton, the northern end of the limestone area, and headed south. I broke the journey roughly halfway at Monyash and camped. Two of the dales – Peter's Dale and Monk's Dale – did not have a right of way, so I walked the road. The following day I carried on and reached the end at Dovedale.

Eight years were to pass before I wrote a book about the walk. In the intervening time, rights of way were made through some of the dales. By adding Lin Dale and ending the walk at Thorpe, I worked out a route based on my original idea, 40 miles (64 km) long and through twenty limestone dales. My book, titled *The Limey Way*, was published in 1979, and, as a challenge, walkers can obtain a red badge if they cover the distance in under twenty-four hours, and a green badge if they walk it in under forty-eight hours. There is a great demand for 'challenge walks', started by the Lyke Wake Walk in the North York Moors. Within the first year of the publication of the book, I had had more than five hundred letters from people who had walked the route. Whilst I walk the route all year round, the months of June, July and August are best for good conditions, weather and long daylight hours.

The majority of people walk north to south, although a few tackle it in reverse. Some have even run it or walked it twice over a weekend! I generally leave Castleton market place at 6 a.m. just as dawn comes. The first part of the route is cruel, for you have a long ascent up Cave Dale onto Old Moor before descending to Peak Forest. The next section to Miller's Dale covers 8½ miles (13.5 km) through four dales – Dam, Hay, Peter's and Monk's. The next 8½ miles to the 'halfway' point at Monyash is through some of the Peak District's finest dales, Water-cum-Jolly and Monsal Dale. A short climb brings you to Monyash. Here you have to decide whether to push on or stay overnight.

Leaving Monyash you descend the striking Lathkill Dale before walking through the dry dales of Gratton and Long Dale. A short walk along the High Peak Trail brings you to Biggin, with 15 miles (24 km) walked from Monyash and the start of the final dale system. Thorpe is now 7 miles away, but by this time you are feeling tired and your muscles are no doubt aching. However, the last dales are also the most beautiful as you descend beside the river Dove through Wolfscote Dale and into Dovedale. The final dale is Lin Dale which you ascend to reach Thorpe. There you can meet up with your support party and head home for a well-deserved hot bath. Although I am biased, there are few walks in Britain that can compare with the beautiful limestone scenery you see on this one. Rather than write more, let me just urge you to come and see for yourself.

In 1983 I devised and inaugurated two new 'Challenges' in the Peak District: first, the Trail-Blazer Challenge Walk, which is a 25 mile (40 km) circular walk from Bakewell, involving 3,600 ft (1,100 m) of ascent, to be walked within twenty-four hours; and secondly, The Rivers' Way, 43 miles (69 km) from Edale to Ilam via the principal rivers of the Peak District. The walk is also an appropriate extension to the Pennine Way (p. 39).

GUIDEBOOKS
John N. Merrill, *The Limey Way* (Dalesman, 1979
– *Peak District Marathons* (JNM Publications, 1982)
– *The Rivers' Way* (JNM Publications, 1983)
– *The Trail-Blazer Challenge Walk* (JNM Publications, 1983)

The Cotswold Way

100 miles (161 km) from Bath to Chipping Campden.
O.S. MAPS 1:50,000 LANDRANGER SERIES
sheets 150 (Worcester and The Malverns), 151 (Stratford-upon-Avon), 162 (Gloucester & Forest of Dean), 163 (Cheltenham & Cirencester), 172 (Bristol and Bath)

I first walked this unofficial long-distance path in 1976 while on a 2,100 mile (3,380 km) walk through England and Wales (p. 58). I was very impressed by its line as it wove along the Cotswold escarpment and through numerous outstandingly beautiful villages. As a result I have walked it twice more. Usually I walk it in four days, but really to appreciate the beauty of the area a week along it would make a most enjoyable outing. I have always backpacked the route, and although there are no official campsites I have always found everyone very helpful and have camped on private lawns as well as at farms. There are youth hostels at Cleeve Hill and Bath, and several more near to the route. There are also numerous places to stay on or close to the Way.

The idea of a long-distance footpath along the Cotswold Hills was first mooted in the 1950s by Anthony Drake and the local Ramblers' Association. It was not until twenty years later that the Gloucestershire County Council designated the route and began waymarking it. With the introduction of a detailed guidebook, the path has become established as one of the loveliest walks in central England.

I have always walked the route south to north, and, to judge from the people I have met on the walk, this appears to be the most popular way. The route-finding is particularly good. On the footpath signs are little stickers saying 'Cotswold Way', and on trees or posts at regular intervals is a yellow painted arrow. If you are going to signpost a route, the Cotswold Way is one of the few which is well done and easy to follow. You should not lose your way!

Bath may seem an odd place to start a long walk, but it sets the theme of fine buildings to be seen. The path soon leads onto Lansdown Hill, providing extensive views down to Bath. Beyond, you walk through Cold Ashton and Dyrham with their attractive buildings. After crossing the M4 motorway you pass through further villages to reach the Somerset Monument at Hawkesbury Upton. You descend again, often passing through delightful woodland to Wooton-under-Edge. I once camped above the village but partway through the night the cows disapproved and forced me to leave! Next is Tyndale Monument before Stinchcombe Hill, Frocester Hill and Haresfield Beacon. Very rarely do you go above the 1,000 ft (300 m) contour line on the whole route. From the Beacon you descend to the magnificent village of Painswick.

Painswick Beacon is next, before Cooper's Hill, Crickley Hill and the long loop high above Cheltenham to Cleeve Hill. The next section, to Chipping Campden, is particularly picturesque, through Winchcombe, Stanway with its gatehouse, Stanton and Broadway. The final hill is

Dover's Hill, before you descend to the journey's end at Chipping Campden, another really attractive market town.

GUIDEBOOKS

R. Kershaw & B. Robson, *Discovering Walks in the Cotswolds* (Shire Publications, 1974)

Ed. David Sharp, *Ramblers' Ways* (David & Charles, 1980)

A. Swale, *The Cotswold Way* (Constable, 1979)

Mark Richards, *The Cotswold Way* (Thornhill Press, 1973)

R. Hodges, *Walks in the Cotswolds* (Spurbooks, 1976)

The Ridgeway

85 miles (137 km) from Ivinghoe Beacon, near Ivinghoe in Buckinghamshire, to Overton Hill, near Avebury in Wiltshire.

O.S. MAPS 1:50,000 LANDRANGER SERIES

sheets 165 (Aylesbury and Leighton Buzzard), 173 (Swindon and Devizes), 174 (Newbury and Wantage), 175 (Reading and Windsor)

It was on the spur of the moment that I walked the Ridgeway, for the first time, in late August 1981. I had heard stories of other people who had walked the route, about the ancient monuments and the distinct lack of water. I decided to walk the route from Ivinghoe Beacon and head westwards, which psychologically would be downhill! I had planned on allowing four and a half days for the route, but in fact the weather was so perfect and there is so little ascending or descending – the highest point on the route is 850 ft (259 m) – that I did it in three days.

The route follows 'the oldest road' and it is believed to be 4,000 years old. The upper half of the route – north of Goring-on-Thames – is mostly along the line of the Icknield Way. The lower half – south of Goring – is along the Ridgeway. It is possible to extend the walk considerably and follow the line of the Icknield Way and Ridgeway, from the Norfolk coast to Seaton in Devon. For the whole time you will be in chalk country, which is why there is a water problem. 'Goring Gap', as it is called, is approximately the halfway point of the route and marks the boundary of the two types of countryside passed through. North to Ivinghoe Beacon is rolling, wooded country, especially beech, and the path weaves its way through extensive woodland. South to Overton Hill, you will see few trees as the path follows the ridges of the Downs.

I arrived late at Ivinghoe Beacon and, after admiring the 360° view, shouldered my 30 lb (14 kg) load and set off to follow the path to Wendover, 12 miles (19 km) away. After the openness of the beacon and its crowds of people, I was soon in some magnificent beech woodland and on my own. In fact I only met ten other people walking the route, mostly from Overton Hill. Wendover, apart from Goring-on-Thames, is the only village or town passed through on the walk where supplies can be purchased. I stayed in Wendover as it was almost dusk when I arrived. Had I known, I would have carried on a little further, carrying water, and camped on Coombe Hill.

Shortly after leaving Wendover, the path skirts Chequers, the Prime Minister's country residence, before encircling Princes Risborough. The next stretch is through trees, beneath the ridges and along a wide track. About 20 miles (32 km) from Wendover the path brought me to the northern edge of Nuffield village. I had found no water all day, and it was a delight to see a small notice on the church stating that a water tap was on the church wall. The path from Nuffield to the river Thames near North Stoke is often described as the worst of the route, for most of it follows Grim's Ditch. In summer it is very overgrown, with shoulder-high nettles. After eleven hours of walking, I reached the banks of the Thames south of North Stoke and camped. The river, with a variety of boats cruising past, makes a pleasant contrast from the dry chalk hills.

The next stage of the walk from the Thames to Overton is waterless – or so I was told. Upon reaching Goring I stocked up with tinned food and bought four cans of coke and a pint of milk – enough for 42 miles (68 km). Virtually at the last house in Goring a woman very kindly filled my water bottle and I was on my way. The path now follows the Ridgeway along a wide fenced track along the crest of the ridges. Up to Goring the path had been for pedestrians only, but from here onwards it is a bridleway open to horse riders. I only met a couple of riders. I was glad I was carrying plenty of drinks, for the day was exceedingly hot – the hottest of the year. By 1 p.m. it was almost unbearable, and I would walk a mile (1.5 km) and find a solitary tree or bush to sit under for a few minutes while I cooled down.

One of the beauties of this section of the Ridgeway is that you come to several ancient monuments. The first was Segsbury Camp, an Iron Age fort, and by evening I was camping beside the path opposite Uffington Castle where there is a white horse. I had found no water all day, and even the water troughs in the fields had their lids bolted. The farms too were not very co-operative, with signs saying 'No Water Obtainable Here'.

Just down from my camp, the next day, I reached Wayland Smithy's

Cave, a long barrow with three chambers, made about 2800 BC. A little further on I came to the aptly named Ridgeway Farm where the owners only too happily filled my water bottle. Two miles (3 km) later, and shortly before crossing the M4, I came to the Shepherd's Rest Inn. It was only 9.20 a.m., but the landlord made me coffee and breakfast – so the route is not as dry as I was told. After the M4, the path continues along the hillcrests, skirts past Ogbourne St George and begins the final ten miles, first along Smeathe's Ridge then Hackpen Hill. Between the two the Ridgeway crosses Barbury Castle, another hill fort. This area is now a country park, with information centre, toilets and a water supply, which will help backpackers considerably.

Having crossed Hackpen Hill, the path begins its very gradual descent to Overton Hill. You can tell that the end is near by the numerous Sarsen Stones lying around. I reached the end with immense regret, for although only a 'short' walk the route is fascinating and requires little effort. I shall certainly come back and walk the route in winter. Before heading home I went to Avebury and wandered round its incomparable stone circle.

GUIDEBOOKS AND FURTHER READING

J. R. L. Anderson, with photographs by Fay Godwin, *The Oldest Road: an exploration of the Ridgeway* (Wildwood House, 1975)
Vera Burden, *Discovering the Ridgeway* (Shire Publications, 1976)
A. Charles, *The Ridgeway Path* (Spurbooks, 1981)
E. Cull, *Walks Along The Ridgeway* (Spurbooks, 1977)
Seán Jennett, *The Ridgeway Path* (H.M.S.O., 1980)
H. D. Westacott, *A Practical Guide to Walking the Ridgeway* (Footpath Publications, 3rd edn. 1977)
– *The Ridgeway Path* (Penguin, 1982)

The North Downs Way

140 miles (225 km) from Farnham to Dover via Canterbury or Wye.
O.S. MAPS 1:50,000 LANDRANGER SERIES
sheets 178 (The Thames Estuary), 179 (Canterbury and East Kent), 186 (Aldershot and Guildford), 187 (Dorking, Reigate and Crawley), 188 (Maidstone and The Weald of Kent), 189 (Ashford and Romney Marsh)

I have not so far walked the Way, but it is on my ever-increasing list of walks to do. As part of my final preparation for my coast walk I walked the Pilgrims' Way from Winchester Cathedral to Canterbury Cathedral, a distance of about 120 miles (193 km), but on the ground nearer 160 miles (257 km). Part of the line of the North Downs Way follows the Pilgrims' Way. I did the walk just before Christmas, camping en route, and although passing through populated areas I found everyone very helpful. Some of the paths were overgrown, little used and poorly signposted, making map-reading essential. However, I enjoyed the walk; the going was easy, with no hard hills to climb, and there were only small areas of open terrain. But the beauty of the walk lies in its historical appeal and buildings. The churches, houses and landmarks all provide colour and interest, and a couple of weeks walking along the route, delving into the past, would be a very rewarding experience.

The North Downs Way begins at Farnham, and for the first 26 miles (42 km) to Dorking via Guildford you pass through the Surrey hills. Just outside Dorking you walk across one of southern England's most famous beauty spots, Box Hill. You continue through woodland and sunken lanes via Merstham and Otford to Rochester in Kent. A further 20 miles (32 km) brings you near to Wye, and here you have to decide whether to go via Canterbury to Dover (27 miles, 43 km) or continue straight on by the shortest way to Dover via Folkestone (18 miles, 29 km). Both have their points of interest: Canterbury for its cathedral, and the Wye Downs are particularly attractive. Either way you can be assured of a good walk to those fabled white cliffs.

GUIDEBOOKS
D. Herbstein, *North Downs Way* (H.M.S.O., 1982)
C. J. Wright, *A Guide to the Pilgrims' Way and North Downs* (Constable, 1977)
J. Spayne & A. Krynski, *Walks in the Hills of Kent* (Spurbooks, 1976, revised edn. 1981)
– *Walks in the Surrey Hills* (Spurbooks, 1974, 5th edn. 1983)
– *Afoot in Surrey* (Spurbooks, 1979)

The South Downs Way

80 miles (128 km) from Eastbourne, across East and West Sussex, to the Hampshire border south of Petersfield.
O.S. MAPS 1:50,000 LANDRANGER SERIES
sheets 197 (Chichester and The Downs), 198 (Brighton and The Downs), 199 (Eastbourne and Hastings)
Being easy terrain and close to many centres of population, the Way has become very popular. It is just the right length for a week's walk as an introduction to backpacking. There is little threat of constant bad

weather; you never go more than 1,000 ft (300 m) above sea level; and once you have gained the crest of the chalk downs you maintain your height where possible. Most people walk in an east to west direction, and the start from Eastbourne must surely rate as one of the finest. You can take the alternative route from Eastbourne inland to Alfriston, but not to walk round Beachy Head and over the Seven Sisters would be to miss one of the most impressive areas of coastal scenery in Britain.

Alfriston is a distance of about 15 miles (24 km) via Beachy Head, and there is a youth hostel nearby. From here you ascend onto the down crest walking along chalk and flint paths which, when wet, can be unpleasantly slippery. You are now confronted with the classic down-land scene of open views with the down edge disappearing into the distance. As you walk you will no doubt see pony-trekkers and horsemen, for the path is a bridleway used by both riders and cyclists. Fifteen miles (24 km) from Alfriston brings you to Newmarket Inn on the A27 road. Nine miles (14.5 km) later is Pyecombe. There are few facilities on the route itself, but you frequently pass close to villages and cross major roads which provide access to many of the principal coastal resorts, such as Brighton.

From Pyecombe you cross further downs to Beeding Hill near Shoreham-by-Sea. For the next 37 miles (59.5 km) to the end of the path at Sunwood Farm on the Hampshire boundary, you keep to the downs, crossing Annington Hill, Chantry Hill, Westburton Hill, Graffham Down, Cocking Down and Beacon Hill. Although the walk officially ends at the farm, most people press on a further 2 miles (3 km) to Buriton, a delightful village with a pond. Two miles away (3 km) is Petersfield, where train and bus services can be found.

GUIDEBOOKS
Seán Jennett, *South Downs Way* (H.M.S.O., 1977)
E. C. Pyatt, *Chalkways of South and South-East England* (David & Charles, 1975)
Derrick Knowlton, *Walks in Hampshire* (Spurbooks, 1977)
Norman Willis, *Walks in Sussex* (Spurbooks, 1977)

The South-West Peninsula Coast Path

A walk of at least 515 miles (830 km) from Studland in Dorset, around the south-west peninsula and Land's End, to Minehead in Somerset. It is made up of five separate footpaths: Dorset Coast Path, 72 miles (116 km); South Devon Coast Path, 93 miles (150 km); South

Cornwall Coast Path, 133 miles (212 km); North Cornwall Coast Path, 135 miles (219 km); Somerset and North Devon Coast Path, 82 miles (132 km).

O.S. MAPS 1:50,000 LANDRANGER SERIES
Dorset Coast Path: sheets 193 (Taunton and Lyme Regis), 194 (Dorchester and Weymouth), 195 (Bournemouth and Purbeck). *South Devon Coast Path:* 192 (Exeter and Sidmouth), 193 (Taunton and Lyme Regis), 201 (Plymouth and Launceston), 202 (Torbay and South Dartmoor). *South Cornwall Coast Path:* 200 (Newquay and Bodmin), 201 (Plymouth and Launceston), 203 (Land's End and The Lizard), 204 (Truro and Falmouth). *North Cornwall Coast Path:* 190 (Bude and Clovelly), 200 (Newquay and Bodmin), 203 (Land's End and The Lizard), 204 (Truro and Falmouth). *Somerset and North Devon Coast Path:* 180 (Barnstaple and Ilfracombe), 181 (Minehead and Brendon Hills), 190 (Bude and Clovelly).

It has always seemed strange to me that this coastal path was split into five sections: I feel that it should be treated as a whole, thereby creating our longest continuous official footpath. With the ever-increasing leisure time and longer holidays, any reasonably determined walker could complete the path in a month. Few areas of Britain, apart from the west coast of Scotland, possess such a sustained and attractive coastline. I have walked the whole path twice, once on my coast walk and another time in its own right. On my Land's End to John o'Groats walk (p. 83) I walked all the coastline to Minehead. Whilst the walk can be done in sections, or even in two halves using Land's End as the break point, for a major backpacking walk in Britain of considerable length with varied coastal scenery all the way, the South-West Way is hard to equal.

Dorset

I always prefer to walk clockwise, and as a result I set off from Studland near Poole. Immediately you come to the stunning scenery of the chalk cliffs and stacks of Old Harry Rocks. Next is the impressive Lulworth Cove and the rock archway – Durdle Door. Near Weymouth the path divides, and you can either head overland to near Abbotsbury or continue around the coast and Chesil Beach to Abbotsbury. Personally I prefer the coastal route, if only to see the beach. At Weymouth is the 'Isle' of Portland, which the path avoids. To me this is a great shame, for Portland is very interesting historically and has a coast path. I always include it on my walk, for from its western side you get an unparalleled view of Chesil Beach. Abbotsbury is renowned for its swannery, and that

too is worth looking at, as is the thatched village. Fifteen miles (24 km) or
more brings you to Lyme Regis and the end of the Dorset path.

South Devon

Leaving Lyme Regis you have some magnificent high-level cliff walking
to Seaton, past the sites of several large landslides. Beyond, the cliffs
begin losing their height as you aim for the mouth of the river Exe via
Sidmouth and Budleigh Salterton. At Exmouth you take a ferry across to
Starcross. The next stage is past the larger coastal resorts of Torquay,
Paignton and Brixham. But it is always surprising how quickly you pass
through them and reach peaceful surroundings to be enjoyed alone. You
are now heading almost due south as you weave your way round the
coast past Dartmouth to Start Point, using ferries across the picturesque
Dart and Salcombe estuaries. Shortly afterwards you head north-
westerly for Plymouth via some aggressive cliffs near Bigbury-on-Sea.
At Plymouth you cross the Tamar river into Cornwall.

South Cornwall

Almost immediately after Rame Head you begin reaching some of the
spectacular coastal scenery and villages that Cornwall is so well known
for: Polperro and Fowey. Inland you can see the huge pyramids of china
clay, and at Charlestown on St Austell Bay you will no doubt see the clay
being loaded onto a boat. All the time now the scenery gets better and
better. The cliffs become more rugged, the villages more attractive –
Mevagissey, Portloe and St Mawes – before you cross to Falmouth. Out
of Falmouth you start the walk around the Lizard peninsula, the most
southerly point of the British mainland. After crossing the Helford river
you begin what I consider to be the finest section of the route as you
make your way around the peninsula to Coverack, Cadgwith, Kynance
Cove, Mullion and on around Mount's Bay to Penzance and finally to
Land's End. All the time the cliffs are impressive and pleasantly broken
up by stretches of beach and quaint villages. It is a section to savour.

North Cornwall

The 'longest county' section of the path. It is not as dramatic as south
Cornwall but the scenery is of a very high standard. Shortly after Land's
End you walk round Cape Cornwall and see the remains of the Cornish
tin mines, especially around Botalloch Head. From here to St Ives it is a
quiet and peaceful section away from everything and with few people.
After St Ives a ferry trip keeps you to the coast as you continue on to

Godrevy Point, Portreath, Perran Beach and Newquay. A little further on and you reach Bedruthan Steps and its magnificent coast scene of steep cliffs and rock stacks. Around Trevose Head and you reach Padstow and its ferry across the Camel river. More picturesque and historical places lie ahead as you reach Tintagel and its fabled castle. Boscastle just beyond is a delightful sheltered village, and another 5 miles (8 km) brings you to Crackington Haven and the impressive cliff walk to Bude. Eight miles (13 km) from Bude at Marsland Mouth you step back into Devon.

Somerset and North Devon
The cliff scenery remains impressive as you press on to Hartland Point and views of Lundy Island. Not long afterwards you reach the stunning village of Clovelly. Although a tourist trap, it is still a village of exceptional character and beauty. The cliffs now recede and give way to huge expanses of sand and beach as you gain Westward Ho! Here you can take a ferry, the last one of the walk, across the river Taw and continue along the sands. Just beyond Ilfracombe you reach Combe Martin and the Exmoor National Park, the only National Park the path passes through. The cliffs from Combe Martin, 1,000 ft high (300 m), demand considerable determination to walk along as you head for Woody Bay, the Valley of Rocks and Lynmouth. From here you begin the final 15 miles (24 km) of the way as you ascend to County Gate and step into Somerset, before descending to Culbone Church and Porlock Bay. One final ascent of Selworthy Beacon remains before descending to Minehead, the end of the walk. The walk can be done carrying the minimum of equipment, for you pass through so many seaside resorts. There are numerous campsites, places to stay and a whole string of youth hostels.

GUIDEBOOKS
Roland Gant, *A guide to the South Devon and Dorset coast paths* (Constable, 1982)
B. Jackman, *Dorset Coast Path* (H.M.S.O., 1979)
B. Le Messurier, *South Devon Coast Path* (H.M.S.O., 1980)
– *Somerset and North Devon Coast Path* (H.M.S.O., 1980)
E. C. Pyatt, *Cornwall Coast Path* (H.M.S.O., 1981)
M. Richards, *North Cornwall: Exploring the Coastal Footpaths* (Thornhill Press, 1977)
Ken Ward and John H. N. Mason, *The South-West Peninsula Coast Path* (Letts Guides, 1977)

Parkland Journey

To round off this chapter, and also to set the scene for the next, I will describe a walk that I completed in 1976, linking together the ten National Parks of England and Wales. It proved to be one of my most enjoyable walks but it was also a tough one, for it took in several long-distance footpaths as well as all the major summits on the way. It marked a new achievement for me, being the first time I had walked over 2,000 miles (3,220 km) without a rest day, at an average of 25 miles (40 km) per day with a 50 lb (23 kg) load. That summer, as many readers will remember, was one of the finest and hottest we have had. Between late May and mid-August I had only four days of rain in the eighty-four days of walking; the rest were unbroken sunshine.

As usual on my major walks, I started at the southernmost point and walked northwards. From Plymouth I headed into Dartmoor, where I picked up the newly-opened Two Moors Way that leads to Exmoor. It took me across rocky tors and clapper bridges, and along delightful, broom-laden river banks. By contrast, Exmoor is gentler in nature, but I still enjoyed the walking. I reached the coast at Lynmouth, where I picked up the Somerset and North Devon coast path to Minehead; again a contrast between the peaceful hills and the coast, with its crowds of people and crashing waves.

Leaving the coast, I passed through the attractive village of Dunster and reached the Quantock Hills, responding at once to their quiet beauty. They offer a magnificent vantage point over the mouth of the river Severn and the South Wales coastline, before the route drops to the flat terrain around Bridgwater, close to the site of the battle of Sedgemoor where the Duke of Monmouth's rebellion was brought to an end in 1685.

Beyond, I passed through the limestone cliffs of Cheddar Gorge, heading for Bath. Here I set off up the 100 mile (161 km) Cotswold Way (p. 48), one of the loveliest 'unofficial' long walks in Britain. The route lies up the Cotswold escarpment, through extensive beech woodland and villages of exceptional beauty.

At Chipping Campden, the end of the Way, I turned left for Wales, heading for the Brecon Beacons via the Vale of Evesham. I ascended the Black Mountains first, crossing Offa's Dyke Path (p. 66), before climbing Pen-y-fan and the other main peaks. On the western side I crossed the Pembrokeshire Black Mountains in total solitude before reaching the coast at Amroth. This coastal path (pp. 64–5) is for me the most attractive stretch of coastline in Wales or England. I never tire of walking it. It has fine sandy beaches as well as rugged cliffs, historical sites both old and new, and an abundance of wildlife and flowers.

From Poppit Sands, the end of the coast path, I continued up the coast to Aberystwyth. Here I left the shore for the next 1,000 miles (1,600 km) as I entered Snowdonia National Park (p. 61). The weather was now so perfect that I was walking very early in the mornings. I was on the summit of Cader Idris at 7 a.m., long before anyone had begun to stir at a campsite which I passed half an hour later. The heat had dried out the ground, and I was able to walk quite safely across land that is often boggy. The rivers were lovely to swim in, and even the mountain tarns were warm; several times I floated in them in the evening to cool down. I climbed Snowdon, the Glyders and the Carnedds before leaving the mountains for the Cheshire plain as I aimed for my home territory, the Peak District (p. 34).

I picked up the Peakland Way (p. 45) and followed it for 40 miles (64 km) through the dales and gritstone hills to Edale and the start of the Pennine Way (p. 39), which I had not previously walked. Little did I know that in the next twelve months I would walk it three more times – in training! I walked the lower half of the Pennine Way to Hawes. Here I left the route and joined the Dales Way (p. 36), which I followed to the Lake District (p. 35). Again in perfect weather, I wove my way over the mountains, climbing the Langdale Pikes, Bowfell, Scafell and Scafell Pike, Great Gable and Skiddaw. It was good to catch my breath again as I crossed gentler terrain in Kelder Forest, striving for the northern end of the Pennine Way. At Byrness I picked up the route and followed it to its end at Kirk Yetholm.

The next morning I turned round and headed back south down the Pennine Way towards Hawes. As always, it was an enjoyable walk through the forests, along Hadrian's Wall and over Cross Fell, England's highest peak outside a National Park.

Back in the limestone scenery of the Yorkshire Dales, I left the Pennine Way to head for my last National Park, the North York Moors (p. 37). At Helmsley I embarked upon the last long-distance footpath, the Cleveland Way (p. 42). This has always been a favourite of mine: you have rugged mountains and moorland to cross before gaining the east coast at Saltburn-by-the-Sea. I walked down the east coast to Whitby, Scarborough and finally Filey, my journey's end.

Perhaps I should have called it a day there, but I couldn't settle. I had had a tumultuous reception at Filey, having walked my way into the

Guinness Book of Records. The press had a field day. They asked what I intended to do next, and, without hesitation, for I knew there was no other training I could do, I replied that I would walk around the entire coast of Britain in fifteen months' time. I had four hours' sleep before putting on my rucksack. I felt I had to get away, and I decided to walk home. First I walked the Wolds Way (p. 44), before weaving my way across Yorkshire. I skirted Sheffield, and entered Derbyshire, and climbed the gritstone edges before finally returning to my cottage. I had walked 2,100 miles (3, 380 km).

CHAPTER 5

Walking in Wales

Wales is renowned for the mountains of Snowdonia, but it has much else to offer the walker. There are the Pembrokeshire Coast Path (p. 63), Offa's Dyke Path (p. 66), and Glyders Way, as well as the unofficial Cambrian Way. When I walked the coast of Wales (pp. 63–5) I was astonished by the beauty of the southern half. Inland were coal-mines, steelworks and industry, but the coast had numerous stretches of golden sands, gentle cliffs and several remote sections. The Gower peninsula was the highlight of the area, with sandy coves and a rugged coastline.

South Wales also has the Brecon Beacons (p. 62) and the Black Mountains, which together form an excellent mountain-walking area. The Pembrokeshire coast has few equals for scenery or coastal walking. And there are numerous castles and other historic monuments on the coast and inland in Pembrokeshire (Dyfed), as elsewhere in Wales. Central Wales is often overlooked, being more rural, but there are numerous walks through delightful countryside where you will be the only walker. Snowdonia is deservedly popular all year round and has a wide choice of high mountains. Offshore is Anglesey, which provides a good circular island walk. Throughout Wales there are many hostels, campsites and other places offering accommodation, which make ideal bases for day-walking or from which to undertake a long walk.

NATIONAL PARKS

Snowdonia

O.S. MAPS 1 INCH TO 1 MILE TOURIST SERIES
sheet 10 (Snowdonia National Park)
O.S. MAPS 1:25,000 OUTDOOR LEISURE SERIES
sheets 16–19 (Snowdonia National Park)
This is the second largest National Park (838 sq miles, 2,171 sq km) with the most rugged and mountainous countryside in England and Wales. It is truly a walkers' paradise, with endless paths to follow and

mountains to climb. There are fourteen mountains over 3,000 ft (900 m) including Snowdon, the highest mountain in England and Wales. To climb this mountain one can follow the superb ridge walk – the Snowdon Horseshoe – or, for a greater endurance challenge, climb all eight 3,000 ft (900 m) peaks in the area in one day. In the central part of the park are the Rhinog mountains; although only just above 2,000 ft (600 m), they are hard and remote mountains away from the more popular areas. At the southern end is one of my favourite mountains, Cader Idris.

Snowdonia is a place that even in a lifetime cannot be fully explored, as there are so many walks through its captivating scenery.

The National Park Office is at Yr Hen Ysgol, Maentwrog, North Wales.

GUIDEBOOKS TO NORTH WALES
S. Ashton, *Scrambles in Snowdonia* (Cicerone Press, 1980)
F. Duerden, *Great Walks of North Wales* (Ward Lock, 1982)
C. Macdonald, *A Visitor's Guide to North Wales and Snowdonia* (Moorland Publishing, 1982)
R. Maddern, *Walks in Magnificent Snowdonia* (Focus Publishing, 1979)
E. G. Rowland, *Hill Walking in Snowdonia* (The Cidron Press, 1958)
– *The Ascent of Snowdon* (The Cidron Press, 1956)
(Both these books have been reissued by The Cicerone Press, 1975)

Brecon Beacons

O.S. MAPS 1:25,000 OUTDOOR LEISURE SERIES
sheets 11–13

On both the eastern and western side of the park (519 sq miles, 1,344 sq km) are a group of mountains known as the Black Mountains. Both provide excellent walking in mountains just over 2,000 ft (600 m). Running through the eastern Black Mountains is Offa's Dyke footpath (p. 66). In the centre of the park are the Brecon Beacons, with Pen-y-fan the highest point at 2,907 ft (886 m).

This is one of the most beautiful walking areas in Britain. Roaming through it are the famous Brecon ponies. The south-western side of the park is limestone country where the longest known cave systems exist in Britain. Towards the eastern side of the park is the only canal in a National Park, the Llangynidr Canal.

The National Park Office is in Glamorgan Street, Brecon.

Pembrokeshire Coast

This is an area of only 225 sq miles (583 sq km). Running around its 168 miles (270 km) of coastline is the Pembrokeshire Coast Path. To me there is nothing to compare with the variety of coastline – sandy beaches, tall cliffs, numerous inlets and fishing villages – that is found in this stretch. It may be the smallest National Park, but it is one of the most beautiful. It also contains Britain's smallest city, St David's, whose cathedral is justly famous. Off the coastline are several islands – Skokholm, Skomer and Ramsey – which are renowned for their sea-bird populations. A good time to walk the coastline is in June, when the cliffs are ablaze with flowers and the lily-ponds at Bosherston (see p. 64) are at their best. For spectacular cliff-walking the area around Strumble Head has few equals, and in the Dale area are several impressive rock folds.

The National Park Office is in Haverfordwest.

LONG-DISTANCE FOOTPATHS

The Pembrokeshire Coast Path

168 miles (270 km) from Amroth in the south to Poppit Sands in the north.

O.S. MAPS 1:50,000 LANDRANGER SERIES
sheets 145 (Cardigan), 157 (St David's and Haverfordwest), 158 (Tenby)

I am often asked which is my favourite section of coastline; without any hesitation I say, Pembrokeshire. I have walked the entire path four times and I am still moved by the beauty I see. The first time I walked it was in 1970, just before it was officially opened. It was strange walking it then, along new paths that had been cut by a small bulldozer. The weather too was strange, one day very hot and the next morning so cold that snow was lying on the ground. The walk can be done in one or two weeks depending on your ability and the distance you walk each day.

Preferring as I do to walk northwards (see p. 150), I start from Amroth, which can be reached by bus from Tenby. It is a pleasant 8 mile (13 km) walk from Amroth to Tenby, and I usually press on a little further to Manorbier, with its Norman castle. I camp nearby or use one of the many bed-and-breakfast establishments. Not far from Manorbier are the magnificent Bosherston lily-ponds. In June several large lakes there are covered with white water lilies, which make a magnificent sight. Close to the headland beyond is a small chapel measuring 8 ft x 12 ft (2.5 m x 3.6 m), known as St Govan's, which can only be reached by fifty steps down the cliff. The cliff scenery from here to where you have to walk inland, around Castlemartin army training area 5 miles (8 km) away, is exceptional. The high cliffs are particularly dramatic, with imposing sea-bird-laden rock stacks and a huge natural archway known as the Green Bridge.

I usually prefer to stop at Castlemartin and camp there, but on two occasions I have pressed on to the Angle peninsula, making it a long day. There is really no alternative, for there is nowhere to stay in between: you are not allowed to camp at Freshwater West. From the Angle peninsula there is no trouble in finding a place to camp, and there are several hostels. Angle has a campsite, and one year I surprised the owner by arriving two weeks before it opened. Angle also makes a good starting point for walking around Milford Haven, the next stage of the walk and a great contrast to what has been seen so far. The Haven, one of the deepest river channels around the coast of Britain, allows huge oil tankers to unload their cargo into one of the many refineries.

After about 12 miles (19 km) through this refinery landscape the path brings you to Pembroke and its impressive castle, the birthplace of Henry VII. Pembroke is a good place to stock up, for once you leave the Haven there are only villages on the route. You can also visit St David's and replenish your supplies there, about 60 miles (97 km) away and 1½ miles (2.4 km) inland. Once back at the mouth of the Haven, now at the northern end, you are again in beautiful scenery, the hallmark of the Pembrokeshire coast. At Dale you approach one of my favourite sections of coast, around St Ann's Head with its numerous spectacular rock folds and along the top of Marloes Sands, a breathtaking slice of beach and cliff; while out to sea are the islands, Skomer and Skokholm.

From the Dale peninsula you begin the 45 mile (72 km) walk around St Bride's Bay to St David's. On a clear day you can see your destination across the wide bay. First you have an impressive steep cliff to walk around before reaching Little Haven, which has a campsite and hostel. When the tide is out you can do a long beach walk here, as you can at Newgale Sands beyond. To reach St David's peninsula you ascend once more to the top of gorse-covered cliffs and head for one of the most attractive villages on the whole route, Solva, perfectly situated in a deep valley reached by a narrow inlet.

The St David's coastline is rugged, especially around its western end, at Ramsey Sound, with Ramsey Island across the water. Around this, past St Justinian's lifeboat station, you gain Whitesand Bay, which is renowned for its surfing breakers and extensive stretch of sand. Inland is a youth hostel, and St David's 'city', with its impressive, small but homely cathedral and ruined bishop's palace – an ideal rest-day spot.

The scenery changes dramatically from Whitesands Bay and becomes more rugged with high cliffs and remote paths. Gone are the gentle scenes and sandy beaches. Apart from Newport, 40 miles (64 km) away, there is no other beach until the end at Poppit Sands. As the path weaves its way around the cliffs you pass through several villages with industrial remains. At Trevine is another hostel, and not far from here you begin working your way to the imposing 400 ft (125 m) cliffs of Pwllderi. The hostel here has one of the finest coastal views anywhere in Britain.

Five miles (8 km) from the cliffs you reach Strumble Head, which even in summer can be a wild place. The lighthouse is reached via a bridge. As you walk here you may well see the Fishguard-Ireland ferry ploughing its way across St George's channel. The next village or town on the route is 8 miles (13 km) away at Fishguard. On the way there the path takes you around numerous pebbled coves and past a monument on Carregwastad Point, where the French landed for an 'invasion' in 1797. They surrendered on the beach at Fishguard. More rugged coast beyond Fishguard brings you to Dinas Head, which is almost an island. On its eastern side is a popular sea-bird colony, and seals pop up and watch you pass. In September baby seals are often seen. Four more miles (6 km) and you reach the beach of Newport.

The final section of the coast path to Poppit Sands, 13 miles (21 km) away, is along a magnificent cliff of exceptional beauty with cascading waterfalls, massive rock folds and distant views. Sadly you walk round Camaes Head and look down onto the sands and the river to Cardigan. I doubt whether any other official long-distance path has given me so much pleasure in walking. I long to do it again.

GUIDEBOOKS
John H. Barrett, *The Pembrokeshire Coast Path* (H.M.S.O., 1974)
Tony Roberts, *A Guide to Walking the Pembrokeshire Coast Path* (Five Arches Press, Tenby, 1976)

Offa's Dyke Path

168 miles (270 km) from Chepstow on the river Severn in South
Wales to Prestatyn on the North Wales coast.

O.S. MAPS 1:50,000 LANDRANGER SERIES

sheets 116 (Denbigh and Colwyn Bay), 117 (Chester), 126 (Shrews-
bury), 137 (Ludlow and Wenlock Edge), 148 (Presteigne and Hay-
on-Wye), 161 (Abergavenny and The Black Mountains), 162
(Gloucester and Forest of Dean)

I first walked the entire path shortly before its official opening in 1971.
Vandalism was already in evidence: the newly carved and erected 'Offa's
Dyke Path' signs had been turned round to point in the wrong direction;
others on trees had been moved and made to point upwards. However,
the weather was kind and I enjoyed the walk as it wove its way along
Offa's Dyke and close to the English border. I decided on this occasion
to do without a tent and just use a nylon hammock. This did not work
well, for trees were scarce and finding two the right distance apart was
almost impossible. I spent several nights squashed into a 'U' shape, and
others lying on the ground; but it all added to the adventure.

The second time I did the walk was on a Land's End to John o'Groats
training walk. I was unwell on reaching Chepstow and remained so all
the way up the path, suffering from food poisoning. Rather than rest and
recover, I walked harder in a weak state. One afternoon at a shop I drank
a large bottle of Lucozade, felt well immediately and walked like a rocket
for three hours before crumpling in a heap. The walk was also memorable for an incident in Montgomery, just off the route. The rain had
streamed down for three days, and my clothes and boots were soaked. I
stayed at a bed-and-breakfast guesthouse in Montgomery to dry out. I
requested the owner to leave my boots in the kitchen, not near the fire, so
that they would dry out slowly. When I asked for them in the morning I
was presented with a pair of steaming boots straight out of the oven!
Another few minutes and the vibram sole would have melted. I set off in
very hot boots.

The beauty of Offa's Dyke lies in its variety of scenery and the fact
that it is a coast-to-coast walk. There are expanses of high mountains to
cross, peaceful remote valleys to walk through, forested areas, delightful
rivers, and numerous historical buildings and castles. For about 100
miles (160 km) of the route you walk along the line, beside or along the
top of Offa's Dyke, which was built by King Offa during the latter half of
the eighth century. The walk can be done in a week, but with so much to

see and appreciate on the way, fourteen days would make it all the more enjoyable.

It is usual to start at Chepstow and walk northwards to Prestatyn. I generally aim for Monmouth on the first day, after looking around Chepstow Castle above the river Wye. Much of the walk to Monmouth is along the Wye valley, past Tintern Abbey, which is well worth looking round. Monmouth has a campsite and hostel, and is renowned for its gated bridge. At various parts on this section you will follow and see the dyke. At Monmouth you leave it and cross rural scenery to Pandy via the impressive Norman White Castle. In the distance you can see the Black Mountains of the Brecon Beacons National Park, across which you next pass. Pandy is my second night's objective; one night here I slept in a horse box!

The crossing of the Black Mountains to Hay-on-Wye, given good weather, is a splendid mountain day with marvellous views. Hay-on-Wye makes a startling contrast, with both a ruined castle and the world's largest second-hand bookshop. Beyond Hay-on-Wye at Knighton you rejoin the dyke proper, and for the next 60 miles (97 km) to Chirk you follow it as it descends, ascends and meanders around the hills. All the time there are extensive views of the dyke making its way across the hills. This is some of the best walking of the route, and the hardest. You pass through Knighton, Clun Forest, Montgomery and near Oswestry to Chirk, having crossed the spectacular Pont Cysyllte aqueduct which carries the Llangollen canal.

From the canal you leave the dyke and head through good mountains and scenery almost due north to Prestatyn, 38 miles (61 km) away. The scenery is different at first as you walk beneath the limestone Eglwyseg Rocks, aiming for 'World's End'. Beyond, after crossing the river Alun, you ascend into the Clwydian Hills, the last major hills of the walk. Upon reaching Bodfari you know that the end is within reach as you cross near to villages and through more rural scenery. Then, quite spectacularly, you come to the crest of the final hill and look down onto Prestatyn and the North Wales coast. It is a sudden and startling contrast to the remote hills you have crossed. Quelling a reluctance to bring the walk to an end, I descend straight to the sands and sea, and don't stop until the sea water is lapping around my boots.

GUIDEBOOKS

John B. Jones, *Offa's Dyke Path* (H.M.S.O., 1976)
Frank Noble, *Offa's Dyke Path* (Queen Anne Press, 1969)
Mark Richards, *Through Welsh Border Country* (Thornhill Press, 1977)

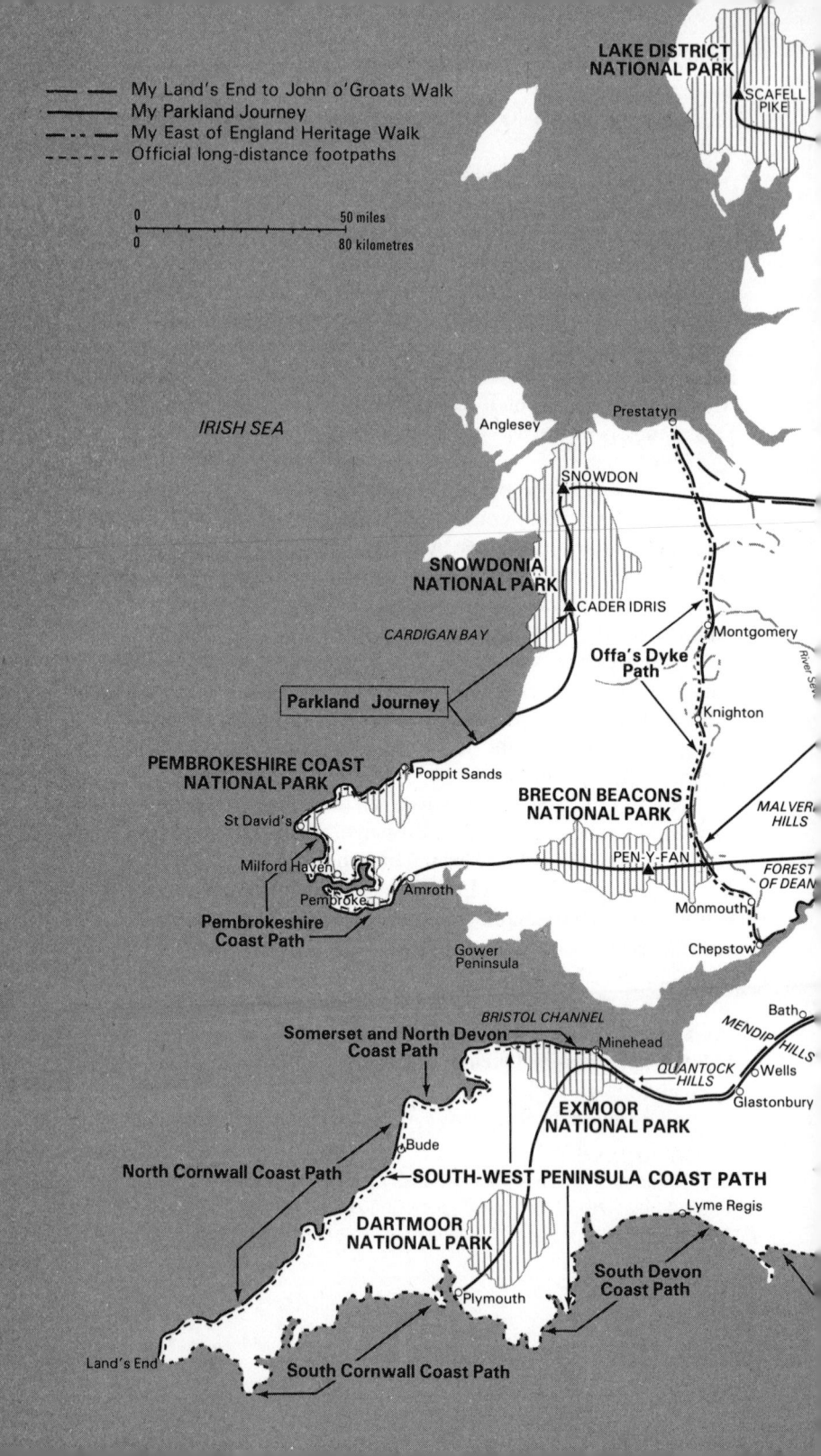

My Land's End to John o'Groats Walk
My Parkland Journey
My East of England Heritage Walk
Official long-distance footpaths

0   50 miles
0   80 kilometres

LAKE DISTRICT NATIONAL PARK

SCAFELL PIKE

IRISH SEA

Anglesey

Prestatyn

SNOWDON

SNOWDONIA NATIONAL PARK

CADER IDRIS

CARDIGAN BAY

Montgomery

Offa's Dyke Path

Knighton

River Seve

Parkland Journey

PEMBROKESHIRE COAST NATIONAL PARK

Poppit Sands

St David's

BRECON BEACONS NATIONAL PARK

MALVERN HILLS

Milford Haven

PEN-Y-FAN

FOREST OF DEAN

Pembroke

Amroth

Pembrokeshire Coast Path

Monmouth

Gower Peninsula

Chepstow

Bath

BRISTOL CHANNEL

MENDIP HILLS

Somerset and North Devon Coast Path

Minehead

QUANTOCK HILLS

Wells

EXMOOR NATIONAL PARK

Glastonbury

Bude

SOUTH-WEST PENINSULA COAST PATH

North Cornwall Coast Path

DARTMOOR NATIONAL PARK

Lyme Regis

South Devon Coast Path

Land's End

Plymouth

South Cornwall Coast Path

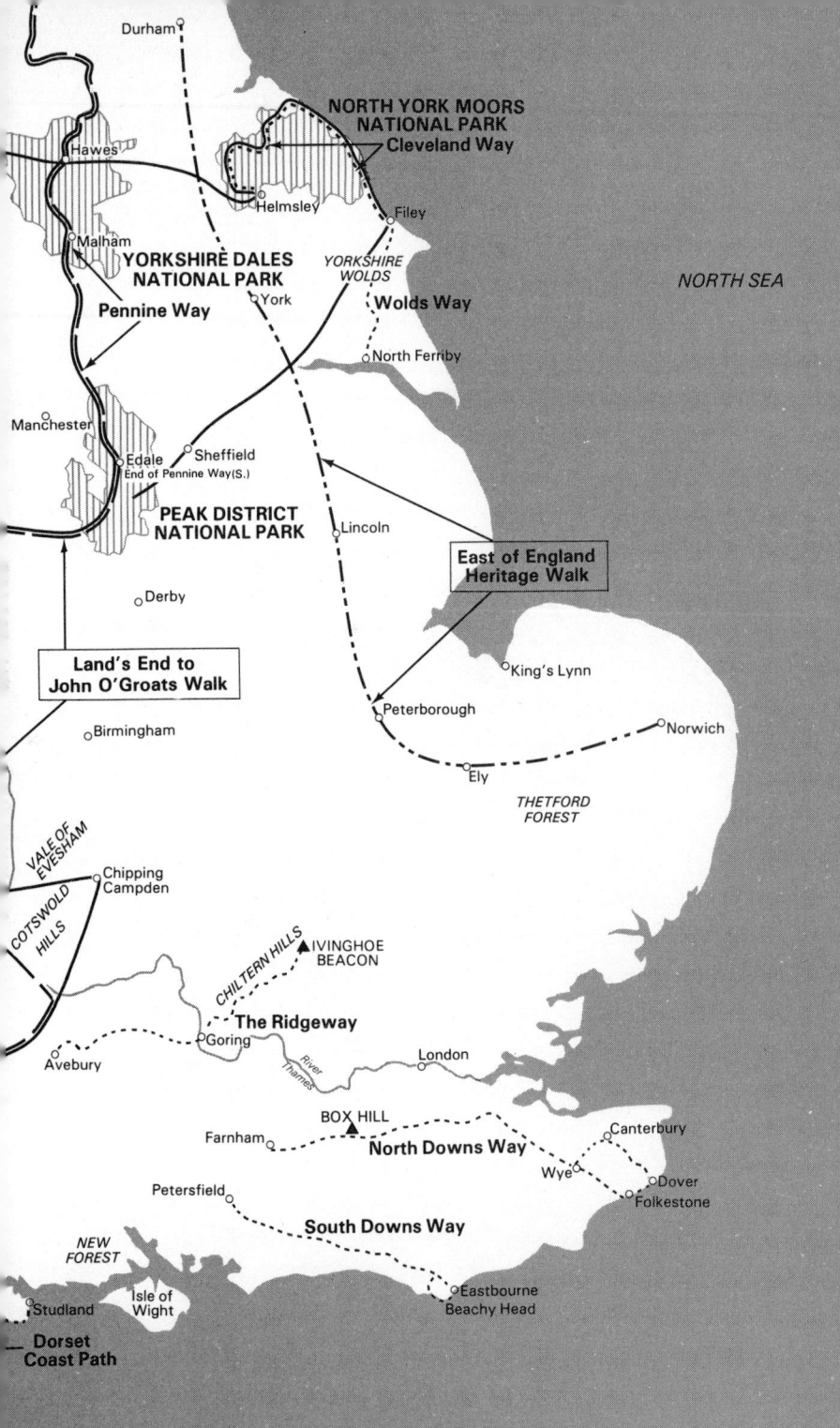

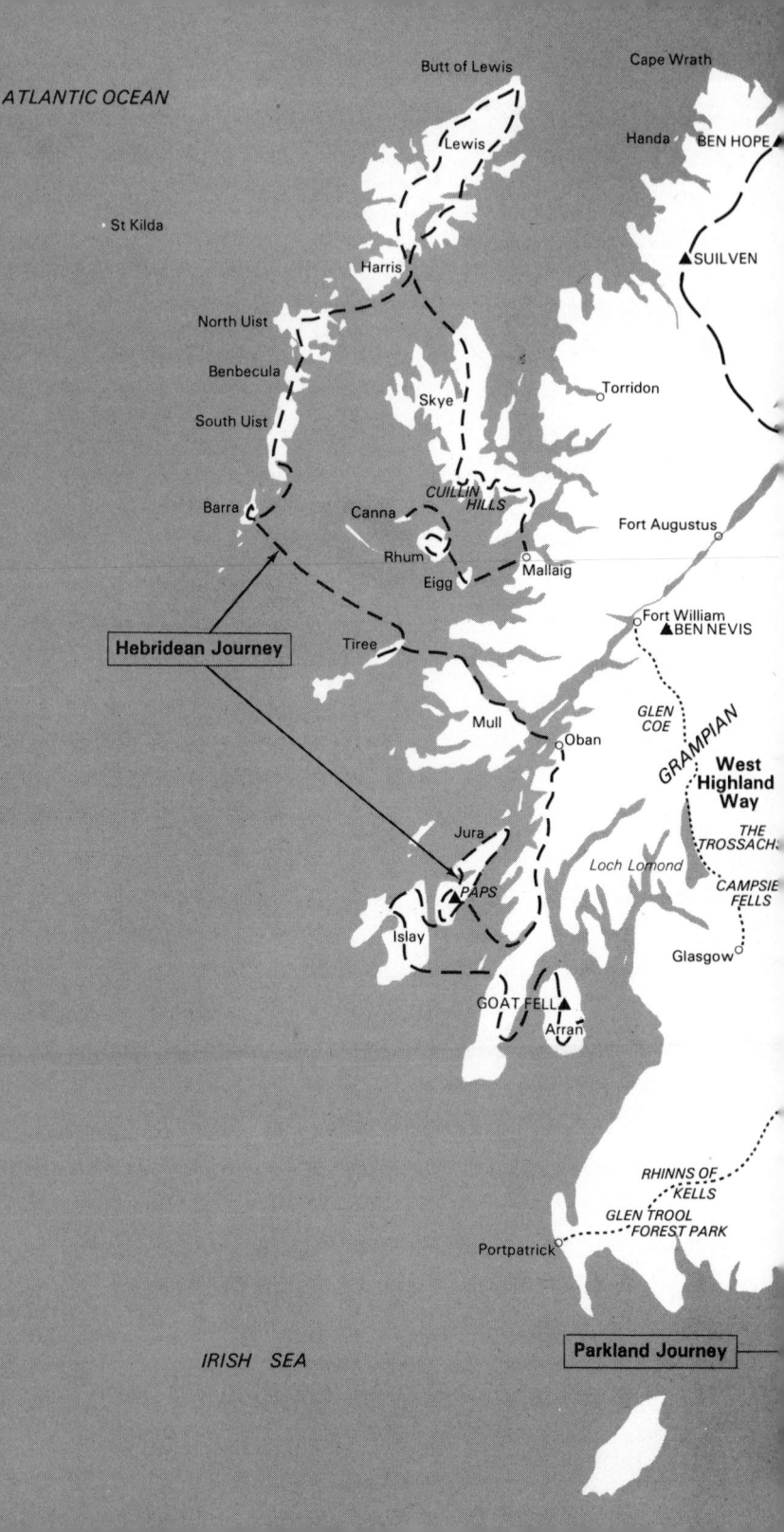

ATLANTIC OCEAN

Butt of Lewis

Cape Wrath

Handa   BEN HOPE ▲

Lewis

St Kilda

SUILVEN ▲

Harris

North Uist

Torridon

Benbecula

Skye

South Uist

CUILLIN
HILLS

Fort Augustus

Barra   Canna

Rhum

Mallaig

Eigg

Fort William
▲BEN NEVIS

Hebridean Journey

Tiree

GLEN
COE

GRAMPIAN

Mull

Oban

**West
Highland
Way**

Jura

THE
TROSSACHS

Loch Lomond

CAMPSIE
FELLS

PAPS

Islay

Glasgow

GOAT FELL ▲

Arran

RHINNS OF
KELLS

GLEN TROOL
FOREST PARK

Portpatrick

IRISH SEA

Parkland Journey

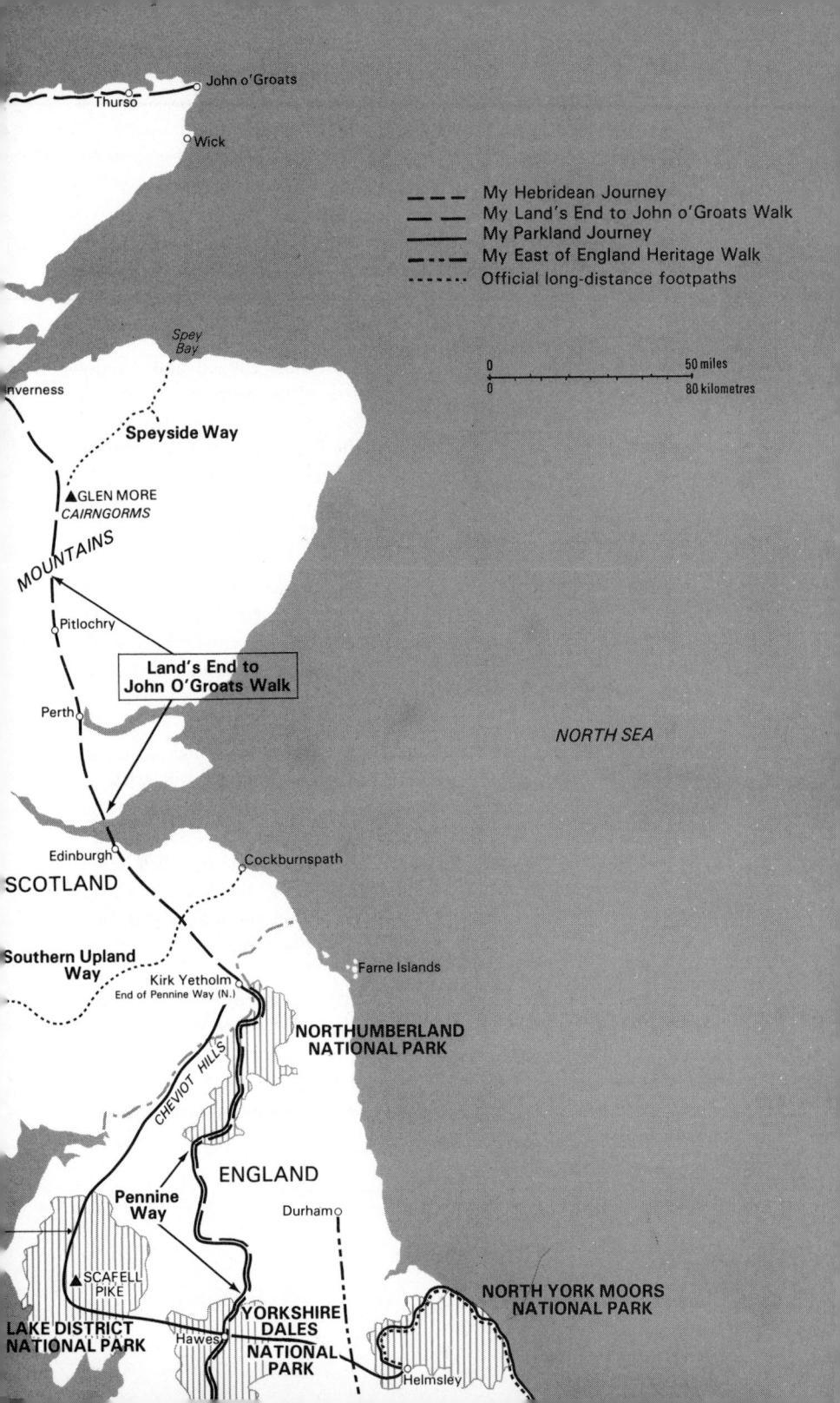

CHAPTER 6

Walking in Scotland

Scotland has always been the mecca of ardent walkers, for here you can get away from everyone and be self-contained as you walk over the mountains and glens. It has some of the most rugged and remote countryside in Britain, and has the fabled 'Munros' (p. 75), of which there are 279 separate peaks. Official footpaths are being planned, to supplement the existing routes such as the West Highland Way, but in the meantime there is limitless scope for making your own route. The Munro mountains present a challenge, and many people keep a book and tick off the ones they ascend; others visit the offshore islands, of which there are more than a thousand.

My first major walk of over 1,000 miles (1,600 km) was in 1970, when I linked together all the islands of the Inner and Outer Hebrides (p. 79). On the Isle of Arran, where I started, the northern mountains have some of the best ridge-walking in Britain. The walk was through a constantly changing scenery rich in wildlife and sea birds. It took me to Harris and Lewis, whose mountains are among the highest in the islands; to the Paps of Jura, three mountains of about 2,500 ft (750 m), which makes an ascent of all three in a day quite a challenge; and to Mull, with its secluded high mountains where few people roam. Approaching the end of the walk I crossed Skye and ascended the mountains of the Trotternish along a ridge which has no equal in Britain. I went on to the Cuillin Hills, whose ridges are the most challenging in Britain. After the walk I went to Fort William to ascend the highest mountain in Scotland, Ben Nevis (4,406 ft, 1,343 m), and to Glen Coe and its magnificent mountains and Aonach ridge.

The following year I explored our northern islands of the Orkneys and Shetlands (p. 81). I saw no other walker as I crossed flatter terrain; the highest point being Ward Hill (1,565 ft, 477 m) on the Isle of Hoy. Unlike many areas of Britain, the islands are covered with ancient monuments and numerous sea-bird colonies. The coastline is captivating and full of rock formations, including the towering 450 ft (137 m) Old Man of Hoy.

On my 1,600 mile (2,575 km) Land's End to John o'Groats walk

(p. 83) I crossed some of Scotland's finest mountains – the Cairngorms and the glens and mountains of the north-west corner. Here is Suilven, which at 2,399 ft (730 m) is not a high mountain, but its shape rising sharply from the surrouding area in isolation makes its ascent one of the best mountain days in Britain.

Scotland has so much to offer the experienced walker who wants to enjoy rugged country and to be self-contained. The scope of walking is huge, from gentle mountain-walking to the magnificent mountains of Torridon. The coast should not be overlooked, and many sections of the west side such as Ardnamurchan or Loch Nevis are among the hardest in Britain. The area deserves attention but needs respect, for even in summer it can snow high on the mountains.

Below is a personal selection of some of the walking in Scotland:

Southern Uplands
The Pentland Hills near Edinburgh provide good walking, as does the border country north of Kirk Yetholm. In the middle of the area are several interesting mountains, including Culter Fell. Across the whole area is the Southern Upland Way, about 204 miles (328 km) from Portpatrick on the west coast to Cockburnspath on the east coast.

Isle of Arran
Often described as Scotland in miniature, the island has few equals for scenery. The northern half contains Goat Fell and a large group of interesting mountains linked by an impressive ridge system. Glen Rosa makes an excellent base for exploring this area.

The Trossachs
This is the valley between Loch Katrine and Loch Achray, and also the surrounding area. Nearby are Loch Lomond and Ben Lomond, whose ascent from near Rowardennan is among the most popular walks in Britain. Starting in the area at Milngavie is the 92 mile (148 km) walk – the West Highland Way (p. 76) – to Fort William. Part of the route is close to the shore of Loch Lomond. Nearby is Arrochar and the Cobbler, a serrated mountain of 2,891 ft (881 m). To the north are Ben Lui, Ben More, Ben Lawers and other peaks.

Central Highlands
These contain two of the most popular areas, Glen Coe and Ben Nevis. Both have excellent walks and climbs. Glen Coe is dominated by

Buachaille Etive Mor, and flanked by Bidean nam Bian and the Aonach Eagach ridge. The ridge is 2 miles (3 km) long and provides, in summer, a most enjoyable rock scramble. In winter it is very tough and should not be attempted unless one is thoroughly experienced. The Ben Nevis area is again excellent walking but in winter the conditions equal anything in the Alps.

The Cairngorms
The largest high altitude mountain area in Britain containing four mountains over 4,000 ft (1,220 m). The plateau is arctic in nature and experiences ferocious weather even in summer. It should be treated with respect. The Lairig Ghru is one of the finest crossings to be made in the area. Ben Macdhui, 4, 296 ft (1,309 m), is the highest mountain here and the second highest in Scotland. The area is a popular ski resort, based on nearby Aviemore. To the east is the Speyside Way, which runs for 60 miles (96 km) from Spey Bay to Glenmore.

The Western Highlands
These contain some of the more remote mountains, some of them over 3,700 ft (1,150 m), which are well worth exploring. The most popular mountains are the Five Sisters of Kintail, just over 3,500 ft (1,100 m), which provide an exceptional mountain day. Nearby are several glens, including Glen Affric.

Northern Highlands
This is one of the few areas in Britain where you can walk all day through magnificent scenery and not see anyone. In the south is Torridon, whose mountain scenery is unsurpassed. Mountains with names such as Liathach, Beinn Eighe, Beinn Alligin and Beinn Dearg provide mountain-walking at its best. To the north are my favourite mountains, for they stand high above the area, in isolation – Suilven, Stac Pollaidh and Quinag, to name but three. Suilven, to my mind, is the most enjoyable mountain in Britain, not just to climb but because of its location and shape. Near the northern coast are Ben Hope and Ben Loyal.

Islands
Jura, in the Inner Hebrides, has the three Paps (approximately 2,500 ft, 750 m) which makes a very hard walk to climb all three in a day, about 20 miles (32 km) and 7,000 ft (2,130 m) of ascent and descent. Mull has a fascinating group of mountains in its southern half, including Ben More

(3,169 ft, 966 m). Skye has the Cuillins, and a camp and climb from Glen Brittle into the heart of them is a must for any mountain lover. Sgurr Alasdair (3,309 ft, 993 m), is the highest. For the rock climber the whole of the Cuillin Ridge in summer is the single finest mountain excursion in Britain. On the northern side of Skye is the Trotternish, which has a superb ridge-walk all the way down to the Storr, near Portree.

The Outer Hebrides have several mountains, such as Eaval on North Uist, which is a walker's nightmare to reach because of the numerous sea and land lochs. The Island of Lewis has a cluster of mountains and glens infrequently trodden, including Clisham (2,622 ft, 799 m), the highest mountain in the Outer Hebrides. One hundred miles (161 km) west of the Scottish coastline is St Kilda, the remotest and most beautiful island in Britain. Off the north coastline of Scotland are the Orkneys and Shetlands, two island groups which provide rugged walking amidst wild compelling scenery.

The Scottish Munros

A Munro is a mountain of more than 3,000 ft (914 m) and named after Sir Hugh T. Munro. In September 1891 his 'Munro's Tables' appeared for the first time in the *Scottish Mountaineering Club Journal*. Until then it was not known exactly how many mountains in Scotland were over 3,000 ft (914 m). Baddeley's *Guide* listed only thirty-one. There are 279 separate peaks and 541 tops. The most southerly one is Ben Lomond, above Loch Lomond; the furthest west is Sgurr na Banachdich in the Cuillins of Skye; the most northern is Ben Hope in Sutherland; and the furthest east is Mount Keen above Loch Lee.

Many people have attempted to climb all the Munros in one walk, but it was not until 1974 that Hamish Brown made the first complete crossing, during the summer months – 1,639 miles (2,638 km), 449,000 ft (136,855 m) of ascent and 289 peaks climbed. No one has done it in winter – yet!

FURTHER READING
M. J. B. Baddeley and C. S. Ward, *Thorough Guide Series*, Nos 1–20 (Dulan & Co, T. Nelson and Ward Lock, 1880–   )
Richard Gilbert, *Memorable Munros* (Cordee, 1978)
J. C. Donaldson and H. M. Brown (eds.) *Munro's Tables* (Scottish Mountaineering Trust, rev. edn. 1981). This book lists all the 3,000, 2,500 and 2,000 ft (914, 769, 615 m) summits in Scotland.

LONG-DISTANCE FOOTPATHS

The West Highland Way

95 miles (152 km) from Milngavie, Glasgow, to Fort William.
O.S. MAPS 1:50,000 LANDRANGER SERIES
sheets 41, 50, 56, 57 and 64

I had long wanted to walk this route, partly for sentimental reasons and partly because it was the first official long-distance walk in Scotland. I had met my wife in Drymen while on my coast walk; the route passes through her favourite part of Scotland. I had covered various sections of the route, having climbed Conic Hill, walked beside Loch Lomond, crossed Rannoch Moor and walked in Glen Nevis. Finding four days free between lectures in the autumn of 1981, I hopped aboard the Glasgow train, with a 35 lb (16 kg) rucksack containing four days' food, tent, stove and sleeping bag.

In Glasgow I switched trains and stations and caught the underground to Milngavie. Leaving the station I was surprised to find an information plaque (one of many on the route) detailing the whole route and the first 12 mile (19 km) section to Drymen. I planned to walk this, although it was now late afternoon and I would cover half of it in the dark. However, the first stretch of 6 miles (10 km) is quite rural as you leave the city environs and walk through forests and tracks beside Craigallian Loch. On the right were the imposing Campsie Fells. The final 6 miles (10 km) were straightforward, alongside an old railway line, then a road, into Drymen. It was a good stage to get the legs working and feel the rucksack on my back. So far the weather had been cool, with a sprinkling of rain.

Leaving Drymen the next morning I couldn't believe my luck. Although it was late October, there was not a cloud in the sky. Soon the route passes through forest before crossing open moorland and leading to the ascent of Conic Hill. The hill, some 1,200 ft (360 m) high, provides a magnificent panorama down towards Loch Lomond, the biggest stretch of inland water in Britain, to the Trossach hills, to Arrochar and to Ben Lomond, the most southern Munro. The summit was lightly covered with fresh snow. It was one of those rare mountain days when you are high up and able to view extensively in crystal-clear weather. It was mild, too, and I walked all day in shorts.

From the hill I descended to Balmaha and followed the path as it weaves its way along the eastern shore of Loch Lomond. It is delightful walking, sometimes through trees, sometimes along the shore, and all well waymarked with a white thistle in brackets on a wooden post. About 14 miles (23 km) beyond Drymen I came to the entrance to the youth hostel at Rowardennan, one of the three hostels on the route. Just before it on the right is the path leading to the summit of Ben Lomond. Here lies one of the beauties of this Way. It can be walked comfortably in a week, but since it passes through spectacular mountain country, one could very easily spend a couple of weeks walking to Fort William and en route ascending several mountains. I carried on to Inversnaid and stayed at the hotel there. Two miles (3 km) before, at Cailness, I could have camped, but time was short and I wanted to reach Fort William in three more days.

By the time I left Inversnaid the next day, the weather had changed considerably and become overcast and rainy. I planned to reach Tyndrum, 22 miles (35 km) away, before dark. First the route hugged the sides of Loch Lomond, passing close to a cave where Rob Roy stayed for a while. In places the path became quite rocky, with numerous bridges. Many people dislike this section, but it is short and at Doune, where there is a bothy for hikers, the worst is over. Three more miles (5 km) bring you opposite the Inverarnan Hotel, and the loch-walking is over. For the next 4 miles (6 km) the route follows paths and tracks beside the Fallock river. In the streaming rain the ground was oozing with water and I was soon soaked. The route does not go into Crianlarich, but passes west of it through forest and moorland. There is a youth hostel here in the summer months.

Two miles (3 km) beyond Crianlarich the Way crosses the A82 to continue up the valley to Tyndrum past the ruins of St Fillan's chapel, with its graveyard on the opposite side of the track. Near the railway station in Tyndrum is a campsite which I had planned to use, but, being wet through, I decided to stay in a hotel and dry out my clothing.

The route from Tyndrum to King's House, 19 miles (31 km) away, is regarded as the finest section of the Way, for you cross the lonely but impressive Rannoch Moor. At first the weather was just dull, but after half an hour's walking the rain began to fall and did not stop all day. I was soaked again! From Tyndrum the route follows the line of the old Glencoe road to Bridge of Orchy, 7 miles (11 km) away, with fine views up a wide valley. A short ascent over a hillside spur brought me to the Inveroran Hotel and the short road walk to Victoria Bridge and Forest Lodge. Beyond, the crossing of Rannoch Moor began along an old road. Although sheeting with rain and very cold, the walk was enjoyable, as I battled against the elements. I saw no one, nor did I see another walker on the whole route. The mountains were all lost in low cloud; even the view of Buachaille Etive Mor was denied me. On reaching the King's House Hotel, I was delighted to find it open and I was able to dry my clothes in their drying-room.

I left early the next day, determined to reach Fort William, 25 miles (40 km) away. As before, the rain poured down, but at least I had dry clothes on this time. Three miles from the hotel the route leaves the entrance of the Pass of Glencoe and ascends the Devil's Staircase, to pass through the mountains to Kinlochleven at the head of Loch Leven, 6 miles (10 km) away. The weather was now very cold, and soon I was walking in snow as I headed for the summit of the pass, which, at 1,800 ft (549 m), is the highest point of the West Highland Way. The ascent up the switchbacks at the staircase was made more interesting by the raging blizzard. I didn't linger on top but pressed on to Kinlochleven and its aluminium works.

I still had three bars of chocolate left so I did not stop in the village, but continued on my way, following an old military road. As across Rannoch Moor, the walk for the next 9 miles (14 km) was wild, remote and lonely. Upon reaching the tarmacked road near Lochan Lunn Da-Bhra, there is an alternative to the route. You can follow the tarmacked road to Fort William, or turn right and cross moorland and forest to reach Glen Nevis and its youth hostel. Although I knew it would be dark before I got there, I turned right and squelched my way through the peat and flooded paths. I descended to Glen Nevis in the dark, but I caught glimpses of Ben Nevis, rising proudly above the surrounding area. Down in Glen Nevis I walked along the road into Fort William, looking forward to a hot bath.

I had to return home the next day, which was a pity, for an ascent of Ben Nevis, Britain's highest mountain, would have made a perfect end to the walk. The West Highland Way is an exceptional route, and my only regret after four wet but most enjoyable days was that it ended at Fort William; I wanted to continue on through the glens. Next time I will walk it in summer, and admire some of our finest mountain scenery; also camp at some of the many wild sites that I passed en route.

GUIDEBOOKS

Robert Aitken, *The West Highland Way* (The Countryside Commission for Scotland – H.M.S.O., 1980) This has a detailed guide plus an official map, using the relevant sections of O.S. 1:50,000 Series maps.

Tom Hunter, *A Guide to the West Highland Way* (Constable, 1979)

The Speyside Way

60 miles (96 km) from Spey Bay to Glenmore.

O.S. MAPS 1:50,000 LANDRANGER SERIES
sheets 27, 28, 35, 36

This route is via Fochabers, Boat O'Brig, Craigellachie, and the Speyside disused railway line (which it follows for 28 miles via Aberlour, Ballindalloch, Cromdale and Nethybridge), with the final section to Glenmore via Abernethy Forest. The route, which should be open to the public in 1984, follows the river Spey much of the time and passes close to the Cairngorm mountains.

Southern Upland Way

204 miles (328 km) from Portpatrick (Wigtownshire), on the south-west coast of Scotland, to Cockburnspath (Berwickshire) on the east coast.

This will be the longest official footpath in Scotland – a coast-to-coast walk – via the Rhinns of Galloway, Glen Trool Forest Park, Dalry, Sanquhar, Wanlockhead, Beattock Summit, St Mary's Loch, Traquair, Melrose, Lauder, Longformacus and Abbey St Bathans. No date has yet been set for opening this path.

SCOTTISH ISLES

Hebridean Journey

O.S. MAPS 1:50,000 LANDRANGER SERIES
sheets 8 (Stornoway and North Lewis), 13 (West Lewis and North Harris), 14 (Tarbert and Loch Seaforth), 18 (Sound of Harris), 22 (Benbecula), 23 (North Skye), 31 (Barra), 32 (South Skye), 33 (Loch Alsh and Glen Shield), 39 (Rhum and Eigg), 46 (Coll and Tiree), 47 (Tobermory), 48 (Iona and Ben More), 49 (Oban and East Mull), 60 (Isla), 61 (Jura and Colonsay), 62 (North Kintyre), 68 (South Kintyre), 69 (Isle of Arran)

For more than twenty years I have been fascinated by our offshore islands, partly because it is an adventure just to get there by boat, and partly because you enter a timeless world which twentieth-century man has not devastated. My first island was Arran in the Firth of Clyde, full of beauty and rugged high mountains. I returned there three times to explore again those quiet sandy beaches and airy ridges. I visited other islands including Mull and Iona in the Inner Hebrides, as well as Skye, with its magnificent Cuillin ridge. To complete my Hebridean wanderings I also went to St Kilda, our remotest island 180 miles (290 km) west of Oban. The wind-battered cliffs there are of such arresting beauty that, for me, a visit to St Kilda is the 'ultimate' island experience.

During the summer of 1969 I walked around the island of Mull. A distance of about 300 miles (480 km), this was my longest continuous walk up to that time. It was then that I finally decided to leave industry and begin a life of walking. I also thought of walking through all the islands of the Inner and Outer Hebrides in one continuous walk. The more I thought about it, the more it appealed. Upon my return from Mull I resigned from my job and began planning my Hebridean Journey.

My route took me first of all around the Isle of Arran in late May 1970. By using the regular ferries I proceeded on to the peninsula of Kintyre, and then to the islands of Gigha, Islay, Colonsay, Jura, Mull, Coll, Tiree, Barra, South Uist, Benbecula, North Uist, Harris and Lewis, Skye, Eigg, Rhum and Canna. It took me fifty-four days to cover the 1,003 miles (1,614 km) on foot. Contrary to normal, the Scottish summer was splendid: in all that time I had only four days of rain! The rest of the time was a heatwave.

Footpaths were scarce, and I crossed the open country by map and sometimes by compass. In my hand were those red-covered 1-inch O.S. maps for which, now that they have been discontinued, I have a nostalgic affection. On each island I walked around its perimeter, visited the main historical sites – the castles and churches – and climbed the highest mountains. I camped out and carried in my metal-framed Bergans rucksack all that I needed – a weight of 45 lb (20 kg).

This was my first major walk, and I relished every moment, meeting the local people and observing their way of life: the peat hags, the whisky, and their easy attitude – 'there's always tomorrow'. The historical buildings, fascinating as ever, I had expected, but I was totally unprepared for the flowers and birds. I became so immersed in them that I bought field-guides and began putting names to the numerous flowers that I saw. Fortunately I carried binoculars and soon learnt the difference between the various sea birds. In June I often came across their nests and was frequently harassed by the swooping mother. Flowers that I couldn't name I photographed, to learn about them on my return.

For me it was a walk of discovery, not just about my surroundings but about myself. For fifteen years I had cherished an idea to make walking my career. Now I began finding out how I adjusted to continuous walking, as I suffered blisters and aching muscles, and learned how to use map and compass, and how to enjoy walking in torrential rain. Emotionally the climax came when I reached the Butt of Lewis, my northernmost point, with just over 700 miles (1,130 km) walked. I broke down and cried, for I knew I had found my true vocation – I just loved it. Wiping my tears away, I came down to earth, knowing I had 300 miles (480 km) still to walk.

I still look upon this walk as one of my most enjoyable, and at some future date I plan to return for another walk along the peaceful shores and lonely mountains.

Northern Isles Journey

O.S. MAPS 1:50,000 LANDRANGER SERIES
sheets 1 (Shetland, Yell and Unst), 2 (Shetland – Whalsay), 3 (Shetland – North Mainland), 4 (Shetland – South Mainland), 5 (Orkney – Northern Isles), 6 (Orkney – Mainland), 7 (Pentland Firth)

Following my success in the Hebrides, I looked at the atlas and thought about another walk. The other main island group lay off the north coast of Scotland, the Orkneys and Shetlands. I decided these were my next target.

In 1971 it was quite an undertaking just to get to the Orkneys. From Sheffield it took thirty-six hours to reach Thurso, where the boat departs for Stromness on the Orkney mainland. But the crossing made up for the hardship; from the boat I passed the 450 ft (137 m) high Old Man of Hoy, Britain's finest rock stack. My first island was Hoy, on the western side of the historic Scapa Flow. Stepping across the island I entered a peaceful world, only to be rudely awakened by a bombarding bonxie or great skua that took exception to my intrusion into his domain. The next day I walked above the Old Man and ascended Ward Hill, which at 1,565 ft (477 m) was the highest point in the Orkneys.

Returning to the mainland, I spent the next three weeks exploring the Orkneys as much as possible. They were not at all the same as the Hebrides, being much flatter and lusher. The Orcadians are said to be farmers with boats, but the Shetlanders are fishermen with farms, for the countryside is much harsher. I worked my way around the mainland, visiting all the key places, such as Yesnaby rock stack, Skara Brae – home of Neolithic man (2500 BC) – and Marwick Head, with its ledges full of nesting sea birds. I walked round the island of Rousay, just offshore but containing an amazing number of brochs, 2,000 years old, and chambered cairns.

From Kirkwall, the capital of the Orkneys, I wandered down the eastern side of Scapa Flow, crossing from island to island via the massive blocks of the Churchill Barriers. To reach the remoter Orkney islands was difficult, and I was not able to link them together to form part of a continuous walk, as I had done in the Hebrides. However, I did manage to visit and walk round Westray, Papa Westray and North Ronaldsay, the most northerly island in the Orkneys, where the sheep have to eat seaweed, as grazing land is precious.

I then flew to Sumburgh Head, the southern tip of the Shetlands. There was a boat service, but it took twelve hours and cost more. Before walking through the Shetlands I caught the weekly boat to Fair Isle, a solitary island between the Orkneys and Shetlands. The week spent there was fascinating. The cliff scenery, with caves and rock stacks, is amongst the finest in Britain. But what I had come to see was the bird life. The island is on the migratory route, and as many as three hundred different species have been sighted here. Two days after my arrival there was great excitement, for a bee-eater had been seen. I eventually watched him through binoculars, and studied his beautiful array of coloured feathers. I came to learn more about the sea birds, the kittiwakes, cormorants, shags, puffins, guillemots and terns. Before leaving the island, I purchased a scarf knitted in traditional Fair Isle patterns.

Back on the Shetland I began to walk through the mainland to Lerwick, its capital before the influx of oil. Offshore was the Isle of Noss, one of the most amazing sights I have ever seen: on its eastern side, with cliffs descending a dizzy 700 ft (213 m), is a gannetry. The gannet, with a wing span of 6 ft (1.8 m), is Britain's largest sea bird, and on this rock face nest some fifteen thousand.

Continuing northwards from Lerwick, I headed for the northernmost islands in Britain: Yell, Fetlar and Unst. On Fetlar I was lucky to see a snowy owl and her three chicks, the only place in Britain where they were nesting at that time. On Unst I walked to Herma Ness, and from the cliffs looked across at Muckle Flagga, the northernmost extremity of that archipelago. London was more than 900 miles (1,450 km) away.

Time was against me. I rushed southwards, back to the mainland to explore the western side of the Shetlands: Fethaland, Ronas Hill, the spectacular cliffs of Esha Ness, and the castled village of Scalloway. The weather had not been good, although it was July, and much of my three weeks in Shetland had been spent in pouring rain. I had walked about 900 miles (1,450 km), and back in Lerwick I caught the ferry to Aberdeen – happy but broke.

This walk and my Hebridean journey are described more fully in my book, *From Arran to Orkney*.

MARATHON WALKS IN BRITAIN

I feel that this is the place to mention two of my major British walks which, although not strictly speaking Scottish, nevertheless owe much to Scotland. They belong here not only because Scotland played so large a part in them both but also because, together, they represent a high point in my own walking achievements on the mainland of Britain. They should therefore come before I conclude this section of the book and turn to other walking areas, starting in the next chapter with Ireland.

Land's End to John o' Groats

The idea of linking the two extremities of the mainland of Britain has been popular all this century, at first travelling by car, but in the last twenty years either by bicycle or on foot. Barbara Moore's walk in the early 1960s was perhaps the first to catch the public's imagination. My own walk, which took almost eight weeks in the summer of 1977, was undertaken partly because I had long wanted to do it and partly in preparation for the coast walk which I was planning for the following year.

The direct route is 874 miles (1,406 km), but mine was over 1,600 miles (2,575 km), for I wanted to walk as many long-distance footpaths as possible. These included, in walking order: the North Cornwall Coast Path, the North Devon and Somerset Path, the Cotswold Way, Offa's Dyke Path, the Peakland Way, and the Pennine Way. My route through Scotland was up the eastern side, before crossing the Cairngorms and the mountains in the north-west. The final 100 miles (161 km) were along Scotland's northern coastline.

I was blessed with good weather and left Land's End in blazing sun.

Although it was late July, the heather was already out. Surprisingly, there were few walkers, except at popular centres such as Bude and Clovelly, and I had the coast to myself. A little beyond Minehead I left the coast and crossed the level ground to Glastonbury and the beautiful cathedral city of Wells. I headed on to Bath and the Cotswold Way. I did not walk all the way to Chipping Campden, for I wanted to walk Offa's Dyke, and near Painswick I left the route and aimed for Gloucester.

To reach Chepstow and Offa's Dyke, I walked down beside the Severn river. At Chepstow I felt ill from a bad tin of peaches I had eaten, but continued on the next day. By the time I had reached Prestatyn six days later, I felt back to normal. A quick walk across the Cheshire plain, crossing the Sandstone Trail, brought me to the Peak District. I resisted the temptation to call at my cottage, and it was not until I reached Edale that my friends found me. The next morning I set off up Grindsbrook and the Pennine Way for the fourth time in twelve months. It felt strange walking on familiar ground, knowing what was around the corner, and seeing places where I had stopped or camped before.

I was now well into my stride, and after ten days' walking I reached Kirk Yetholm. From here I was in new country. First I made for Edinburgh before crossing the Forth road bridge. To reach Perth, my next principal city, I entered my first glens and small mountains. After Perth I aimed for Inverness. The weather, although it was September, turned out to be excellent, with the autumn colours already much in evidence. My route too was of a high quality as I began threading my way through the mountains and glens of Cairngorm. I had planned to traverse the tops, but as I approached the Lairig Ghru the weather changed, with driving rain and gale-force winds. I kept to the glens instead.

Beyond Inverness I strode into a timeless landscape: there seemed to be nothing moving except for deer. For four days I wandered over the mountains and down the glens in perfect weather. The remote country-side was brought alive by the sun glowing in golden colours. On the fourth evening I looked across at my favourite mountain, Suilven, in Sutherland. Other solitary mountains came into view – Canisp, Stac Pollaidh, and Fionhaven in the far distance.

I reached the northern coastline of Scotland at Bettyhill. The camp-site owner, seeing me, asked where I had walked from. Land's End, I said. With true Scottish hospitality I was asked in for tea and a hot bath – my first for weeks.

The coast walk of 100 miles (161 km) via Thurso to John o' Groats was very pleasant walking, although nostalgic. Offshore across the Pentland Firth were the Orkneys, the scene of my second major walk. I reached John o' Groats after walking 1,608 miles (2,588 km) in fifty-seven days. Whilst this is always assumed to be journey's end, the true north-eastern point of mainland Britain is a mile away at Duncansby Head. I walked there and admired the view over to the Orkneys and down the east coast of Scotland and those magnificent rock stacks close to Duncansby Head.

Two days later, having managed to hitch a lift, I was in Fort Augustus. Everything was happening too quickly. I didn't want to return home just yet! I walked along the Caledonian Canal and Loch Ness to Fort William. That really was journey's end, and a group of friends 'rescued' me and took me home.

British Coast Walk

My walk in 1978 around the entire British coastline, and the three highest mountains of England, Wales and Scotland, was the culmination of my walks in Britain – for a while. The walk and preparation are well-documented in my book, *Turn Right at Land's End*, but as that walk was undertaken five years ago, I think it should now be seen in relation to my more recent walks.

The walk was a hard one, not because of the rugged terrain, but the sheer physical fact of walking nearly 7,000 miles (11,000 km) – more than 25 miles (40 km) per day, seven days a week, for ten months, carrying 50 lb (23 kg) of equipment. The whole exercise was like a military undertaking, with a master schedule and numerous commitments and appointments every day. The weight of this was also a heavy burden. The publicity arrangements, which I made myself, were daunting; I wish I had known what I was letting myself in for.

Today, I do not look upon the coast walk as the pinnacle of my achievements. Instead I view it as part of my progression.

Since the coast walk I have completed several other walks which are far harder and more demanding. My walking skill across all manner of terrain and in contrasting climates has improved; my physical strength has grown; and my mental approach, my ability to drive myself on, has become more effective. Each walk I perform better, and I complete the journeys in faster times than are normally reckoned. As I enter my fortieth year, I believe that for the next five years or so I shall be at my peak performance.

CHAPTER 7

Walking in Ireland

There is excellent walking in both Northern and Southern Ireland, but it is neglected by most walkers. In 1974 I walked the whole of the west coast from Cape Clear to Malin Head: in those 1,500 miles (2,400 km) I followed the coast, crossed mountains and visited more than fifty islands. Surprisingly, in four months I did not meet another walker and only four English people. I say 'surprisingly' for I found the people extremely helpful, and I passed through scenery that nowhere else in Britain can equal. The Ring of Kerry, the Dingle peninsula, the Burren, the Cliffs of Moher, Connemara and Donegal were all very impressive places.

Ireland has many 'Munros' – mountains over 3,000 ft (914 m) – and these are listed on p. 87. Like Scotland, Ireland has fewer footpaths than there are in England and Wales, but the maps are good and will help you to make the most of your visit. The numerous youth hostels and the Irish way of life will make your stay even more enjoyable. Peaceful walking in unfrequented and uniquely beautiful countryside is the reward for those who take the trouble to discover them.

On my west coast walk I went wherever I wished along paths, tracks, and across wild mountains. Not once did I meet any hindrance. Everyone was eager to show me the way. As one might expect in a place which has 'soft rain' every day, I crossed some of the boggiest land I have ever seen. But on these walks I saw a wide variety of flowers in abundance, the like of which has disappeared from most areas of the British countryside. The villages had many old churches of historical importance, and numerous Celtic crosses. I camped often on private land, where permission was gladly given. Only in the more popular areas, such as the Ring of Kerry, are there official campsites. At night I would walk along to the local pub, which had been open since mid-morning, and drink a glass of 'holy water' (Guinness) and join in an impromptu sing-song or listen to a fiddler playing. Southern Ireland is a place where a walker can enjoy solitude amidst a charming and very hospitable people.

Maps

I INCH TO I MILE MAPS (1:63,360 THIRD SERIES)

Nine sheets cover the whole of Northern Ireland and adjoining parts of the Republic of Ireland. These are produced by the Ordnance Survey of Northern Ireland, 83 Ladas Drive, Belfast, BT6 9FJ.

I ¼ INCHES TO I MILE MAPS (1:50,000 SERIES)

This series replaces the existing 1 inch maps, and they will cover the whole of Ireland. Eighteen sheets will cover Northern Ireland. The Ulster Way is being shown on these sheets.

APPROX. I INCH TO 4 MILES (1:250,000) HOLIDAY MAPS

sheet 1, Ireland North, showing the Ulster Way, is one of four sheets covering the whole of Ireland; sheet 3 (Ireland East) shows the Wicklow Way.

Eire (the Republic of Ireland) is also covered by ½ inch to 1 mile (1:126,720) maps and some areas by 1 inch to 1 mile maps (1:63,360 Series). The new 1:50,000 series (1¼ inch to 1 mile) is being introduced. The maps are available from The Ordnance Survey, Phoenix Park, Dublin, Ireland.

The Irish Munros

There are eleven summits in Ireland over 3,000 ft (914 m) high, and all lie in the southern half of the country (see p. 92 for guidebook details). They lie in four distinct groups: Lugnaquillia Mountain (3,039 ft, 927 m), in the Wicklow Mountains; Galtymore (3,018 ft, 920 m), south of Tipperary; Brandon Mountain (3,127 ft, 953 m), on the Dingle peninsula; and Carrantuohill (3,414 ft, 1,041 m), in Macgillycuddy's Reeks, near Killarney.

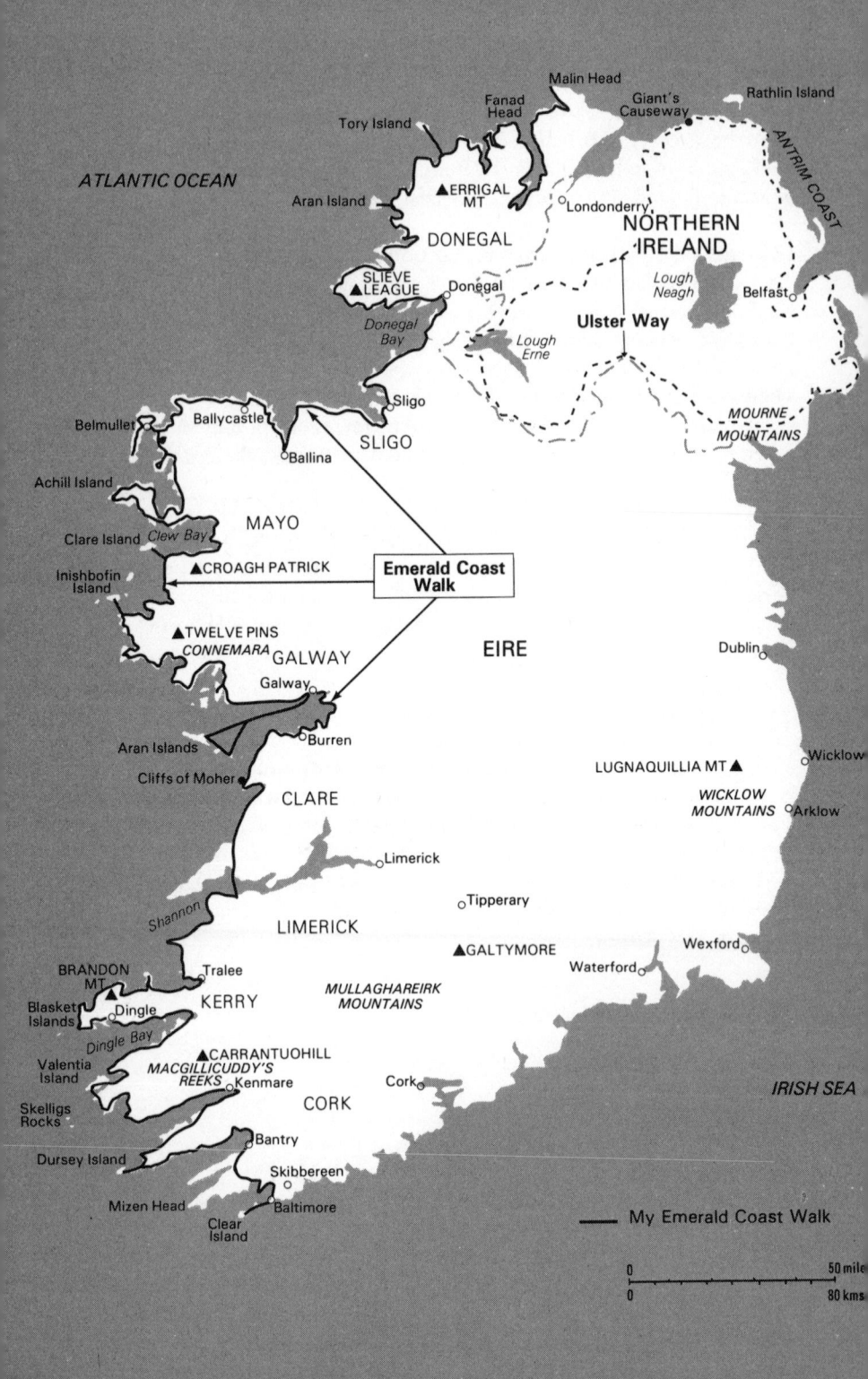

ATLANTIC OCEAN

Malin Head

Fanad
Head

Tory Island

Giant's
Causeway

Rathlin Island

▲ ERRIGAL
MT

Aran Island

Londonderry

NORTHERN
IRELAND

ANTRIM COAST

DONEGAL

SLIEVE
▲ LEAGUE

Donegal

Lough
Neagh

Belfast

Ulster Way

Donegal
Bay

Lough
Erne

Sligo

SLIGO

MOURNE
MOUNTAINS

Belmullet

Ballycastle

Ballina

Achill Island

MAYO

Clare Island

Clew Bay

Inishbofin
Island

▲ CROAGH PATRICK

Emerald Coast
Walk

EIRE

Dublin

▲ TWELVE PINS

CONNEMARA

GALWAY

Galway

Burren

Aran Islands

Cliffs of Moher

CLARE

LUGNAQUILLIA MT ▲

Wicklow

WICKLOW
MOUNTAINS

Arklow

Limerick

Tipperary

Shannon

LIMERICK

▲ GALTYMORE

Wexford

Waterford

BRANDON
MT

Tralee

KERRY

MULLAGHAREIRK
MOUNTAINS

Blasket
Islands

Dingle

Dingle Bay

▲ CARRANTUOHILL

Valentia
Island

MACGILLICUDDY'S
REEKS

Kenmare

Cork

CORK

IRISH SEA

Skelligs
Rocks

Dursey Island

Bantry

Skibbereen

Mizen Head

Clear
Island

Baltimore

My Emerald Coast Walk

0   50 mile
0   80 kms

NORTHERN IRELAND

The Ulster Way

A circular route of 450 miles (720 km) round the perimeter of Northern Ireland.

O.S. MAPS I INCH TO I MILE (1:63,360 THIRD SERIES)
sheets, 1 (North Coast), 2 (Londonderry), 3 (Mid-Antrim), 4 (Omagh), 6 (Belfast), 9 (South Down), 10 (Derry and Fermanagh)
1 inch to 1 mile strip maps are being made for sections of the route, as the Way becomes finalised.

The Ulster Way samples the best scenery in Northern Ireland and passes through the six counties that comprise the country. The path crosses mountainous country, including the Mountains of Mourne, wild moorland, forests, cliff paths and along the shore, and skirts Belfast. On the Antrim coastline, one of the finest in Great Britain with the Giant's Causeway, the route follows the National Trust's Antrim Coastal Path. Offshore is Rathlin Island. All the Northern Ireland youth hostels are very close to the Way. In some places the route is not completed, but most of it is waymarked with yellow arrows and signposts at roads. Numerous link paths take you into central Northern Ireland, especially to the shores of Lough Neagh.

Further details can be obtained from: The National Trust, Rowallane, Saintfield, Ballynahinch, Co Down, N Ireland; and Sports Council for Northern Ireland, 49, Malone Road, Belfast, BT9 6RZ.

SOUTHERN IRELAND (Eire)

The Wicklow Way

A route of 58 miles (93 km).

O.S. MAPS I INCH TO I MILE (1:63,360 SERIES)
sheets 'Dublin District' and 'Wicklow District'

The first account of the Wicklow Way was published by J. B. Malone in 1966. The route is being made a permanent feature by the long-distance walking routes' committee of COSPOIR (The National Sports Council). In 1980 the first stage was opened, and in 1981 stage two. The route traverses the eastern edge of the Dublin and Wicklow mountains, the largest unbroken area of high ground in Ireland. Much of the route is above 1,600 ft (500 m).

Details about the walk may be obtained from the Irish Tourist Board, PO Box 273, Dublin, 8.

Emerald Coast Walk

1,500 miles (2,400 km) up the west coast of Ireland, from Skibbereen in County Cork to Malin Head in northern Donegal.

In 1974 I spent June, July and much of August walking up the whole of the west coast of Ireland. Off this coast are more than three hundred unspoiled islands full of fascinating features, and my plan was to include as many of them as possible in a walk from the farthest point in the south-west, Cape Clear, to Malin Head, the farthest point in the north-west. The walk was inspired by the film, *Ryan's Daughter*. After seeing the extensive beach of Inch Strand and the vertical cliffs of Moher, I couldn't wait to see for myself the treasures of the Emerald Isle.

As always, it rained – soft rain – every day, but this did not detract from the enjoyment of the walk. I camped often, and was invariably made very welcome. Many times the locals were over-generous, walking ¼ mile (400 m) to give me eggs or plying me with pints of Guinness. At other times I stayed at youth hostels, whose basic rules and easy atmosphere made hostelling a pleasure. On a few occasions, to dry out, I stayed at bed-and-breakfast establishments.

I could find very little to read about walking in Ireland, and at that time no guidebooks existed. I was therefore unprepared for the breathtaking beauty of the landscape I was to see day after day. Even more surprising, in three months of walking I met no other walker. The roads were quiet, and if a car passed you, you looked at it in amazement.

I started off from Skibbereen in County Cork. A short walk brought me to Baltimore and the ferry to Clear Island. Heading north three days later, I crossed rugged mountains to Bantry Bay and the beautiful garden island, Garinish Island. After further mountain ascents across unfrequented terrain I reached the cable car to Dursey Island, a place which, ten years ago, had no post office, shop or pub. I continued around the coast to the abandoned copper mines at Allihies and on beside the Kenmare river.

The next section was particularly attractive coastal and mountain walking as I came round the shore and over the mountains to Ballinskelligs and the remarkable 700 ft (215 m) Skelligs Rocks offshore. Next I stepped onto Valentia Island and caught the ferry to the mainland from its northern end. I now embarked upon the walk around Dingle Bay and peninsula. Here at last I could see the fabled 4 mile (6.4 km) expanse of golden sand of Inch Strand. Later at Dunquin I visited the school used in the film, *Ryan's Daughter*. Offshore were the Blasket Islands, now abandoned, but I persuaded a boatman, after three pints of Guinness, to take me across. The sun shone brilliantly, and I was able to explore one of the most beautiful islands I have ever visited. Beyond was the Atlantic, and the next land mass was America.

I continued on along the shore to Tralee before crossing the Shannon river to gain County Clare. Here I entered some of the finest scenery, unmatched anywhere else in Great Britain. First were the towering cliffs of Moher, along the top of which I walked for 4 miles (6.4 km). Beyond, I stepped on the limestone pavement of the Burren. The pavement covers a huge area, and I spent a whole day crossing it. At Galway I boarded a boat to the Aran Islands, which I had seen from the Burren.

The Aran Islands are an extension of the limestone plateau, and are barren and windswept. The islanders have a struggle to exist and to grow crops there. The Islands are of course famous for their knitwear patterns, although many of the sweaters are made on the mainland. The ancient monuments are extensive, and I spent a considerable time passing from ruined church to cliff-top fort as I walked round. The islanders have their own special boats, called 'curraghs', which are extremely buoyant and are made from a wicker frame covered with tarred canvas. Because they are so delicate they cannot be dragged along the ground and have to be carefully lifted and carried.

Back on the mainland, I pressed on into Connemara, but bad weather ruled out an ascent of the 'Twelve Pins of Connemara'. I visited Inishbofin Island before continuing to Clew Bay and Clare Island. From there I could see Achill Island, one of the largest islands off the west coast, which I reached six days later, having walked around Clew Bay and ascended Croagh Patrick. In July each year the ascent is made, usually barefoot, by as many as 50,000 people on the annual pilgrimage.

North of Achill Island I crossed more mountains and peaceful coastline to Belmullet, Ballycastle and, after the Ox mountains, reached Sligo. For the first time, I had walked more than 1,100 miles (1,780 km) without a rest day. At Donegal, three days later, I decided to extend the walk by 200 miles (320 km), thus enabling me to walk more than 1,500 miles (2,400 km).

Donegal was the 'gem' of the walk. The scenery was devastatingly beautiful: Slieve League and its 1,600 ft (500 m) sea cliffs; the perfect deep U-shaped valley of Glengesh; Aran Island with steep spectacular cliffs, caves and rock stacks; Errigal Mountain; and Tory Island, a small but very attractive island.

Northern Donegal was also impressive, with extensive beaches at Tranarossan and Fanad Head. I was now on the final stage as I walked around Lough Swilly for Malin Head, which I reached with mixed feelings – intense sorrow that this long and magnificent walk had come to an end, and a firm resolve that one day I would walk the entire British coastline. As I stood on Malin Head I could just see the Hebrides, where my marathon walking began. Half an hour later the mist rolled in, like a curtain. I turned round and began walking south.

The Ring of Kerry

The route – a walk around the fabled ring – is only in the planning stage, but it is hoped that the project will go ahead and be completed in a few years' time. The walk will largely use old coaching roads. *An Taisce* (The National Trust for Ireland), together with the Laune Mountaineering Club, have been the prime movers in this project.

Other walks

COSPOIR, The National Sports Council, is planning to develop long-distance walks all over Ireland, using the Ulster Way as its model. There is every reason to hope that these plans will materialise, for the scenery is excellent and remote areas abound in Ireland, especially on the western side.

An information sheet, 'Hill Walking and Rock Climbing', can be obtained from the Irish Tourist Board (Dublin and London).

BOOKS ON WALKING IN IRELAND

J. C. Coleman, *The Mountains of Killarney* (Cordee)
J. S. Doran, *Hill Walks in the Mournes* (Cordee)
Joss Lyman, ed., *Irish Peaks* (Constable, 1982)
H. Mulholland, *The Irish Munros*; Guide to Eire's 3,000 ft mountains (H. Mulholland, 1980)
Irish Walk Guides: 1 South West, 2 West, 3 South East, 4 North West, 5 East (Gill & Macmillan, Dublin)
John Merrill, *Emerald Coast Walk* (Walking Boots, 1982)

CHAPTER 8

Walking in Europe

All European countries provide excellent walking, whether through high mountains or on gentler ground. In this chapter I will describe the principal walks that I have done, and then give information about walking in countries which I myself have visited. The emphasis, as before, will be on major long-distance footpaths, and there is a map on pp. 102–3 which indicates the six routes, known as E-paths, established by the European Ramblers' Association, as well as some of the French Grande Randonnée (GR) routes, and one of my own which links the E2 and the GR10 – a 2,800 mile (4,500 km) walk from Holland to the Atlantic coast of Spain via the Alps, the Mediterranean and the Pyrenees.

My first experience of walking in Europe was when, at the age of sixteen, I went to Norway as a member of a twelve-man expedition. We travelled by train from Bergen to Finse on the Hardanger glacier where, for a week, we learnt about glacier travel – how to move in rope parties across the ice, wearing crampons and carrying ice-axes, how to cut steps, and test snow-bridges for strength, and how to rescue someone from a crevasse. It was all absorbing work, and I enjoyed it to the full. The final two days were spent crossing a large part of the glacier by compass.

The next section of the trip was a 150 mile (240 km) walk through the mountains, carrying all our gear and staying in huts. Here I was introduced to the excellently run and maintained Norwegian hut system as we crossed the mountains. After two days in Oslo, seeing the Kon-Tiki raft among other things, we returned home.

Captivated by the Norwegian mountains, I came back the following year and spent another week at Finse. The glacier guide, with whom I had struck up a friendship the year before, began preparing me to qualify for a guide's certificate. I had come for a month, and in order to get further experience, I planned a long walk and glacier climb through the Jotunheimen area. Few places have fascinated me more. In three weeks I crossed thirty-two glaciers and climbed many of the highest mountains, including Norway's highest, Glittertind and Galdopiggen.

Although only just over 8,000 ft (2,450 m), they were a fitting climax to the walk. The feelings I experienced of being alone in mountains, depending on myself only, have never left me. Sadly, it was several years before I could go back there again.

My second experience of European walking was in 1960, when I headed for Switzerland with the intention of 'having a look' at the Eiger and its notorious north wall. I was not equipped for such a route but, with a couple of Germans, reached 10,500 ft (3,200 m) on the eastern flanks. I wandered around the Grindelwald valley for a few days, but the weather was unsettled, so I decided to move on. I hitched a lift to Zermatt to see that pinnacle of mountaineering, the Matterhorn.

The first night there I stayed at the Hornli Hut, and before dawn was ascending the 'tourist' route. There was considerable snow and ice, and it took us five hours to reach the Solway Hut at 12,500 ft (4,810 m). Here everyone, including the guides, turned back; so did I. I had two days' rest before an Australian joined me for another attempt. The weather was better this time but the route was still ice-covered. After eight hours' ascent from the Hornli Hut we were within 1,000 ft (300 m) of the top, but my companion was suffering badly from altitude sickness and we descended back to Zermatt after a 23-hour day. Reluctantly I went home, not realising that it would be nearly twenty years before I set foot in the Alps again.

When I did go to Europe again, in 1979, I decided to walk the Tour of Mont Blanc, a circular route of about 100 miles (161 km) which traverses the seven valleys bordering Mont Blanc – and which is one of the most beautiful walks I have ever experienced. Two years later I was back in the Alps, following the E4 for 700 miles (1,100 km) across Austria. The next year, 1982, was the year of my long European trek from Holland to the Atlantic coast via Nice, which took me through some of Europe's finest mountains and scenery. And most recently, in October 1983, I walked across Corsica along GR20, a little-known but remarkably enjoyable route.

These are the walks that I shall now describe.

The Tour of Mont Blanc

A circular walk of about 100 miles (161 km) around the base of Mont Blanc through France, Italy and Switzerland.
MAP: DIDIER & RICHARD 1:50,000 SERIES (Massifs du Mont Blanc Beaufortain)

Mont Blanc, the highest mountain in Europe at 15,771 ft (4,807 m), is surrounded by seven valleys. The massif borders France, Italy and Switzerland. The walking is hard and involves long ascents and descents, and frequently requires crossing passes that are over 8,000 ft (2,438 m) high. The weather is a constant factor, and it is not until late August usually that the route is entirely snow-free. In my opinion the walk is the finest in Europe, and the scenery will provide you with memories of remarkable beauty, day after day. Most of the route is waymarked by a red-and-white stripe on a rock or tree. It is not a walk to be taken lightheartedly because of the altitude, weather and rough terrain. It is essential that an ice-axe be carried and that you are equipped for mountain walking with good boots and adequate clothing.

To 'guide' me round the walk I used Andrew Harper's book, *Walking Guide to the Tour of Mont Blanc*. There are several maps, of different scales, to the area: I used the Didier & Richard edition – Massifs du Mont Blanc Beaufortain – 1:50,000 series. This map covers the whole of the walk and details the route with a blue line marked 'TMB' (Tour du Mont Blanc). All the variation routes are also marked, and the average times needed to walk between given points. This is the most significant difference from British walking. In Britain we can estimate how long it will take to cover a certain walk by the number of miles. In Europe, because of the difficult terrain and long ascents and descents, the sections are worked out in hours.

The following is a day-by-day account of my walk, and I hope it provides an insight into alpine walking. I set off on Wednesday, 22 August, and finished the walk ten days later on Saturday, 1 September, 1979.

DAY ONE – *Col de Voza to Les Contamines – 8 miles (13 km), 6 hours*
The guide recommended starting from Col de Voza because the majority of people would be coming on the direct train from Paris to St Gervais, and could then take the Mont Blanc tramway and alight at Col de Voza. This is what I did. It is normal to walk the tour anti-clockwise and, although it is against my usual practice, I agree that it is the best way. By starting from the col you have a magnificent view up the Chamonix valley. To descend into it would be wrong. It is far better to walk anti-clockwise and reach the breathtaking scene from the other side, bringing the walk to a stunning climax.

From Col de Voza the principal route of the TMB descends to the valley floor and mainly follows road walks to Les Contamines. I chose the variant route, as this brought me straight into high mountains. Two miles from the col, with largely gentle ascending, brought me to the mouth of the Bionnassay glacier. An alarming swing bridge, upon which no more than two people are allowed at a time, hung over a steep drop, down which the melting glacier water poured. The view up the glacier to the Aiguille du Goûter was stunning and gave me a foretaste of the scenery to be expected on the walk. After another mile of steady ascending I reached the summit of Col de Tricot, 6,955 ft (2,120 m).

The descent to the Chalet de Miage was steep and hard on the knees. At the chalet, where you can stay, I joined other walkers at the tables, sat in the sun and ate a huge sandwich. From my seat I gazed across at the glacier and the Dômes de Miage. To reach Les Contamines from the chalet needed another ascent, thankfully brief, to the Chalets du Truc. Again, food can be obtained here; indeed, throughout the whole walk there are chalets and refuges where food and overnight accommodation are available. I then descended through the trees to Les Contamines. Most villages had a Tourist Office, and from them I learnt where the campsite was. Although I did not need to carry full backpacking equipment, because of the abundance of places to stay, I felt it would give me greater freedom and would certainly be much cheaper. The campsite fee was modest, and the site was excellent, with showers, tables and chairs under cover where one could prepare and eat a meal.

DAY TWO – *Les Contamines to Les Mottets Refuge – 14 miles (22.5 km), 6 hours*
The first 2 miles (3 km) were relatively flat walking along the valley floor to the church – Notre Dame de la Gorge. Like many alpine churches, this one has beautiful paintings under the eaves, while, inside, the altar and surrounding area are exceptionally ornate. The next 4 miles (6.5 km) were steady climbing to the summit of the Col de Bonhomme, 7,641 ft (2,329 m). In the final stages several large expanses of snow had to be crossed. As always, the view from the col was absorbing and well worth the effort. A further mile of walking, basically maintaining height, brought me to another col – Col de la Croix-du-Bonhomme, 8,123 ft (2,476 m), my first col over 8,000 ft (2,438 m). Here is a magnificent refuge, reminiscent of a Scottish castle. Its location, offering a wide vista, is second to none.

As it was early in the day, I pressed on and took the variant route over Col des Fours, 8,743 ft (2,664 m). Again, large areas of snow had to be crossed. I left my rucksack at the col and climbed Tête Nord des Fours, which, at 9,045 ft (2,757 m), is the highest point on the whole walk. I had noticed the weather beginning to deteriorate as I left the refuge an hour before. While I was on the summit the clouds moved in at an incredible speed and, after taking a few photographs, I raced down to my rucksack and began the steep descent to La Ville des Glaciers. On the descent the cloud obliterated everything and it poured with rain. One hour previously it had been a perfect sunny day. Now the conditions were wild. I hurried on to Les Mottets refuge and stayed there. Moments later a thunderstorm erupted. That night I slept in my sleeping bag in the barn. On the floor were wooden boards, forming a long continuous pattern along both sides. A passageway ran up the middle. For washing you used the water trough outside. The barn could accommodate seventy people. Rather than eat meals prepared by the refuge owner I cooked my own, as I had set off with several days' food.

DAY THREE – *Les Mottets Refuge to Chalets Purtud – 14 miles (22.5 km), 8 hours*

The morning brought little change in the weather. Mist swirled around, it was damp, and there were no views. From the refuge a steady ascent brought me to the Col de la Seigne, 8,254 ft (2,515 m). The col is on the French/Italian border, and as I began descending I walked into Italy. The ascent had all been in cloud, but on the way I was fortunate enough to see a 'broken spectre'. This is an extremely rare phenomenon. With the sun behind me and cloud in front, a circular rainbow lit up the cloud and my shadow reached out to the centre of it. In the last twenty years I have only seen this happen twice: once on Scafell Pike at Easter, and the other on New Year's Day when I ascended the Paps of Jura. On all three occasions the temperature was just above freezing point.

As I descended from the col the miserable weather conditions evaporated and an exceptionally beautiful day emerged. Almost 2 miles (3 km) from the col I ascended the slope to the Elizabetta refuge. Of all the refuges I met on the tour, this was by far the most attractive, being perched close to a glacier. From the refuge balcony, and as the clouds dispersed to expose a rich blue sky, for the first time on the walk I could see Mont Blanc itself. After a short descent from the refuge the path accompanies a straight road past the Lac de Combal.

Although not really a lake, the waters from the melting glacier have formed numerous channels, creating a large area of marshy ground. Rising above this is the moraine wall of the Miage glacier. I left the route to have a look at this and the Lac du Miage, on which large chunks of glacier ice float.

The next part of the tour, from the lake to where I camped at Chalets Purtud, was spectacular. The perfect weather, coupled with the high path overlooking Mont Blanc and the Brouillard and Freney glaciers, made it an unforgettable experience. At Col Chécroui, I could look down onto Courmayeur. Seeing no campsites nearby, and plenty in the valley below me at the base of Mont Blanc, I descended to them. Walking through three countries meant that currency was a problem. Wherever possible, I used French francs, which were accepted in both Italy and Switzerland. At the campside that night they gladly accepted francs.

DAY FOUR – *Chalets Purtud to Lavachey via Courmayeur – 11 miles (17.5 km), 5 hours*

Most of the day was spent walking along roads. First I went past the church, Notre Dame de la Guérison, with the Brenva glacier opposite. Next I looked across at the Italian mouth of the Mont Blanc tunnel before curving round into La Saxe and Courmayeur. If time allowed, a whole day could be spent exploring Courmayeur and ascending Mt Chétif above the town. The view from the summit is quite exceptional over Mont Blanc. I returned to La Saxe, then pressed on to Entrèves and up the Val Ferret valley to Lavachey, where I camped.

DAY FIVE – *Lavachey*

The morning brought a complete contrast in the weather. Gone were the clear blue skies and hot sun. Instead it was grey and overcast, with low cloud and pouring rain. Ahead of me was the Col du Grand Ferret, 8,323 ft (2,536 m). In these conditions it was foolish to attempt the col. I stayed put and set off the next day in better weather.

DAY SIX – *Lavachey to Champex – 21 miles (34 km), 10 hours*

I was away early, at 7 a.m. The weather was much improved. To reach the col meant first of all walking along the valley to Arnuva before ascending past the Pré de Bar glacier. Here the ascent began to become steep and more awkward. The rain had fallen as snow at higher altitudes, and I soon found myself walking and climbing through 12 inches (30 cm) of snow. The final ¾ mile (1 km) to the col was an alarming experience: one slip and I would fall several hundred feet, and

I was glad I had an ice-axe to reassure me. The col kept disappearing in the cloud, and the temperature was extremely cold. My beard was frozen. I had gone by compass to the col, which is on the border with Switzerland. To continue, I took another bearing and began descending in atrocious conditions, with a strong wind and a 'white-out', when the snow and sky merge as one, offering no horizon. An hour later I was out of the clouds and snow and was being warmed by the sun. In fact I changed into my shorts!

Down in the valley I followed the road to the villages of Ferret and La Fouly, enjoying to the full the delicate beauty of the flowers growing all around in the alpine meadows. The scenery was dramatic, for, all the time I was descending, the sheer walls of Mont Blanc rose higher and higher. From La Fouly I pressed on to Praz de Fort, and the next couple of miles were a joy, the Swiss villages delightful with their wooden chalets. Near Issert I left the valley floor and climbed steeply up the side to reach the village of Champex, beautifully situated beside a lake and surrounded by high mountains. I camped at the northern end of the village.

DAY SEVEN – *Champex to Trient – 12 miles (19 km), 6 hours*
Instead of walking the usual TMB route over Bovine to Trient, I decided to take the variant route over the Fenêtre d'Arpette, 8,743 ft (2,665 m). It is a hard walk and one not to be taken lightly, but the scenic rewards are well worth the effort. From Champex it was steady ascending up the Val d'Arpette. After 3 miles (5 km) the ascent began in earnest as the path zig-zagged its way up and wove through a maze of boulders. In the final stages several small snow slopes had to be crossed before the final sheer slope to the col. It is really a small dent in a high ridge, and it gets its name from a boulder that straddled two others, forming a window. The view when reaching the summit over the Trient glacier is breathtaking.

The route down from the col to the valley floor is steep and cannot be rushed. As I descended, I kept stopping to admire the crevasses and séracs, towering ice pinnacles, of the Trient glacier. Two miles' walk along the valley floor brought me to Trient village, where I stocked up with food before camping on the village outskirts.

DAY EIGHT – *Trient to Argentière – 12 miles (19 km), 5 hours*
Almost immediately after leaving Trient I began the gradual ascent to Col de Balme, 7,188 ft (2,191 m). After only an hour of walking I was

uncomfortably hot and changed into shorts. Two hours earlier the tent had a layer of ice on it, and a thick frost had covered the ground. Most of the ascent to the col was across alpine meadows giving no hint of what lay beyond the col.

Gaining the col, the boundary of Switzerland and France, a breath-taking scene opened up before me. In front lay the whole sweep of the Chamonix valley to Col de Voza. To the left was Mont Blanc, the Bossons glacier, whose tongue reaches far down into the valley, and, crowning all, was the intricate jumble of the Aiguilles. It was a feast to the eyes as I looked at Aiguille Verte, Les Drus, Aiguille du Grépon and Aiguille du Midi, to name but a few. On the right-hand side of the valley were the smaller but impressive Aiguilles Rouges. This is the reason why you are advised to walk the tour anti-clockwise; for you reach this stunning view in the morning with the sun behind you. I stayed a long time, admiring the incomparable scene. Reluctantly I turned away and descended to the valley to Le Tour and Montroc, and I camped at Argentière.

DAY NINE – *Argentière to La Flégère – 8 miles (13 km), 5 hours*
Not a long day's walk, but one that included the *passage dangereux*, the hardest part of the tour. I retraced my steps from Argentière to Montroc and began the ascent up the valley side. The sides of the Chamonix valley are steep and high, and walking in them is a tough proposition. In Britain we have nothing equal in severity. Even the simplest walks become very exposed. As I approached the *passage dangereux*, a brown marmot sat on a nearby rock cleaning itself. I had seen several of these mammals but this was the closest I had been to one. The *passage dangereux* was an alarming climb, requiring metal ladders, hand rails and hanging ropes. The actual climbing is straightforward, but awkward with a load. Everything is heightened by the scale of the mountains and the 3,000 ft (900 m) drop that yawns between your legs. I was glad when after fifteen minutes I had completed the ½ mile (1 km) crossing.

The path from the top of the *passage* basically maintains height around the side of the valley to La Flégère, 6,158 ft (1,876 m). Before making my way there I continued ascending to 7,716 ft (2,352 m) to see the Lac Blanc. Unfortunately mist was swirling around, but the lake provides a lovely view on a clear day with the reflection of Mont Blanc in the water. I retraced my steps and followed the path to La Flégère.

DAY TEN – *La Flégère to Les Houches – 10 miles (16 km), 6 hours*
My last full day on the tour, and what a spectacular one. From La Flégère I contoured round the valley sides before beginning the ascent to Col du Brévent. On the way I saw a viper. Several signs during the last couple of days had warned that they were in the area and to take care. I was able to photograph it hurriedly before it disappeared under a boulder. At the col I walked into snow and, with my ice-axe ready, began the ascent of Le Brévent, 8,284 ft (2,525 m). Of all the beautiful views I had seen on the tour, I don't think any surpassed the one from the summit of Le Brévent. From here you can gaze right into the heart of the Mont Blanc massif; while Chamonix lies almost dizzyingly at your feet far down below.

After an hour of total absorption, I left the summit and descended to Bel Achat and Merlet, eventually crossing the river and entering Les Houches, where I camped. Two hours' walk the next morning would bring me to Col de Voza and the end of the walk. I visited the local supermarket and indulged in a roll of delicious new French bread and a litre of wine to celebrate. Sitting outside the tent, I soaked up the view to the Aiguilles.

DAY ELEVEN – *Les Houches to Col de Voza – 2 miles (3 km), 2 hours*
A short but steady climb brought me to the col, ending the circuit. As the day was still young, I continued ascending to the end of the Tramway du Mont Blanc, the station at Le Nid d'Aigle, 8,852 ft (2,698 m). From here I could look closely at the Bionnassay glacier. As a sort of finale to the walk, I continued ascending to the Tête Rousse refuge at 10,390 ft (3,167 m). The views were extensive on the ascent. Tired but well pleased at walking the Tour of Mont Blanc, I began the descent of several thousand feet back to Les Houches.

Looking back on the walk, I don't think I have ever enjoyed a walk more. The ever-changing grandeur of the scenery makes the effort a never-ending pleasure. This is one walk I can hardly wait to do again.

GUIDES
A. Harper, *Walking Guide to the Tour of Mont Blanc* (Cicerone Press, 1977)
T.M.B. (Topo Guide) French edition but with maps.

EQUIPMENT LIST
See p. 104.

EQUIPMENT LIST

The following is the basic equipment I carried on my walk round the
Tour of Mont Blanc (weight 50 lb, 22.5 kg):

1 Berghaus Cyclops Sérac No. 3
  rucksack
1 Black's insulation mat
1 Black's Icelandic Mummy sleeping
  bag
1 pair of Scarpa Bronzo boots
2 thick cotton shirts
1 pair of climbing breeches (Rohan –
  Superstriders)
1 pair of shorts
6 pairs of Norwegian ragg socks
  (3 long, 3 short)
Vest and pants
1 North Cape pullover
1 Berghaus Scirocco Gore-Tex jacket
1 Black's Merrillite tent

1 Camping Gaz globetrotter stove
7 Globetrotter gaz cylinders
1 pair of Gore-Tex gaiters
1 pair of Gore-Tex overtrousers
1 pair of gloves – nylon with fleecy
  lining
1 woollen hat
Large and small metal spoon
Silva compass, whistle, torch, first-aid
  kit, sewing kit, log books, guide and
  map
Cameras, film, lenses and tripod
Ice axe and crampons
7 Raven Foods Regal Range Main
  Meals
7 Raven Foods Regal Range Desserts

Across Austria

MAPS: FREYTAG UND BERNDT 1:50,000 AND 1:100,000
WANDERKARTEN SERIES

I set off in late June 1981 to spend five weeks on a fact-finding walk
across Austria, covering 700 miles (1,100 km). My plan was to walk the
alpine section of the European Route E4. The total route is from the
Pyrenees to Rust beside Neusiedler See on the Austria/Hungary
border. The Austrian section takes in some of the best mountain scenery
in the country, and includes the Kaiser and Karwendel Alps.

I decided to carry and use some different equipment from the usual.
My rucksack was made in Spain and was primarily a climbing sack of
about 70 litres capacity. It had no metal frame but was well padded. I
found the capacity restricting, with no side pockets, but the rucksack was
comfortable to carry and served me very well. For a tent I decided to go
as lightweight as possible and used a Phoenix Phoxhole, a one-person
tent made of Gore-Tex and weighing 2½ lb (just over 1 kg). The tent is
barrel-shaped and no more than 2 ft (60 cm) high at the front. Whilst I
like the principle of the tent, I found its size too small. I nicknamed it 'my
envelope', for I had to enter it feet first.

Getting information on the route proved difficult, and it was not until I went on a skiing holiday near Innsbruck that I was able to track down a guidebook to the route. It was written in German, which was a problem for me, but it did give basic maps indicating the route. I then purchased all the necessary 1:50,000 maps that cover the walk, and most of them had a red line with the number 4 beside it, indicating the line of the path. This was all the information I had, and it proved quite inadequate as the book route and map route differed frequently. Even out on the walk itself information was hard to come by, although I often found path signs with the route number on. The paths too are individually numbered and this number is also on the map. Typically, where the walk began, at Rust, the information office knew nothing about the walk or where it started! I did finally locate the route – 6 miles (9.5 km) from Rust.

I flew to Vienna and the next morning caught a bus to Rust. The weather was excellent – hot, sunny and a crystal blue sky. Rust was attractive, with storks nesting on the chimney pots, and the early part of the route was very pleasant. Starting almost at sea level I headed for the mountains, and it was a good six days' walking through vineyards and rural scenery before I came to any sizeable peaks. The paths were well signed, and I very rarely went wrong. There were no campsites, and the two youth hostels I had passed were full, so I had to stay in small hotels or pensions. However, I thought this would change once I was in mountainous country. It did not. The mountains were all limestone and provided some excellent walking across high alpine meadows and through rugged peaks along narrow paths. Before arriving in Austria I had joined the Austrian Alpine Club so that I could use their huts. I stayed at a few, but I did not like the extortionate prices they charged nor the total dependence upon them for mountain travel. In the whole walk there were only two campsites on the route.

To reach Eisenherz, renowned for its iron-ore mountain, the route crossed spectacular mountain scenery. Although well into July, the weather was bad, with freezing conditions and the summits covered with snow. Beyond Eisenherz were the Totes Gebirge mountains. The crossing of this range over steep snow-fields and through some wild limestone scenery was by far the best and most enjoyable three days of the whole walk. Here I was thoroughly enjoying it, although the weather had so far been mixed. The next day brought rain, and for the remainder of the walk – three and a half weeks – it rained eight hours every day.

I headed on through the Salzburger Kalkalpen, crossing mountains, through forests and past several impressive castles. By now the signposting of the route had deteriorated, and it was only guesswork as to whether I was on the right path. Information on the ground differed greatly from what the map and guide said. Because of the continuous rain, I could not attempt the high mountains, and instead I began walking through the valleys, making my own route. It became extremely frustrating, for I should have been walking through some of Austria's finest mountain scenery, in the Kaiser and Karwendel Alps. I saw little as they were lost in cloud. Snow was now a problem, and was as low as 2,000 ft (600 m) although it was late July. Warnings were given out over the radio not to go into the mountains because of the risk of avalanches.

It was proving to be the worst summer for years, and I had no option but to keep to the roads and stay in hotels to dry my clothes every night. I also adopted the Austrian way of walking and carried an umbrella! At the Rhine in Liechtenstein I ended the walk.

I left with mixed feelings. I was not impressed by the signposting or the information about the walk, and I disliked the hut system, which denies one the freedom that camping affords. I had been unlucky with the weather and perhaps with the route, but surprisingly I had not met another hiker, apart from a few weekenders, on the whole walk. I knew, though, that the Alps offer glorious possibilities for walkers, and I would not allow myself to be deterred by a single disappointing experience.

GUIDE
Europäischer Fernwanderweg E4 (Kompass-Wanderführer) (Deutscher
   Wanderverlag)

European Trek

I had long wanted to do a walk in Europe that included as much alpine walking as possible. Following my abortive walk in Austria the year before, therefore, I returned to the continent in 1982 to embark on a route of over 2,000 miles (3,200 km). I started in late May at Bergen op Zoom on the coast of Holland, and my route (the European long-distance footpath E2, which coincides for much of the way with the French GR5) took me first through Belgium and Luxembourg, and then across the Jura Alps in France to Lake Geneva.

It took me three hours to reach Belgium after leaving the Dutch coast. The weather was exceptional as the continent sweltered under a heatwave. I had nine days of heat before two weeks of rain and storms. The walking for the first 400 miles (650 km) was flat, and I met no other walkers, just hundreds of cyclists. I carried 45 lb (20 kg) on my back and camped out almost every night. Having passed through Liège, the terrain became more hilly as I walked through the 2,000 ft (600 m) hills of the Ardennes.

Luxembourg came as a surprise. This small principality was a scenic gem, with delightful walking through wooded river valleys and past romantic castles perched high up in the hills. On gaining the river Moselle, which is the border between Germany and Luxembourg, I entered the fabled wine-growing area. At first I drank little, but with a litre of wine costing no more than a litre of milk, I soon began to drink more. The camping was also enjoyable, for one could pitch the tent in a vineyard and sample the different wines.

I entered France with regret, for I had really enjoyed the walk through Luxembourg. But my spirits quickly revived as I began ascending higher mountains and climbed my first 1,000 m (3,280 ft) peak of the route. My reason for choosing to walk across the flat first, before reaching the mountains, was to build up my fitness. The plan worked well, for although I had had five weeks in the Himalayas before this walk, I was still not as fit as I wanted to be. Walking 26–27 miles (42–43 km) a day soon caused me to shed weight, and by the time I had reached the Jura Alps (which are not very high or rugged) my muscles were nicely toned, my back was used to the load, and my mental attitude was ready for the long climbs ahead. At the Ballon d'Alsace, another wine-growing area, on a mountain well over 1,000 m (3,280 ft) high, I had the cherished view across to Lake Geneva and the high snow-capped wall of the Alps. I knew that in ten more days I would be there.

At Nyon, on the shores of Lake Geneva, I turned away from the GR5 and the red-and-white blazes. I could not resist entering Switzerland to do a high-level traverse across her mountains. I walked around the shore to Montreux, where I began ascending 8,000–10,000 ft (2,500–3,000 m) passes, first to Château-d'Oex, before Gstaad, Kandersteg, Mürren, Grindelwald and on to the Grimsel pass. The scenery was outstanding and, being mid-June, there was still plenty of snow on the passes, making an ice-axe essential. The Lauterbrunnen valley and the Eiger north face were the finest sights – both seen in the best of weather. From the Grimsel pass I descended the Rhône valley for two days of relatively flat walking to Martigny. Here I began ascending once more into France and Chamonix, picking up the GR5 again to do the 'Grande Traverse' of the French Alps to the Mediterranean at Nice.

This traverse is supposed to take thirty days. It is a hard mountain-crossing of unyielding passes, with long ascents and descents to the valleys. I felt in top form, and the weather was glorious – exceptional for July. Apart from a thunderstorm at the Col de Bonhomme I had nothing but sun. I walked long and hard every day, causing the locals to shake their heads in wonderment. They had never before seen a walker doing in one day what they did in three. Fourteen days after entering France I reached Nice, with a little over 60 miles (100 km) walked in the last thirty-six hours. I was tired, but there was a reason for my haste. I had a mail drop at the Post Office; I wanted to get there before Saturday lunchtime. I arrived on Friday evening.

I had one major problem which I had never experienced before: my boots had split in two. The trouble began in Switzerland, but I pressed on. In the French Alps the boots became a serious worry, as the metal shanks had split. I had to reach Nice, for I knew I would be on flatter terrain and could walk in training shoes while I began the task of breaking in a new pair of boots. I searched Nice, eventually succeeding in finding a pair, and continued on my way.

The routes inland were parched from the relentless heat, so, rather than walk along waterless trails, I hugged the French coast as far as the Spanish border. It was a startling contrast, going from the rugged loneliness of the high Alps to the crowded beaches of the Mediterranean and the topless beauties. After four days of walking my new boots were causing me discomfort. The upper cuff was higher than in my previous pair and was rubbing uncomfortably, with the result that both my ankles had become swollen. I walked in trainers for a day, but found that I became much more tired wearing lightweight footwear than heavy boots. At Toulon I bought another pair of boots, lighter and more comfortable. I reckoned that they would at least enable me to keep walking 26 miles (42 km) a day. Two hundred miles (320 km) further on at Arles I finally found a good pair of boots that fitted well. I moved into these and began breaking them in. Seven hundred miles (1,100 km) later, and halfway through the Pyrenees, the boots at last felt comfortable.

Five hundred miles (800 km) of Mediterranean walking brought me close to the Spanish border at Banyuls. Here, after a final swim in the warm sea, I set off across the Pyrenees, following part of GR10 and the High Level route. I had always felt that to walk through Europe you should not only cross the Alps but traverse the Pyrenean mountain chain, from the Mediterranean to the Atlantic at Hendaye. Whilst these mountains may not be as high or as rugged as the Alps, they are certainly a great challenge and a splendid mountain crossing from coast to coast. I met very few walkers, and no one at all attempting the whole crossing. (I had met only about thirty walkers in the French Alps.) The scenery was impressive, and the route wove its way through the mountains, across high passes with numerous options, which I quite often chose, to ascend the nearby 9,000–11,000 ft (2,750–3,350 m) peaks. Again I surprised the locals at my pace. Fifty days is the accepted crossing time; I did it in twenty-six.

Whilst I still camped most nights, I did stay in several *gîtes-d'étape*. These very well maintained and accommodated huts are largely cared for by the Randonnée Pyrénée Organisation. Most are run by local families who reside there, and although you can cook for yourself, meals with the family are very cheap. There are showers, bunk beds, and sometimes a washing machine. I did not make reservations in advance.

After two months of constant sunshine, it seemed almost an affront that rain should come. The weather became highly volatile, and on one occasion I was caught on a mountain summit in a thunderstorm. I put the rucksack and ice-axe well away from me, and huddled under the tent to keep dry. For three hours the storm raged and lightning flickered all around me. During a lull I quickly descended to a mountain hut 2,000 ft (600 m) below, which was crowded with walkers taking shelter. I never quite understood the weather pattern. Whereas in Britain a storm normally only lasts an hour or two and then disappears, in the Pyrenees it would hang around for twenty-four hours or more. A little over halfway I retreated back to the *gîte* where I had stayed as the storm and torrential rain cascaded down. It rained for thirty-six hours.

Although I originally planned this as a 2,000 mile (3,200 km) walk, I had soon realised that distances in the guidebooks, especially in the Pyrenees, were grossly understated. I reached Hendaye on 12 September, seven days behind schedule but having walked 2,800 miles (4,500 km) in 107 days; my best performance so far. I was tired, very tired, with over 500,000 ft (152,000 m) of ascent behind me. I felt little elation – just awareness that this was journey's end. The next morning I walked into Spain and boarded the boat back to Britain.

Across Corsica

In October 1983 I set off along GR20, a short but demanding walk across the island of Corsica, and one that I enjoyed greatly. I had heard about the walk from many French people, but it is little-known in Britain. The route starts in the north near Calvi, at Calenzana, and traverses the mountains of the National Park to Conca near Porto Vecchio on the south-east coast. Although only 104 miles (167 km) long, the guidebook states that it takes fifteen days to walk. I do not accept that: I did it comfortably in nine days, and three of those were half-days. However, the walk is hard, very rugged, remote, and prone to vicious thunder-storms. Because of its mountainous nature you have about 50,000 ft (15,240 m) to ascend, often rock-scrambling, and several very steep descents. It is not a walk for the unfit.

As the walk is in a French National Park, camping is allowed only in emergency, such as a storm. The route has fifteen refuges (huts) between five and seven walking hours apart. They are fully equipped, with calor gas, cutlery, crockery, tables, chairs and bunk beds. It is a splendid hut system, each hut having space for twenty-four people. During the busy months – mid-June to mid-September – a guardian looks after the building and collects your money. In 1983 this was 20 French francs a night – about £2.00.

You will need to carry all your equipment, including a stove, sleeping bag and tent for emergencies. Food is a problem as the route only passes close to one village, Vizzavona. You will therefore have to carry about four days' food and eat where you can, or even drop off the route to resupply.

In July and August the route is very popular, with as many as 1,000 people walking it at one time. After 15 September most people have gone and it is quiet again, but still very warm at 26°C (79/80°F). For this reason I went in early October. I had excellent weather – T-shirt and shorts everyday – and met only twenty other people walking the route.

Before I set off I heard numerous stories about the difficulty of the route and the queues at the fixed ropes and chains. The route is certainly hard physically because of its continuous ascents and descents. The fixed chains are only in one place – Col de la Solitude. Here you have to descend 600 ft (183 m) of steep rock, and, after a traverse, ascend 800 ft (244 m). Much of it is safeguarded by fixed ropes and chains. Like the rest of the route, it is well located and easy to follow, and you should experience no problem.

As with all the Grande Randonnée (GR) paths, the whole route is well blazed with red-and-white markings on rocks and trees throughout its length. The guidebook has detailed maps and trail profile and these, together with the estimated walking time, give a clear picture of what the walk entails. You can get more detailed maps for different areas of the walk but I found the guidebook quite adequate. For those wanting a walk in good mountains with the Mediterranean sun, I cannot think of a better location than Corsica.

GUIDEBOOK
GR20 (Fédération Française de la Randonnée Pédestre)

OTHER WALKS IN EUROPE

So far in this chapter I have described only those walks in Europe which I have undertaken myself. Fortunately for readers who may be tempted to explore other parts of the vast network of European footpaths for themselves, there is no shortage of information which can be obtained easily enough, if one knows where to seek it, from books, clubs and other such organisations. Partly for this reason, and partly because it is not possible in a single chapter to offer more than a few signposts to European walking, I shall devote the remaining pages to sharing information which I have learned from my own experiences and enquiries over the years, and which I hope may help to point others in the right direction.

E-paths

I have already referred to the six major long-distance footpaths established by the European Ramblers' Association. Their routes, which may be seen in outline on the map on pp. 102–103, are as follows:

E1 from Flensburg in West Germany, on the border with Denmark, to Pegli near Genoa in Italy, i.e. from the North Sea to the Mediterranean, via Lake Constance and the Gotthard pass – 2,422 km (about 1,500 miles).

E2 from Bergen op Zoom in Holland to the Mediterranean at Nice, via the Ardennes, Luxembourg, the Vosges, the Jura and the Alps – 1,957 km (about 1,300 miles).

E3 from Royan, on the Atlantic coast of France, to Marktredwitz in West Germany, close to the frontier with Czechoslovakia, via the Ardennes, Luxembourg and Bavaria – 2,295 km (about, 1,400 miles).

E4 from Rust in Austria, near the Hungarian border, to the Pyrenees at Bourg-Madame, via Salzburg, Lake Constance and Grenoble – 2,200 km (about, 1,350 miles).

E5 from Lake Constance in Switzerland to Venice in Italy, via the Austrian Alps, Bolzano and Verona – 600 km (about 400 miles).

E6 from the Baltic at Copenhagen, Denmark, to the Adriatic at Rijeka, Yugoslavia, via Germany and the Austrian Alps – 2,796 km (about, 1,700 miles).

Books with sketch-maps giving details of these walks, printed in German and known as *Kompass-Wanderführer*, are published by Deutscher Wanderverlag, Dr Mair & Schnabel & Co, Haussmannstrasse 66, D-7000 Stuttgart 1, West Germany.

France

Grande Randonnée (GR) routes

The whole of France is criss-crossed by a series of long-distance footpaths called *sentiers de grande randonnée*, each with its own number. The routes are too numerous to list here – I have already referred to GR5 (the French designation for the E2), GR10 (which traverses the Pyrenees from the Atlantic to the Mediterranean), and GR20 (which crosses Corsica) – but details may be obtained from the Fédération Française de la Randonnée Pédestre, Comité National des Sentiers de Grande Randonnée, 92 rue de Clignancourt, 75883 Paris, France, which has information about all the routes, and offers a free map as well as advice about the guidebooks and regional maps needed for each walk.

Walkers in France are exceedingly well catered for, with around 25,000 km (about 16,000 miles) of paths marked. A good general guide to exploring France on foot is Rob Hunter's *Walking in France* (see Bibliography).

The Alps

Seven European countries have their own Alpine Club – Austria, France, Germany, Italy, Liechtenstein, Switzerland and Yugoslavia. Before my walk across Austria I joined the Austrian Alpine Club, the headquarters of which are in Innsbruck but which also has a branch in England (address: 13 Longcroft House, Fretherne Road, Welwyn Garden City, Herts). The club was founded in 1862 and now has more than 200,000 members. The UK branch was formed in 1948 and is the largest mountaineering club in Britain.

Membership of the club gives access to 983 huts in Austria, which are normally open from the beginning of July to mid-September. There are other benefits too, including reduced hut fees and rail fares, and the club arranges alpine tours and courses. The UK branch publishes a quarterly newsletter, holds lectures, and has an outdoor activities programme.

The address of the Austrian Alpine Club, which also has an office in Vienna, is: Österreichischer Alpenverein, Wilhelm Greil Strasse 15, A-6010 Innsbruck, Austria.

The Swiss Alpine Club also has a branch in England (address: Swiss Centre, 1 New Coventry Street, London, W1V 3HG). Most members of the Swiss Club are climbers, but there are benefits for walkers too. Lectures and meetings are organised regularly, including an annual summer meeting held in the Alps, and members (of whom there are two kinds, full and affiliate) have the use of a hut in Patterdale in the Lake District, and of a cottage in North Wales.

The address of the club in Switzerland is: Schweizer Alpin Club/ Club Alpin Suisse, Helvetiaplatz 4, 3005 Bern, Switzerland.

The other European Alpine Clubs do not have branches in Britain, but their local addresses are as follows:

Club Alpin Français, 8 rue de la Boétie, 75008 Paris, France.

Deutscher Alpenverein, Praterinsel 5, D-8000 Munich 20, West Germany.

Club Alpino Italiano, Via Ugo Foscole 3, 20121 Milan, Italy.

Liechtensteiner Alpenverein, F1–9490 Vaduz, Liechtenstein.

Planninarski Savez Jugoslavia, Dobrinjska 10–1, Belgrade, Yugoslavia.

Austria

The Austrians operate an award system – gold, silver and bronze – based on the length of time taken to complete a walk, and subject to control stamps being obtained at the various specified places. Long-distance footpaths include:

1. The Nordwaldkammweg (NWKW), opened in 1960, was the first waymarked long-distance path in Austria. The walk is 140 km (87 miles) long, and it runs from Dreisselberg to Harbach. Part of the route follows the Austria/Czechoslovakia border, and walkers must keep to the waymarked route. It usually takes six days.

2. The Kamptal-Seenweg, which is 100 km (62 miles) long, runs from Rosenburg to Nebelstein, and five days are normally allowed.

3. The Northern Alpine East-West Footpath, inaugurated in June 1975, begins at Bregenz and ends at Vienna. It is approximately 1,000

km (624 miles) long, and 50–60 days should be allowed to walk the whole route. There is a guidebook, *West-Ost Weitwanderweg '01'*.

Full details of these walks, and of available guides and maps, may be obtained from the Austrian Alpine Club (see under *The Alps* above). Another useful source of information is the Austrian National Tourist Office, 30 St George Street, London w1.

Switzerland

There is an extensive footpath system in Switzerland, and about 35,000 km (22,000 miles) have been signposted. The Swiss Footpath Association, which has been responsible for this work, has also indicated difficult walks with additional red/white symbols, and provides details of the average time needed to reach your destination. The address of the Association is: Schweizerische Arbeitsgemeinschaft für Wanderwege, In Hirshalm 49, CH-4125 Riehen, Switzerland.

Information about walking tours may be obtained from local tourist offices in Swiss towns. The seven long-distance routes listed below were suggested by the Swiss National Tourist Office in London, which will also give details of relevant maps and guidebooks:

1. A central lowlands itinerary from Romanshorn to Geneva (eight to ten days).

2. A tour along the alpine foothills from Rorschach to Vevey (about eight days).

3. The Alpine Pass route, which takes in fourteen passes between Sargans and Montreux (twelve to sixteen days).

4. The Jura Ridge itinerary, from Zürich to Crassier (ten to fourteen days). This is the ridge route of the Swiss Jura Association.

5. A north to south itinerary from Lugano to Basle (ten to fourteen days).

6. The Rhine-Rhône itinerary from Coire to Lausanne (ten days).

7. La Haute Route, the classic high-level traverse from Chamonix in France to Zermatt in Switzerland, 175 km (110 miles) with 10,633 metres (34,899 ft) of ascent. Allow about ten to fourteen days.

The address of the Swiss National Tourist Office is the same as that of the Swiss Alpine Club referred to above: Swiss Centre, 1 New Coventry Street, London, w1v 3HG.

Sweden

Often referred to as 'one enormous national park', Sweden is criss-crossed with waymarked footpaths and routes, and is a hiker's paradise. The law of *Allemansrätt* (Everyman's Right) allows the walker to wander anywhere without permission (as long as landowners' privacy is respected).

The southern half of the country contains several long-distance routes, including:

1. Sörmlandsleden, south of Stockholm, the longest route in Sweden (500 km, 320 miles), and divided into thirty-eight stages.
2. The East Coast route, near Oskarshamn (160 km, 100 miles).
3. Skaneleden, in the southern corner (220 km, 137 miles).
4. Siljansleden, near Lake Siljan (340 km, 212 miles).

The northern half of Sweden, Lapland, is one of Europe's last great open spaces. It contains several National Parks, including Sarek, which is the largest wilderness area in Europe. No huts or trails exist here: you have to be competent and self-sufficient to explore the area. In other parts of Lapland there are huts run by the Swedish Touring Club, and many long-distance marked routes. The name and address of the club are: Svenska Turistforeningen, Stureplan 2, S-103 80 Stockholm, Sweden.

A leaflet, *Hiking in Sweden*, may be obtained from the Swedish National Tourist Office, 3 Cork Street, London, W1X 1HA.

Norway

Like Sweden, Norway is still largely unspoilt and is a marvellous country for walking. Not only does it have a great variety of walks, with good maps and paths and an excellent hut system, but it also has mountains to ascend and impressive glaciers to cross or climb (some of them the largest in Europe), as well as lakes, rivers and fjords. Among the finest walking areas to explore are the Hardanger plateau, Jotunheimen, Rondane, and northern Norway.

The Norwegian Mountain Touring Association, formed in 1868, has done much to make walking both safe and enjoyable for its members, with an efficient system of reasonably priced huts and lodges to stay at, and cairned routes connecting them. Advance booking is not accepted – accommodation will be found for everyone – and the lodges are open from late June until mid-September. Membership of the Association, which is called Den Norske Turistforening (DNT), is obtainable from the Norwegian State Railways Travel Bureau, 21/24 Cockspur Street, London SW1, or direct from the DNT at Stortingsgaten 28, N-Oslo 1, Norway.

A guidebook, *Mountain Touring Holidays in Norway* by Erling Well-Strand, published by the DNT, is available from Stanford Ltd, 12–14 Long Acre, London, WC2E 9LP. Further information may be obtained from the Norwegian National Tourist Board, 20 Pall Mall, London, SW1Y 5NE.

I am well aware that this short account of walking in Europe is incomplete, for it is based almost entirely on my own experiences and on the knowledge that I have gained from them. That it should end with Scandinavia does not mean that there are no other countries worth exploring on foot, merely that I have not myself been to them yet and therefore feel unqualified to offer advice about them. I am conscious, for example, that I have only referred in passing to Germany, where the habit of walking is perhaps more deeply rooted and of longer standing than in any other European country, and where the facilities for walkers are, I understand, at least as good as those to be found elsewhere. But I cannot speak of them from first-hand experience, any more than I can speak of Italy, Spain or Portugal, and I therefore prefer to let this chapter end where it began, with Norway, the country where I had my first few formative weeks of walking outside Britain almost twenty-five years ago, and for which I have retained a special affection ever since. Norway is certainly a country to which I shall hope to return whenever the opportunity comes my way.

1 *a* Self, on an outward bound course, aged 16; *b*, after my first solo walk in Norway, 1961 (see p. 93); *c*, ready for my first major walk, Hebridean Journey, summer 1970 (see p. 79).

2 *a* Walking near my home in Derbyshire, through Chatsworth Park to Edensor; *b*, camp at North Lees on the Peakland Way (see p. 45).

3   On my Derbyshire boundary walk, July 1976 (see p. 30).

4 *a* My favourite rocks, Cratcliffe Tor, close to where I live; *b*, Handa Stack, on Handa, my favourite island, off the coast of north-west Scotland

5 *a* Suilven, my favourite mountain, in north-west Scotland (see p. 73);
b, the French Alps, from Aiguille du Midi (see p. 100).

6 In the Himalayas, bound for Everest, with Ama Dablam in the background, May 1980 (see p. 119).

7 *a* On top of Mt Katahdin, the northern end of the Appalachian Trail, July 1979 (see pp. 131–40); *b*, half-way along the Pacific Crest Trail, in the state of Oregon, July 1980 (see pp. 140–45).

8 On the summit of Mt Whitney in California, September 1980, after
walking the Pacific Crest Trail from Mexico to Canada (see p. 144).

CHAPTER 9

Trekking in the Himalayas

I have completed three treks in the Himalayas so far, and have also been to the Indian Himalayas in preparation for a future major walk.

The first trek was as a 'leader' to Everest on an organised trip in 1980. I enjoyed the company of the group as we worked our way to Everest base camp. It was, as you will read, very easy walking. I had pictured the Himalayas as being suitable only for the hardest and fittest people – a myth that had grown up about our highest mountains. The Everest trek broke the myth and revealed it as an excellent walking area.

I returned to Nepal the following year on my own, to walk around the Annapurna massif and to the Annapurna sanctuary. I was totally self-contained, carrying 60 lb (27 kg) of food and equipment. The contrast between the two trips was extreme. On the Everest trek we walked in luxury and had little contact with the local people, whereas on the Annapurna trek I learnt much about them and their way of life, and greatly enjoyed trekking in these high regions. I went again to the Himalayas in 1982, and this time explored the Helambu and Langtang region, alone, to the immediate north of Katmandu.

The story of these three treks follows.

A walk to the Everest Base Camp

In April 1980 I spent three weeks leading a trek to base camp, organised by Sherpa Expeditions of London.

'Trekking' in the Himalayas, means walking along paths and reaching an altitude of 18,500 ft (5,639 m); 'one never uses one's hands'. Trekking is very easy in a group, as you have little to do and carry no equipment, except what you are likely to need during the day. Being a trekking party of six visitors, we had a 'Sirdar' (a head Sherpa, who was the guide), one other Sherpa, one cook and two assistants, six porters and four yaks. Between them they carried the equipment (see p. 121). The porters, for instance, carried about 70 lb (32 kg) each, and wore no shoes even when crossing a glacier at 18,000 feet (5,500 m)! At around 6 a.m. the cook would awaken us with a mug of tea. We would then leisurely get up and sit down to breakfast half an hour later. Our only chore was to pack our sleeping bag and other personal effects into our own kit bags. The Sherpas would take the tents down and see to the loads.

As a rule we were walking by 8 a.m. The cooks would have dashed ahead to a pre-arranged lunch halt and would be waiting for us to arrive with a hot meal about four hours later. In the afternoon we walked two or three hours to our campsite. Again the cooks would be waiting with a hot drink, and the tents were being erected by the Sherpas. All we had to do was walk!

However, while the walking was relatively straightforward over rocky terrain and often very exposed paths, we did have to contend with altitude. Up to 11,000 ft (3,350 m) there is not likely to be any problem. Above this, the altitude begins to have an effect. The secret is not to go 'too fast too high'. If, as we did, you spend a couple of nights at around 11,000 ft (3,350 m) and another couple around 15,000 ft (4,600 m) before pressing on to 18,000 ft (5,500 m) or 19,000 ft (5,900 m), then your body is better prepared for the rarefied air. Most people suffer from headaches and nausea above 12,000 ft (3,650 m). I know I did! We even took sleeping pills at night to relax and have a good night's rest. If you ignore the information and simply press on, you risk facing serious consequences, for hospitals are scarce.

There are two severe forms of mountain sickness: pulmonary oedema (waterlogged lungs) – basically this is extreme breathlessness even when resting; and cerebral oedema (waterlogged brain) – this is when people stagger along, are drowsy and often drop into unconsciousness. In both cases there is only one thing to do, and that is to lose altitude as quickly as possible. There is a Himalayan Rescue Association which publishes information for trekkers. They also operate a rescue service; a helicopter is charged at about £1,000 per hour. Medical insurance for treatment and rescue is available in Britain and is part of the tour operators' deal. Individual policies are obtainable.

Before leaving Katmandu we had to obtain our trekking permits from the Department of Immigration. The permit includes a passport photograph, details of where one is allowed to trek, and the duration. At Police Posts permits are shown, but in fact Namche Bazar was the only place where we were asked to produce ours. From Katmandu we flew with our loaded kit bags and food to Lukla, where the landing strip at 9,300 ft (2,835 m) is one of the most difficult in the world. There is no second attempt! Fortunately, our twin-engined Otter plane made a perfect landing. Our Sherpas, porters and cooks were waiting. After sorting out all the equipment, the trek began.

Our route to Everest base camp was not the normal route via Namche Bazar, Thyangboche Monastery, Pheriche and Lobuche. Instead, from Namche Bazar we went further west to Gokyo before crossing the Nyimagawa Pass (17,800 ft, 5,425 m), to reach Lobuche and Gorak Shep. Two days' walking from Lukla brought us to Jorsalee Bridge at just over 9,000 ft (2,750 m). Here the real work of the walk began as we ascended steeply to Namche Bazar, the Sherpa capital. Part of the way up the path we stopped and admired our first glimpse of Everest, sixteen miles away. By the time we reached Namche Bazar at 11,300 ft (3,450 m) we all had headaches. Three hours later we reached Khumjung. Now at well over 12,000 ft (3,650 m), I was feeling the effects of the altitude – a splitting headache and nausea – and later I was violently sick. After a night's rest I felt perfectly all right again and we headed on, maintaining height, until we camped near Phortse.

The views that day were huge and dramatic. For much of the time the symmetrical shape of Ama Dablam (22,494 ft, 6,856 m), filled our horizon. It is one of the most beautiful mountains in the world and also a very hard climb. Two days later, and with half the party now suffering from the altitude, we reached Gokyo, a cluster of buildings and stone walls at around 16,300 ft (5,000 m). The next day we slowly climbed an 18,000 ft (5,500 m) mountain, Gokyo Kang, and sat absorbed, hardly able to take in the grandeur of the mountain panorama – Cho Oyu, Pumori, Everest, Nuptse, Lhotse and Makalu.

The next day we moved across a glacier to the foot of the Nyimagawa Pass. The following day, with the crossing of the 17,800 ft (5,425 m) pass, was, for me, the best day of the trek. We walked steeply up the scree slope and helped the porters over the awkward sections. It seems incredible, but one of them, carrying 70 lb (32 kg) held on his back by a head band, calmly climbed up and crossed snow and ice in his bare feet! His feet were like those of an elephant: thick-soled and immensely durable. The top of the pass was a snow and glacier field. We put on crampons and, using ice-axes, made our way across and descended steeply down a valley to Duglha, where we camped in a snow-storm.

The next day we began ascending, once more, to Lobuche, more than 16,000 ft (4,900 m). Here was our base for two nights while we climbed Kala Patar, visited Gorak Shep and Everest base camp. The ascent of Kala Patar was slow but the effort was worth it, for the view from the 18,192 ft (5,545 m) summit across to Everest is unequalled. There in front of us was the south-west face and the Khumbu icefall.

Our plan from Lobuche was to ascend another 18,000 ft (5,500 m) pass, the Kongma La, and descend to Chukhung. Unfortunately the weather was against us and we walked round the valleys to Chukhung (15,535 ft, 4,735 m). It was a splendid little diversion, for the following day we explored the southern slopes of Nuptse, and I went across glaciers to the northern side of Ama Dablam. We had now almost run out of time, and had three days left to get back to Lukla and the plane. From Chukhung we began descending to Dingboche and picked up the usual Everest Trek route and headed on to Pangboche. Near here we called in at our first tea shop, and while the Sherpas downed *chang*, we sipped our hot tea. To get across the nearby river we crossed an alarming swing bridge over a deep gorge. Because of the nature of the ground it was at an angle which heightened its precarious position. Once safely across, we began steady climbing to Thyangboche Monastery (12,715 ft, 3,876 m).

Here there is a trekkers' lodge built by the New Zealand Government. Because of Sir Edmund Hillary, New Zealand has close ties with the Sherpa community and has done a considerable amount of work for them – building schools, hospitals, air strips, etc. The monastery is a fine building, and we were taken round it by one of the Lamas. It is here that all Everest expeditions call and receive the Head Lama's blessing. From the monastery the view of Everest, Ama Dablam and nearby Kangtega (22,340 ft, 6,811 m) makes a fitting end before the steep descent to Namche Bazar.

As we descended we came into another world; it was late April and the rhododendrons were just coming into flower. The path to Namche Bazar is one of the most impressive I have ever walked on. Only about 3 feet wide (just under a metre), the path cuts its way round steep valley sides. Often there is 1,000 ft (300 m) above you and 2,000 ft (600 m) below, plunging down to the river.

From Namche Bazar we retraced our steps to Jorsalee Bridge and left the Sagarmatha (Everest) National Park. When we had come through fifteen days earlier we paid an entrance fee. We were now walking about 12 miles (19 km) a day, for about eight hours, including lunch break. With regret we reached Lukla later the next day. Our trek had ended, but I am sure we all felt grateful for having had the experience, and I for one was eager to get back into those mountains. It didn't take me long to realise that, for high-altitude walking, where other ranges end the Himalayas begin.

The best time to go trekking is in October/November, or March April. The equipment I took with me was basically the same as I use for walking in Britain. I had a heavy sleeping bag, Black's Highland Extreme, for the nights at high altitude, and certainly appreciated its warmth. For extremely cold nights I had thermal underwear with me, but I never used it. At 14,000 ft (4,250 m) and over in the evenings and early mornings I wore a Black's Snowgoose duvet, but during the day I wore just shorts and a shirt. I carried and used an ice-axe and crampons. I also carried waterproof clothing, but the weather was kind and I did not have to use it. My boots (Scarpa Bronzo) were fully broken in, and my day sack was Berghaus Cyclops Guide. We camped every night and used Vango Force 10 tents.

On the trek itself we slept two to a tent, and washed ourselves in the cold streams; at high altitudes we didn't bother. Whilst it was a predominantly male party, I noticed that other groups had many female members. Apart from the hot drinks given to us by the cooks, I drank very little. Below 9,000 ft (2,750 m) the water was discoloured, and without boiling it or adding purification tablets (which I don't like doing) I would not drink it. There are few public toilets, and everyone carried a toilet roll in their day pack. At high altitudes the sun's rays are strong, and I applied sun cream liberally to my face, neck and arms.

Before the trip I had several visits to the doctor for vaccination against cholera and typhoid and, just before I left, gamma globulin against hepatitis. As a precaution, I took a weekly malaria pill, which I had to continue taking for six weeks after my return. Apart from altitude sickness, the most common complaint was dysentery. I always carried 'Lomitol', which I found soon brought me back to normal.

Around Annapurna

The Himalayas are the ultimate area for trekking or walking; not so much because of their remoteness but because you are trekking at the highest altitude. I had long wanted to walk in them on my own. In April 1981 I flew to Katmandu, intending to trek right round the Annapurna massif, cross the Thorung La Pass (17,700 ft, 5,400 m) and ascend to the Annapurna base camp and Sanctuary. I was a little cautious at trying something like this on my own, but once I had set off my doubts disappeared.

I obtained my trekking permit, and at 6 a.m. the next morning I was down in the square getting my bus ticket to Dumre, more than 100 miles (161 km) away. This was where the walk begins and, contrary to my usual practice, I would be walking the route anti-clockwise – the 'devil's way'. The main reason for attacking the route from Dumre is because the pass is best negotiated from the Dumre side, and once over it you should, in theory, soon reach water. To do it the other way is exceptionally hard, and no drinking water will be found for at least a day. The bus, and there were many of them bound for Pokhara via Dumre, was lavishly painted with the words 'Express Service' or 'De luxe Seating'. In reality the buses were dilapidated and held together with wire and string. The bus to Dumre, a journey of six bone-shaking hours along dusty roads, had to be pushed to start every time we stopped. The bus I came back on from Pokhara, the walk's end, had to have gearbox attention frequently and two wheel changes! But this kind of thing is really part of the fun of being in remote parts, and adds to the adventure.

I was the only person to get off at Dumre. It felt strange shouldering my heavy load and not really knowing what the route ahead would be like. The temperature was close to 38°C (100°F), hardly the ideal walking weather, but I set off nevertheless. I did 10 miles (16 km) in the heat, walking past thatched houses, water buffalo wallowing in muddy pools, banana trees growing in profusion, and a lot of friendly people. For most of the time on the first few days I was walking up a river valley, slowly gaining height. Upon reaching the summit of the pass, I would have ascended more than 16,000 ft (4,900 m).

Gradually, as the days passed, the walking became more enjoyable in cooler temperatures, and the path began winding its way high above the river to small villages, often reached by a large suspension bridge. By now I was in a routine, and occasionally stayed in 'lodges' at the cost of about five pence for the night. I had set out with fourteen days' food, and unless one wanted a rice meal with lentils, it was better to cook for oneself. Sometimes I camped and met other trekkers, including a French group and a small German expedition. I learnt about 'tea houses'. Every couple of hours along the trail would be a tea house, where one could rest the 60 lb (27 kg) load and drink a glass of hot sweet tea around a smoky open fire for two pence. At these stops you came to know the local people, their joy of life and their primitive surroundings. The houses were impeccably tidy, with the basic necessities – an open fire, kettle and pans, a few plates, cutlery, a large water jar, and a mat to sleep on. Outside would be the cattle and hens, which often walked in through the open doorway.

Six days from Dumre I stayed at Lower Pisang. The wind was too strong to camp, and there was no suitable sheltered spot, so I slept in a house porch. I joined the French party, but found there was nothing for breakfast: the village could only provide two eggs for four people. The day's walk from here was very attractive, with a small pass to ascend, providing distant views to the Annapurna massif and to Pisang Peak. Now, at more than 10,000 ft (3,050 m) above sea level, the walking was taking a little longer, and a slow but steady pace was the day's rhythm. By early afternoon, after skirting round several small lakes, I came to Braga village, a small settlement with tiered houses lining a sheltered curve in the valley side. The houses were all made of stone, with the cattle on the ground floor. To get to the first floor, a ladder carved out of a tree trunk acted as the stairs. Lining the upper walls were large rows of chopped firewood.

The trail climbed again as I headed for Manang at a height of 12,500 ft (3,800 m). The village is famed for its archery contests but I saw none as a blizzard blew up and I sought shelter in one of the lodges for the night. The snow fell all afternoon, and by the following morning, after freezing conditions overnight, a good 3 inches (7.5 cm) of snow had carpeted the area. Originally I had planned to visit Tilicho Lake nearby, at about 17,000 ft (5,200 m). It is reputed to be spectacular, being surrounded by high mountains and glaciers descending to the water's edge. But, in these conditions it was not worth attempting to get there, for the trail is tricky in the best of weather. I had hoped to have reached the lake from the Kali Gandaki gorge, but this too was denied me as the area was out of bounds.

From Manang I ascended through the snow past the last settlement, Tengi, and headed for the 'base camp' of the Thorung Pass at 14,500 ft (4,420 m). At first the day was bright and sunny, but by lunchtime it had turned cold and there was driving snow. I reached the camp after quite a battle through deep snow, often having to guess the route. The camp was busy as two trekking parties had been waiting for three days in the bad weather for the right conditions to cross the pass. The morning brought clear blue skies and everyone set off up the pass. For me, with my heavy load, it was a long haul. Fortunately the porters ahead were breaking the trail, making route-finding easy. The path wove its way upwards, often steeply, and with only an ice-axe to arrest a fall I crossed several exposed snow-fields. The porters were an inspiration;

some wore tennis shoes, and some just crossed the snow in bare feet!

I reached the summit of the pass after seven hours of gradual ascent, and was rewarded with spectacular views over many beautiful nameless mountains. I was feeling unwell, though, and was suffering from dehydration. I had melted a pint of water (just over half a litre) before setting off, but had soon used this up. It was another four hours of steep descent before I came to a river and simply drank and drank. The clear blue sky caused another problem, and many porters, who had no snow goggles, suffered from snow blindness. Although I had goggles, my face puffed out from the merciless glare from the snow. I learnt later that two people froze to death on the pass – not a place to take lightly even in good weather.

On the descent I had my first glimpse of Dhaulagiri, the sixth highest mountain in the world, and one of the most difficult to climb. I reached Muktinath, the first village on the other side of the pass, after nearly fourteen hours' walking. It had been a hard crossing with a heavy load: and the altitude, although I had suffered no headaches, had made me very lethargic. I amazed the porters by coming over with a 60 lb (27 kg) load and they exclaimed: 'A white skin doing that!' Muktinath is a pilgrimage centre, to which many Hindus make the long climb from Pokhara and beyond. The monastic buildings are fascinating, and one of them has 108 water spouts. At another the women wore special head-dresses with jade stones. Inside the building the holy flame burnt natural gas from a hole in the ground, but I was banned from entering.

I pressed on the next day, although tired, and decided I would descend to the Kali Gandaki gorge and Jomson. The gorge is the deepest in the world, with 26,000 ft (8,000 m) mountains on either side, towering some 18,000 ft (5,500 m) above. During the monsoon the river bursts its way down the valley, but in late April just a small stream flowed down the middle of a huge expanse of pebbles and boulders. Had I been able to turn right upon reaching the gorge I could have walked to Mustang, but that region is closed to trekkers. Walking in the gorge after 11 a.m. is a battle. Up till then the air is still, but after that strong gale-force winds funnel their way down the gorge.

Jomson, at 8,500 ft (2,600 m), came as a surprise, with its modern houses, landing strip and bakery. I stayed at a lodge and ate locally-made apple pie. I even had a hot shower, which consisted of a bowl of hot water and a ladle. It was my first wash for days, and my last until I reached Pokhara three weeks later. My next village was a startling contrast to any I had seen or was to see on the whole trek. Named Martha, it was extremely tidy, with paved streets and an intricate water system. The outlying ground was extensively cultivated, with small areas of fruit trees. Many of the house fronts were whitewashed, and on the flat-topped roof were rows of firewood.

Leaving Martha the next day, the walk down the gorge provided magnificent views to Dhaulagiri, Tukche Peak and Nilgiri. I had planned to ascend the valley side and get a close look at the Dhaulagiri icefall, but the weather dictated otherwise, with low clouds and thunder-storms. Instead I continued down the gorge to Tatopani and its hot springs. I arrived there the next day but the water, although hot, looked filthy and not in the least inviting. From Tatopani I left the gorge and began heading for Annapurna base camp, four walking days away. First I had to ascend 5,000 ft (1,500 m) to Chitre and Poon Hill. From the summit of the hill at 6 a.m. the next morning I watched a spectacular sunrise as the golden rays of the dawn flashed on to Dhaulagiri and the Annapurnas. Just sticking above the high ridges was the fishtail summit of Machhapuchhre, one of the world's most beautiful mountains.

From Poon Hill my next objective was Ghandrung, which I reached via a virgin forest where agile monkeys swung through the trees. From Ghandrung it is a one-way route to the base camp. I was advised to have a short day and walk to the Captain's Lodge. The ex-Gurkha captain was very affable, and gave me the best room. From my window I could look up the valley to Machhapuchhre and to Hiunchuli close by. Until recently, the ascent continued up a steep narrow gorge to Hinko Cave. But instead of spending the night in the cave I stayed at the Himalaya Hotel, a bamboo hut. There I ate the last two eggs as an omelette.

The gorge ahead to base camp is tricky, and I was advised to get through it by 11 a.m. The danger is from avalanches, and I had to cross eleven avalanche slopes. Three days later, when I came down the gorge, several of the slopes had fresh avalanche snow upon them.

Annapurna base camp was certainly worth the trouble to reach. Here at 13,500 ft (4,100 m) is the last running water, and I camped close by. There were many people here, a Japanese expedition attempting a nearby peak, and a French expedition on Hiunchuli which had just given up because of an exceptional depth of snow above 20,000 ft (6,000 m). The beauty of the site lay in the spectacular surroundings of the Annapurna massif and its descending glaciers. Alas, the weather was bad. During the night the temperature dropped to minus 26°C (−14°F) and by 11 a.m. it was 35°C (95°F). The mornings were usually bright and sunny, but by midday the clouds had rolled in and it snowed for the rest of the day. However, I didn't mind; I had achieved what I had set out to do, and after two nights here I packed up and descended back to Ghandrung.

From Ghandrung I descended more than 2,500 ft (750 m), crossed the river on a very unstable bridge, and began ascending to my final pass before Pokhara. In torrential rain later in the day I reached Dhampus and looked across at Machhapuchhre, swathed in cotton-wool clouds that rolled around its ramparts. The holy mountain looked stunning. In 1954 Wilfrid Noyce came to within 50 ft (15.4 m) of the summit but turned back in a storm. Since then no expedition has been granted permission to ascend it.

From Dhampus it was downhill all the way to Pokhara, where I stayed in a small hotel and had a hot bath. Pokhara is famed for Phewa Lake, and for a few pence I hired a canoe and went out on to the lake to photograph the magnificent vista of all the major mountains I had walked beneath, reflected in the water's surface. The water was quite warm and I dived in from the canoe, almost sinking the boat.

My trip was nearly over, and I boarded an 'express' bus the next morning for Katmandu, eight hours away. I had been lucky to have suffered from no illness or dysentery, which plays havoc with many people. Although the weather had not been as good as usual, the walk of about 300 miles (480 km) had been through some of Nepal's finest scenery and amidst some of the friendliest and happiest people I know.

Helambu and Langtang

To the immediate north of Katmandu lie these fascinating trekking areas, and I returned to Nepal in April 1982 intending to visit them both. I planned to walk through the Helambu region first and then to cross the Tharepati Pass (11,125 ft, 3,400 m). From there I would continue ascending to just over 14,000 ft (4,250 m) to the Gosainkund Lakes, a popular pilgrimage goal. A long descent would bring me to the Langtang River and the Langtang National Park. Several days of ascent to 16,000 ft (4,900 m) would take me up the river valley to the 26,000 ft (8,000 m) mountain wall separating Nepal from Tibet. Rather than retrace my steps, I hoped to ascend the Ganja La Pass – 16,000 ft (4,900 m) – and return via the Helambu region back to Katmandu.

I allowed a full month for the trek, and on paper the plan was feasible and through unspoilt Nepal scenery. In the event, bad weather frustated my plans and I never crossed to the Gosainkund Lakes or the Ganja La.

Instead I did two really excellent treks, one around the Helambu region and one through the Langtang valley. This was my third Himalayan trek – my second alone. The Everest trek had been very popular, and I had seen numerous Westerners every day. The Annapurna trek had also been popular in places, but I had met the locals more and had had a chance to learn about their way of life. But the Langtang trek was by far my most enjoyable Himalayan experience of the three. Although the weather did not enable me to cross the high passes, I saw more of the area than I had originally planned, only met a handful of Westerners in a month, and met and lived with the locals in their houses.

One can walk straight out of Katmandu to Sundarijal, the start of the trek in Helambu. Instead, I took a taxi along the rough road rather than suffer walking in the hot weather. The route lay first beside the giant water pipes of the electricity generating station before ascending past numerous thatched houses and terracing. The views were extensive over ridge after ridge of terracing. Two days of hot walking brought me to the Malemchi River, which at only 3,000 ft (900 m) was refreshing to swim in. The next day I walked close to the river, past banana trees and numerous corn mills driven by an ingenious system of hollowed tree trunks bringing the water steeply to the mill wheel. That night I stayed with a local family at Thimbu in their two-roomed house. Outside were a water buffalo and a few hens. I kept the whole family entranced as they watched me at my gas stove, while I cooked my evening dehydrated meal. I am not keen on rice, and almost the only food you can obtain locally, apart from eggs, is *dal bat* – rice and lentils.

A steep ascent brought me to Tarke Ghyang at 9,000 ft (2,750 m), with a small monastery and a prayer-wheel. Originally I planned to return there from the Langtang valley via the Ganja La pass, but the locals all said it was an impossible three-day crossing because of the excessive amount of snow. That night I stayed with a Sherpa family, ate some dried buffalo meat, which I didn't much like, and churned butter by hand with the owner's wife. To reach Tharepati Pass required a very steep descent to the river, 3,000 ft (900 m) below, before a 3,000 ft (900 m) ascent to Malemchigaon. I reached the village tired, and in the midst of a thunderstorm and falling snow.

I arrived at the pass after another 3,000 ft (900 m) ascent, through a forest where monkeys ran through the high branches. The pass summit was snow-covered and not at all inviting. I continued on, still hoping to get to Gosainkund. Two hours' walking brought me to a large cave where I planned to spend the night. Shortly afterwards a Canadian and his guide arrived and suggested we stay in a small hut a little higher up. We moved in and, because the roof leaked, put our tents up inside. We all spent a very uncomfortable night at 12,000 ft (3,650 m), with the sound of massive boulders crashing down around us; it snowed heavily, and during the night the roof collapsed, crushing our tents! The pass was out of the question, and as the maps were only sketches we could not rely on any compass readings; we all decided the only wise decision was to retreat.

We retraced our steps back to Tharepati and Tarke Ghyang. Here we took an alternative route along a ridge to Sarmathang, where we camped close to a monastery with magnificent views to snow-capped peaks, notably Gauri Sanker. The next day we descended 6,000 ft (1,825 m) to a river and had a swim. That night we roasted two hens bought locally and got drunk on 'rakshi', locally brewed rice wine. Two days later we reached Panchkhol and caught a bus to Katmandu.

There I spent a frantic afternoon getting my trekking permit extended and my flights confirmed, and obtained the last seat ticket for the morning bus to Trisuli Bazar. I was still determined to get to the Langtang valley. At 7 a.m. I was on the way to Trisuli, in a bus designed to hold fifty people but which had a hundred inside and seventy-five on the roof! Five hours later, after driving along twisty and very exposed dirt roads, the bus reached Trisuli. At only 1,500 ft (450 m) it was devastatingly hot, but I set off to walk a couple of hours to Betrawati, where the climb begins. In an effort to beat the heat I was walking again by 6 a.m. the following morning, for I had been told that once I reached Ramche, the entrance to the National Park at 6,000 ft (1,825 m), the air would be cooler. I paid my park entrance fees of 60 rupees – about £2 – and passed on along the trail, winding its way high above the Trisuli River.

The rhododendrons were out, monkeys swung through branches, and the locals walked along the trails in bare feet carrying bamboo baskets on their backs. In the distance mountain summits began to appear. As in the Helambu region, after gaining a height of about 9,000 ft (2,750 m) at Syabru I had to descend steeply to the Langtang River. This heavily forested narrow river gorge gave no indication of the splendours beyond. Five hours of walking and I approached Ghora Tabela. Quite dramatically the valley opened out into a large U-shaped valley with high snow-draped mountains on either side, especially the Langtang Himal at around 23,000 ft (7,000 m).

The next day I continued ascending to Kyangjin at 13,000 ft (4,000

m) and stayed in a government lodge. It was now very cold at night and there was snow on the ground. Tibet was close by, and I had passed two military check posts to reach this point. On the valley floor was a landing strip. Kyangyin is a small cluster of buildings, including a cheese factory and a monastery. I bought half a kilo (1 lb) of yak cheese, which tasted good. Behind the village were three glaciers from the Langtang peaks, and after a short climb I had a good view of these frozen tracts.

Leaving my gear in the lodge, I set off early the next day to walk up the remainder of the valley to Langsisa. The weather was perfect, with clear blue sky and shimmering snowy high peaks on either side. Yaks grazed in the valley floor, and an eagle kept me company for a while. Of all my Himalayan days so far, I enjoyed this one the most, alone amidst one of the finest displays of mountain splendour to be seen anywhere. The journey from Trisuli was worth all the effort to get there. At the valley end I sat on the glacial moraine and gazed at the towering walls of snow and ice rising to Gosainthan, one of the 26,000 ft (8,000 m) peaks. On the other side of the ridge was Tibet. Late that morning I retraced my steps, fearful of being caught in the usual afternoon storm, but for once none came. The sunset that evening filled the valley with orange light.

I retraced my steps to Ghora Tabela, and part of the way down the gorge, rather than return along the route I had come, I turned right and ascended steeply up the gorge side. The trail is narrow and very exposed as you walk 3,000 ft (900 m) above the gorge. One slip can seal your fate. It is the most exhilarating Himalayan path I have been on, and at one point becomes positively alarming; to get round a rock wall, wooden poles had been jammed into the cracks and stones placed on top to form a path. I hurried round, not looking at the drop below. Three hours later I was in Syrabrubensi, sitting in a hot spring! What amazing contrasts there are in Nepal. From my warm natural bath I could see the snow. Up river was Tibet, and the village had a large Tibetan refugee camp.

Time was now running out. I completed two days of hard walking to get back to Trisuli. Alas, the bus was full, but at the last minute the driver relented and I climbed on top and began the journey back to Katmandu. The next day I raced around buying gifts, and collected my Tibetan rug before boarding the plane for Delhi. I had cut things fine in the end, but it had been a memorable training walk. Two weeks later I began my European walk (p. 106).

REFERENCE BOOKS

Stan Armington, *Trekking in the Himalayas* (Lonely Planet Publications, PO Box 88, South Yarra, Victoria 3141, Australia, 1979)

S. Bezruchka, *A Guide to Trekking in Nepal* (Cordee, 1981)

Mario Fantin, *Wonderland of Nepal Everest Trek* (The English Book Store, New Delhi, 1975)

Robert and Linda Fleming, *Kathmandu Valley* (Kodansha International Limited, Tokyo, 1978)

T. Iozawa, *Trekking in the Himalayas* (Yama-Kei, Tokyo, 1980)

John A. Jackson, *Sonamarg (Kashmir). Climbing and Trekking Guide* (Department of Tourism, Jammu and Kashmir, 1976)

Takehide Kazami, *The Himalayas* (Kodansha International Ltd, Tokyo, 1973)

Dorothy Mierow and Tirtha Bahadur Shrestha, *Himalayan Flowers and Trees* (Sahayogi Press, Tripureshwar, Katmandu, Nepal, 1978)

Prakash A. Raj, *Kathmandu and The Kingdom of Nepal* (Lonely Planet Publications, see above, 1978)

Robert Rieffel, *Nepal* (Sahayogi Press, Tripureshwar, Katmandu, Nepal, 1978)

Hugh Swift, *Trekkers' Guide to the Himalayas and Karakoram* (Hodder, 1982)

MAPS
1:50,000 SERIES (Freytag-Berndt und Artaria, Vienna, 2nd edition, 1978)
Sheets 1 (Kathmandu), 2 (Khumbu Himal), 3 (Lapchi Kang), 4 (Rolwaling Himal), 5 (Shorong/Hinku), 6 (Tamba Kosi), 7 (Dudh Kosi)
This series of maps covers the main trekking areas in Eastern Nepal, which includes Everest.

COMPANIES OPERATING HIMALAYAN TREKS
Sherpa Expeditions, 3 Bedford Road, London w4.
   Treks to Everest Base Camp, Annapurna Sanctuary, Manang, Tomoson, Langtang Valley and to Kashmir and Ladakh.
Ramblers Holidays Ltd, 13 Longcroft House, Fretherne Road, Welwyn Garden City, Herts., AL8 6PQ.
   Treks to Helambu, Manang and Langtang.
Thomas Cook Holidays, Thorpe Wood, PO Box No 36, Peterborough, PE3 6SB.
Exodus Expeditions, 167 Earls Court Road, London, SW5 9RF
Kashmir Himalayan Expeditions (M. S. Baktoo Group of Houseboats), 17 Stanthorpe Road, Streatham, London, SW16 2DZ
Trailfinders Travel Centre, 46 Earls Court Road, London, W8 6EJ
Woodcock Travel Ltd, 25–31 Wicker, Sheffield, S3 8HW

CHAPTER 10

Walking in America

Walking conditions in the u.s.a. are very different from those in Britain. In general, the terrain is not to be taken lightly for it is more rugged and remote, the climate has greater extremes, and the wildlife can be dangerous. But America does have some of the world's finest walking, through stunning scenery, and there are wilderness areas where another human being may not be seen for a week or more. There are plans to create several major long-distance walks, and in my opinion America is likely to become the foremost walking area of the world.

I have so far completed two major walks in America – the Appalachian Trail and the Pacific Crest Trail. Over the next few years I intend to do further major walks here, and I am about to undertake a 4,500 mile (7,250 km) coast-to-coast walk from Virginia to California (see map on pp. 132–3). I also have plans for a 3,500 mile (5,600 km) walk down the Continental Divide, from Canada to Mexico. In 1983 I set off to walk this trail but after 100 miles (160 km) the trails and the National Parks were closed because of man-eating grizzly bears. I road-walked 250 miles (402 km) around the danger area but was not allowed in because one camper was mauled and escaped whilst his companion was eaten alive. I decided to return home and walk another year.

The Appalachian Trail

A continuous footpath running through the entire chain of the Appalachian Mountains was the idea of Benton Mackaye, a naturalist. In 1921 he published a paper on the Appalachian Trail, a project of regional planning. But it was not until 1931 that a trail ran from Georgia to Maine: just over 2,000 miles (3,200 km).

Today, the original route has changed and is about 2,400 miles (3,850 km), and is in fact the world's longest footpath. The southern terminus is Springer Mountain in Georgia, 3,782 ft (1,152 m) high. The trail passes through fourteen states which, in walking order, are Georgia, North Carolina, Tennessee, Virginia, West Virginia, Maryland, Pennsylvania, New Jersey, New York, Connecticut, Massachusetts, Vermont, New Hampshire and Maine, to Baxter Peak, 5,267 ft (1,605 m),

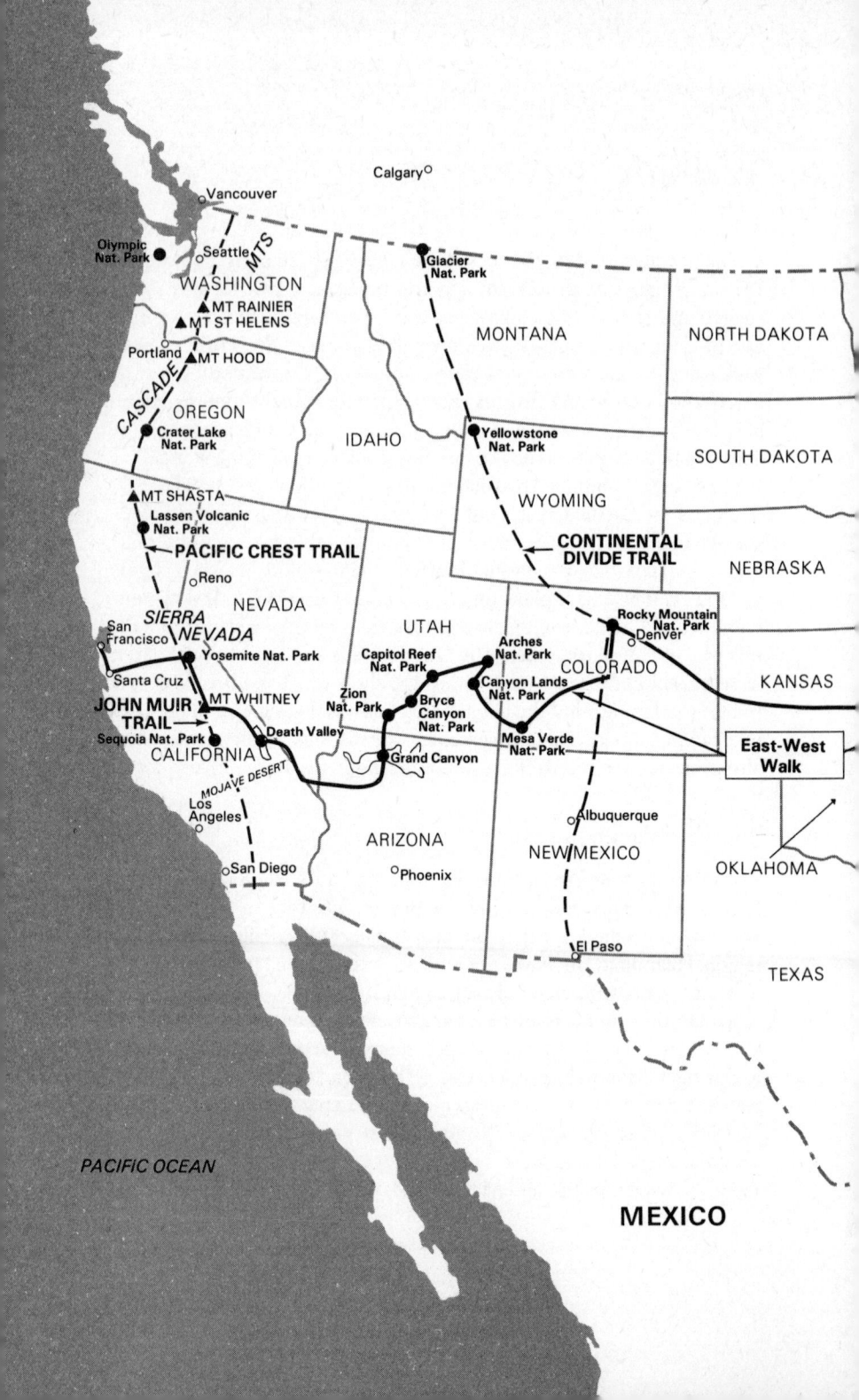

on Mt Katahdin, the northern terminus. Much of the route is around the 4,000 ft (1,219 m) contour level, and it passes through numerous National Forests and two National Parks. Where the trail crosses the Hudson River in New York State, the elevation is just over 100 ft (30 m), whereas in the Great Smoky National Park in North Carolina it reaches its highest point at Clingman's Dome, 6,442 ft (1,963 m). The other National Park, the Shenandoah in Virginia, is more than 400 miles (6,400 km) away and is gentler, with summits around the upper 3,000 ft (900 m) mark. In New Hampshire are the White Mountains which, in my opinion, are the finest part of the trail: magnificent jagged mountains above timberline, rising to Mt Washington at 6,288 ft (1,886 m).

Because the trail is so long, remote and wild, it is a backpackers' route only, so a tent, cooking equipment and food for several days have to be carried. At regular intervals along the trail there are wooden shelters, three-sided, where you can stay. A spring is usually not far away. The walking is basically straightforward and is in many ways like walking a very long Pennine Way. The one aspect that an Englishman finds hard to adjust to is being among trees almost all the time. This is all right for a while, but as the days pass one longs for a view. As a result, the Appalachian Trail is often referred to as 'the long green tunnel'.

Apart from its remoteness – often I went eight days without seeing anyone – what distinguishes the Appalachian Trail from British walks is the number of hazards one must expect. All the time I was walking along the trail I watched where I put my feet. Two poisonous snakes abound, the copperhead and the rattlesnake, and a bite from one of these can have very serious effects. Some people carry a snake-bite kit, but I didn't: the mere thought of making an incision and sucking out the venom was enough to put me off. I saw both these varieties of snake and seven others. Black bears are also a problem. In the Great Smoky National Park they are such a nuisance that everyone has to stay in a shelter with a metal grid across at night. Many people encourage them by giving them food, and the trash cans are made 'bear proof'.

I did have one nasty skirmish with a bear, when I was camping high up a mountain in Virginia. Around 10.30 p.m. he came, grunting and growling, in search of the food in my tent. I frightened him away by making as much noise as possible, banging my pots and pans. He came back four hours later, more determined. I shouted for all I was worth, and luckily he went away. I had had enough by this time and, finding a small hut nearby, I moved in and barricaded the door! It really was all my own fault, for I should have hung my food up from a tree – 10 ft (3 m) above the ground and at least 5 ft (1.5 m) from the bough. Other nocturnal animals came around my tent, such as skunks and porcupines. In shelters, mice ran across my face, and chipmunks and squirrels were quite tame and came seeking food.

Also to be avoided are two plants, poisonous ivy and poisonous sumac. If you brush against them with bare skin a rash forms and will spread. I was advised to wear long trousers to safeguard my legs. I didn't; I wore shorts all the time and kept clear of the plants when I came to them. Not once was I caught.

The worst hazard of all is the weather. Mt Washington in the White Mountains, New Hampshire, is notorious and is one place where it can snow any day of the year. Large signs give you warnings as you walk in the area. On the summit of Mt Washington the highest wind speed ever recorded was in 1934: the wind reached a velocity of 231 miles (372 km) an hour. I experienced very little wind on the trail. Rain, yes. At one point it rained hard and continuously for twelve days. Everything was soaked. But the most alarming problem of all was thunderstorms: I suffered eight in a seven-day period. These storms make ours seem like nothing. I was caught several times high on a ridge, in the most ferocious storms possible. There was no escape, and I just had to sit them out. I moved my rucksack, cameras and watch well away from me and watched the lightning flash down and explode disturbingly close to where I was! There was nothing I could do, for the storms came at speed and often lasted as long as three hours. In one storm ¼ inch (19 mm) diameter hailstones fell. I didn't mind the snakes and bears so much, but the storms were frightening. I was alone; no one knew where I was; and I needed to keep a tight grip on my mind to carry on, knowing that I might not see anyone for another two or three days.

Since the trail passes through such remote countryside, the waymarking must be good and dependable. It is, and, except in National Parks and Forests, most of the waymarking (blazing) is done voluntarily. For long stretches the Appalachian Trail is the only trail through the area, and, the trees being dense, foliage blazing is vital. At regular intervals there is a 2 in x 6 in (51 mm x 152 mm) white blaze painted on a tree bough or stone. If I hadn't seen one for ¼ mile (0.5 km) I knew I had lost my way! Although there are guidebooks to the trail, one must at all times follow the white blazes even if they differ from what is indicated in the guide. The route is often changed or relocated to avoid private property, and this information cannot always be found in the guidebooks. Whenever there is a change of direction to the trail there is a double blaze. As soon as you see one of these you must take care to find the right route to follow. In the low-lying states such as New Jersey and New York, the trail is not walked often and I found the waymarking very poor. I had to check carefully that I was heading in the right direction. At road junctions there is usually a wooden Appalachian sign giving the mileage to the next shelter or peak. And in the very few towns that the trail goes through, the white blazes can be found on the telegraph poles. Foot-bridges across the main interstate highways have Appalachian Trail signs on them.

In some of the towns there were hostels run by the local church. The first one I came to was after about 300 miles (480 km) from Georgia at Hot Springs in North Carolina. This was by far the best-run hostel on the trail, with showers, bunk beds, cooking facilities and eating-room. There are six in all, on or close to the trail. The one at Pearisburg, Virginia, although 2 miles (3 km) off the trail, is situated in the grounds of the Catholic church and is a perfect little haven in which to rest and lick your wounds. Usually the hostels are free, but you are expected to contribute a nominal amount towards the running costs. These stops in the hostels or at a town enabled me to collect mail from the post office, catch up with the news, re-stock with food and supplies, and visit the Laundromat to wash clothes.

One thing that did take a bit of getting used to was the American way of life – their zest for life, dependence on a car, hamburger stands, motels and 24-hour TV etc. After living off dehydrated food while on the trail, it was a treat to go down town to the diner and have a steak or a substantial meal. Usually on reaching a town I just ate and ate. I soon became used to visiting the chain fast-food houses such as Dunkin Donut, McDonald's, Wendy House or the Pizza Hut.

Well over a year before I set off on the walk, I joined the Appalachian Trail Conference and received their *Trailway News* at frequent intervals. This kept me informed about the trail and its problems. I also read as much as I could about the trail, including the books listed at the end of this section. I purchased the necessary ten guides and maps, and began my planning. All the information suggested that the best time to start the walk was at the beginning of April, and one could then follow the arrival of Spring northwards. Therefore, I planned to set off from Springer Mountain on 5 April 1979; which is what I did.

I flew to New York, and by Greyhound bus, a journey of twenty-one hours, I reached Gainsville, Georgia, the nearest town to the start of the trail. From here I took a taxi to the approach walk from Amicola Falls

Park. Before leaving Gainsville I mailed five parcels to post offices along the trail. These parcels contained dehydrated food for seven days, and the guidebooks needed at the various stages. It was far simpler and cheaper to parcel them up in England and then mail them in America. On each parcel I marked 'To be called for – Englishman walking the Appalachian Trail'. The post office then held it for me until I arrived. I also put on the approximate date I would arrive there and was never far wrong. All the parcels arrived safely, as did all the maps and guides that I sent back to England.

For much of the time during the first few weeks on the trail I was walking through an almost lifeless world around 4,000–5,000 ft (1,220–1,520 m). Spring had not arrived up there. After the first week I descended into a valley 3,000 ft (900 m) below, and the contrast was amazing: new leaves unfurled and spring flowers were about to bloom. Later, this wealth of wild flowers – trout lily, trillium and lady's slipper to name but three – was one of the most rewarding sights on the trail. I met many people in the first three weeks; in fact I overtook 400. I learnt later that something like 1,500 people set off from Springer Mountain in April with the express purpose of walking all the way to Mt Katahdin. Out of that figure of 1,500 only about 400 would actually make it. Since 1931 only about 250 people have covered the entire route in one continuous walk. Many have walked the whole trail over several years, doing a section at a time. The average American walks 15 miles (24 km) per day and takes 5–6 months to do the whole walk.

It was not long before I began to realise that the distances indicated on the guides were inaccurate, largely because of the route changes. For instance, one sign stated that a shelter at Moreland Gap was 10 miles (16 km) away. An average person would reach the shelter in three and a half hours, yet on the ground it took me more than six hours! The true distance was nearer 18 miles (39 km). This resulted in a major problem for me because I had only ninety days at my disposal. I was walking an average of 28 miles (45 km) per day and should have completed the trail within eighty days. As it turned out, though, the true distance was nearer 2,400 miles (3,860 km) than the supposed distance of 2,055 miles (3,307 km). In the end I had no option but to miss out 150 miles (240 km) in the final three states, and reach Mt Katahdin before heading home, having walked 2,200 miles (3,540 km). For me it was a very hard decision, for never have I had to 'miss out' a section before. However, because of the shortness of time, I felt justified. The Appalachian Trail was for me an introduction and training walk before tackling the Pacific

Crest Trail. I had come with the intention of walking 2,000 miles (3,220 km), and I had in fact easily surpassed my target in the time available.

There were other serious inaccuracies in the guides and the maps. I, along with the others I met on the route, soon found even the new guides to be very misleading. For example, one guide specified a store at a given point: reaching where it should have been, I found it had been pulled down eleven years before. Another gave details of a place to stay which, when I arrived, I was told had not been operating for five years. In the end, apart from using the guides as an 'introduction' to a section, I did not rely on them much. Also the maps were extremely poor, and the scale was too small: generally 1 inch to 5 miles (25 mm to 8 km). Only in the two National Parks were the maps 1 inch to a mile (1 cm to 0.63 km). In places of danger, such as during a thunderstorm, there was nothing on the map to give me any idea of what lay in my vicinity, which could have helped me out of a difficult situation.

Safety on the trail was another worry. No one knew where I was, and if anything serious had happened I would have been in trouble. There are registers along the trail at odd intervals, and where possible I signed in.

The Great Smoky National Park was a magnificent section of trail, about 70 miles (110 km). I was high up all the time, often above timberline, enjoying extensive views over the wooded hills. Through Virginia, which has almost a third of the trail in it, the walking was delightful, especially in the Shenandoah National Park, which offers magnificent views from the 'overlooks'. In both National Parks I had to obtain a backpacker's permit to walk through the area and to use the shelters or camp. I stayed at the camp grounds in the Shenandoah, but the bears were a nuisance, coming round the tents at night for food. Special 12 ft (3.6 m) high poles were littered around the area so that I could hoist my food away from the tent.

In Pennsylvania I had one of my worst experiences on the trail, yet it is one that I now look back on with amusement. It had been raining extremely hard for thirty-six hours. My tent and much of my equipment were soaked. After walking 33 miles (53 km) I crossed a road and saw the sign for Darlington Shelter – 1½ miles (2.5 km). I hurried on but after more than an hour I still hadn't reached it. Half an hour later I found it and had no option but to sleep on the wet earth floor beneath a leaking roof. Around 2 a.m. I awoke and, on lighting a match, discovered that I was lying in 6 inches (152 mm) of mud and water. I blew the match out, rolled over and went to sleep! At first light I was off and reached Duncannon in mid-afternoon. Here I stayed at the Fire Station, where they thoughtfully allowed trail hikers to use their facilities. Donning clean clothes, I went to the Laundromat and washed and dried all mine, including the smelly wet sleeping bag.

Despite what I have said about the trail and its faults, I do not want to give a wrong impression of my walk. The truth is, I thoroughly enjoyed it and relished the challenge of a totally different environment. When I reached Baxter Peak on Mt Katahdin, I suffered a powerful feeling of loss, for the trail had taught me a great deal about America, her climate and people. I had seen a wide range of wildlife: white-tailed deer that were almost tame, the friendly chipmunks, strikingly beautiful butterflies, both small and large – and a whole spectrum of wild flowers. I had walked through wilderness areas, watched woodpeckers tapping at trees, seen wild turkeys and heard their startled cry, identified both box- and snapping-turtles, photographed a black eastern diamond rattlesnake, witnessed memorable sunsets and sunrises, and enjoyed, for the first time, meeting people walking a long-distance path.

I would unhesitatingly encourage others to go and walk part or the whole of the trail. A good five months is needed, and if I were to do it again I would start no earlier than mid-April. This would mean that I would see more of Spring emerging, have less capricious weather, miss the tiresome mosquitoes which plagued me for five days in May while crossing the swamps of New Jersey and New York, would also miss the June black-fly season, and would reach Maine in late July or early August.

I had two days at Baxter State Park, which contains Mt Katahdin. The area is exceptionally beautiful, and I saw several moose in the park. Once you reach the northern terminus of the trail, Baxter Peak, you have the finest ridge walk anywhere as the exciting conclusion. Knife Edge ridge from the Peak is better than our own Crib Goch (in Snowdonia) or Striding Edge (Helvellyn, The Lake District). If time allows, a few days exploring this wilderness area would prove a fitting end to your walk.

EQUIPMENT LIST

The following is a list of the main items of equipment I used on the walk, all of which were supplied by British manufacturers. The MSR stove, made in America, was very kindly lent me by Field and Trek Ltd. This stove is the only one suitable for the entire walk: obtaining gas cylinders or a specific type of fuel is hard. The MSR stove will burn any kind of fuel, and I used kerosene (paraffin), colman's fuel (rather like methy-

lated spirits), white gas (petrol), and barbecue starter fuel! It functioned
well on all these fuels and did not let me down.

1 Berghaus Cyclops Sérac No. 3 rucksack
1 Black's Insulation Mat
1 Black's Highland Extreme Sleeping Bag
1 Black's Ventile Highland Jacket
1 Berghaus Scarpa Bronzo Boots
1 Black's Gore-Tex Tunnel Tent

GUIDEBOOKS

The organising body for the Appalachian Trail, from whom to obtain
the guidebooks, maps and other books, as well as membership, is:
Appalachian Trail Conference, PO Box 236, Harpers Ferry, West
Virginia 25425, U.S.A.

The ten guidebooks (which include relevant maps) are: *Maine*; *New Hampshire
and Vermont*; *Massachusetts and Connecticut*; *New York and New Jersey*;
Pennsylvania; *Susquehanna River to Shenandoah National Park*; *Shenandoah
National Park*; *Southern Virginia*; *Tennessee and North Carolina*; *North Carolina
and Georgia*

SELECTED BIBLIOGRAPHY

Ed Garvey, *The Appalachian Hiker II* (Appalachia Books, 1978). This is the
    'Bible' of the walk.
National Geographic Survey, *The Appalachian Trail* (1972)
C. Ross, *A Woman's Journey* (East Woods Press, 1982)
Earl Schaffer, *Walk with Spring* (Appalachian Trail Conference, 1983)
Ann & Myron Sutton, *Wilderness on the Doorstep* (Lippincott, 1967)
Katahdin to Springer Mountain (Rodale Press, 1977)

The Pacific Crest Trail

I first learnt about the Pacific Crest Trail while on my second major walk
in 1971 through the Orkneys and Shetlands. While in Kirkwall, I
happened to come across the June 1971 issue of the *National Geographic
Magazine*, which included an extensive article on the trail. I resolved that
some day I would walk the trail, from Mexico to Canada.

I began my preparation for it in 1979 (the year after my British coast
walk) by walking the Appalachian Trail, which served as my introduction both to the American way of life and to the special problems of
walking in America. But as the Appalachian Trail only reached a height

of 6,800 ft (2,070 m), and as the Pacific Crest was over 13,000 ft (4,000 m), I also needed experience of high mountains. Soon after returning from America, therefore, I went to the Alps and walked the Tour of Mont Blanc (see p. 94). As part of my final preparation in April 1980, I went to the Himalayas and led a trek to Everest base camp (see p. 117), reaching a height of well over 18,000 ft (5,500 m). Within ten days of my return from Nepal I was heading across the Atlantic to begin the Pacific Crest Trail.

The idea of having a continuous trail, hugging the high mountains of California, Oregon and Washington, was first suggested by Clinton Clarke in 1926. Soon to come into existence was the John Muir Trail (see guidebook list, p. 145) in the Yosemite area of California, the Cascade Trail through Oregon and the Skyline Trail in Washington. But it was not until 1968 that the Pacific Crest Trail was adopted as a National Scenic Trail. Although a trail was already in existence then in Oregon and Washington, even now, out of about 1,600 miles (2,600 km) only a little over 500 miles (800 km) of permanent trail exists in California. Originally the plan was to have the trail finished by 1980, but it will be another ten years before it is fully complete. The trail from the Mexican border to Canada will eventually be 2,600 miles (4,200 km) long.

I reached the Mexican border, just south of the small village of Campo, approximately 50 miles (80 km) east of the San Diego, on 14 May. After photographing myself on the border, I headed north to Campo and signed in the Pacific Crest Trail register in the post office. I was about the four-hundredth person to have done so already that year. The first 500 miles (800 km) of the route were mostly through desert scenery, and a couple of days from the border the temperature soared to 35°C (95°F). This caused problems, for although my feet were hard and my boots had walked more than 600 miles (over 1,000 km) and were fully broken in, I got a blister that simply grew and grew.

The route combines desert with several 9,000 ft (2,750 m) mountains, and it made a startling contrast to be one day scorching in high temperatures and the next day camping in the snow. Most people set off at the beginning of April, when the temperatures are milder. I had planned to start in mid-May on purpose, for I average more than 25 miles (40 km) per day, which is a faster walking pace than usual (see p. 137). With such high temperatures I was worried about the Mojave Desert. Normally the temperature there is over 38°C (100°F), and it is advisable to cross the desert at night. Fortunately the temperature never rose any higher than 30°C (85°F), and I was able to cross in daylight in early June. I never carried any water and often went more than 16 miles (26 km) between watering points. I found this no hardship, but the Americans were rather astounded!

After about 550 miles (880 km) I reached Weldon and called at the post office to collect my food parcel containing fourteen days' food. I had brought across dehydrated food for 100 days from Britain, packed in parcels ready for mailing to a dozen post offices on or close to the trail. Not one was lost. From Weldon I began the ascent into the High Sierras, with some trepidation, for there was a good deal of snow. Everyone I met told me of the unusually high level of snow, but, undeterred, I pressed on. Sixty miles (96 km) from Weldon I had to leave the mountains and take the 'alternative' route up Owens Valley. The High Sierras were snowbound and had experienced their worst snowfall for many years, with twice as much snow as usual. I couldn't fight my way through, nor could I even find the trail. The rivers too were a problem: they were bursting from the melt water, which made them impossible to cross. I followed one river for 10 miles (16 km), but found no safe way across.

I headed out to the Owens Valley and walked up Highway 395. It was the worst road walk I have ever done. I could see the snow-draped mountains on my left and vowed I would be back. I checked in at the Forest Ranger Stations to learn of the current snow position, but all advised me not to go in. I trudged on to Lake Tahoe and ended up walking more than 300 miles (500 km) of road. I had chosen the wrong year to walk the trail, for I soon encountered another problem – St Helens. It had erupted on 18 May, and a month later I learnt that the trail was closed in Washington.

North of Lake Tahoe I was able to get back on to the trail, although I was still having to cope with a lot of snow. In northern California I reached Lassen Volcanic National Park and could see at first-hand many examples of volcanic activity, with thermal springs, geysers, a boiling lake, volcanic mountains, expanses of lava and cinder-cone hills. One of the most pleasurable aspects of the volcanic areas were the hot springs. On several occasions I stripped and lay in pools steaming with hot water. On one occasion the pool next to me was too hot to lie in. Instead, I put some tinned food to cook while I lay in my slightly cooler pool!

Approaching the Oregon border, with 1,600 miles (2,575 km) walked, I crossed the Marble Mountain Wilderness. Never have I seen so much evidence of black bears; their droppings were everywhere. I walked round a bend in the trail to find a black bear and cub walking in front of me, gently ambling up the hillside. That was one of the most wonderful sights I saw in America. They knew I was there – they have good noses to compensate for poor eyes – but they ignored me. Later that day three bears came down to the tent seeking food. I frightened them away by banging my cooking pans. Bears have little fear, and will rip the tent or rucksack for food, and should always be treated with respect.

In Oregon the scenery of the trail changed and became more wooded, with many high volcanic mountains such as Mt Jefferson and Mt Hood. At around 10,000 ft (3,000 m) they were very impressive, with glaciers on their upper flanks. In central Oregon I walked through the Three Sisters Wilderness – three glaciated mountains of exceptional beauty. For me they provided some of the finest scenery of the whole trail. After eighty-five days walking with only four days of rain, otherwise hot sun, I reached the Columbia River, the border of Oregon and Washington. I had walked just over 2,000 miles (3,220 km). In front of me was the Giffard Pinchot National Forest containing Mt St Helens. The trail, closed because of the recent and continuing volcanic activity, was not open again before Mt Rainier, 150 miles (240 km) north. Rather than road walk to Mt Rainier, I headed south to the Oregon coast and walked the coast trail to the mouth of the Columbia River. There I had to hitch a lift across a 4 mile (6.4 km) bridge, as it was closed to pedestrians, and reached Washington State.

Heading for Mt Rainier, I did a very lengthy walk around the Olympic Peninsula and through the rain forests to reach Seattle via two ferries. The next day I reached Mt Rainier and had a go at climbing this 14,500 ft (4,420 m) mountain, the most heavily glaciated in America. I gave up at 12,000 ft (3,650 m) because heavy rock falls had rendered the route very hazardous. The snow on the mountain up to about 9,000 ft (2,750 m) was covered in ash from Mt St Helens, and from my camp at 10,000 ft (3,000 m) I could see Mt St Helens steaming away. I picked up the trail again and headed north for the last 350 miles (565 km) to the Canadian border. I had eight days of very hard rain, but as I neared the North Cascades National Park my luck changed, and for the final few days in early September I had perfect weather.

The scenery was breathtaking. The trail wove its way through the mountains, averaging a height of 6,000 ft (9,650 m), with extensive views over numerous glaciated mountains. Two days from the border I met a group of climbers from the Seattle Mountaineers Club and joined them on a 1,000 ft (300 m) rock climb up the 8,500 ft (2,600 m) peak named The Tower. It is rarely climbed, and I signed in the summit register before reversing down the exposed rock face. The following day I pressed on and walked 29 miles (47 km). I knew the end of the trail, just inside Canada at Manning Park, was 37 miles (60 km) away. I thought the best way to do it was to walk it in one day. With my 60 lb (27 kg) pack on my back I left my final camp at 5.00 a.m., and eleven hours later, feeling tired but exceptionally sad, I reached Manning Park. I had made an illegal entry into Canada and spent the next twenty-four hours looking for a Customs and Immigration post to allow me to enter officially!

The walk from Mexico had taken 118 days and, because of Mt St Helens, I had walked much further than the official route: 2,700 miles (4,345 km) in all. I had grown to love the trail, and on reaching Canada felt totally dejected. As soon as I arrived in Vancouver, I immediately purchased air tickets to get back to the High Sierras. Although I had walked from Mexico to Canada there was still one thing left to do, and that was to climb Mt Whitney, the highest mountain in the contiguous states of America at 14,496 ft (4,418 m).

I headed back to the Owens Valley and at Lone Pine began the ascent of the mountain. It is not technically a difficult mountain, but the altitude does cause problems. Also it had snowed and was very cold. I camped a couple of nights at 12,000 ft (3,650 m) to acclimatise before ascending. There was a lot of snow and ice, which made the ascent tricky, but at 1.00 p.m. on 15 September I stood on the summit, in a temperature of −20°C (−6°F). The next day I descended to the Owens Valley, 10,000 ft (3,000 m) below, where the temperature was 35°C (95°F).

The following day, after having spent five months in America, I began the journey home. I am left with incredible memories of wonderful walking through the remote areas of Northern America. It was an experience I shall never forget.

Equipment

My rucksack was a new Berghaus Cyclops Scorpion which withstood the continuous punishment very well. I carried a 100 ft (30 m) rope for river crossings and for any climbing, and was thankful to have it. I also carried an ice-axe which proved invaluable, and saved my life at one point when I fell on a steep snow field. My boots were Scarpa Bronzo: they had to be re-soled after 2,000 miles (3,220 km), but certainly were the best type of boots for such an undertaking. I used a Black's (new)

'Icelandic Mummy' sleeping bag which kept me warm and snug even in my highest camps. My tent was a 'special' of hooped design and had been made for me out of Gore-Tex by Black's of Greenock. For food I used Raven's Regal meals, and I never grew tired of them. For cooking I used a Primus Grasshopper stove with propane cylinders. It functioned faultlessly, and the American subsidiary firm sent me cylinders to my pick-up points.

GUIDEBOOKS
The Pacific Crest Trail, vol 1: California (Wilderness Press, 1977)
The Pacific Crest Trail, vol 2: Oregon & Washington (Wilderness Press, 1979)
F. Beckey, *Challenge of the North Cascades* (The Mountaineers, 1977)
L. & G. Clark, *John Muir Trail Country* (Western Trails, 1977)
D. Green, *A Pacific Crest Odyssey* (Wilderness Press, 1979)
S. L. Harris, *Fire & Ice: The Cascade Volcanoes* (The Mountaineers, 1980)
C. Long, *The Pacific Crest Trail Hike Planning Guide* (Signpost, 1976)
National Geographic Society, *The Pacific Crest Trail* (1975)
E. Ryback, *High Adventure of Eric Ryback* (Bantam, 1971)
A. & M. Sutton, *The Pacific Crest Trail: Escape to the Wilderness* (Lippincott, 1975)
T. Winnett, *Guide to the John Muir Trail* (Wilderness Press, 1978)

AMERICAN TRAILS

I firmly believe that America will become the magnet for walking in the future. The vast spaces, the numerous National Parks, wilderness areas and diverse scenery provide a huge variety of walking opportunities. America already has some excellent trails, two of which I have described, and many others are proposed and are being actively looked into.

National Scenic Trails

The Appalachian Trail – 2,200 miles (3,540 km) from Springer Mountain in Georgia to Mt Katahdin in Maine. Designated 2 October 1968.

Pacific Crest Trail – 2,500 miles (4,000 km) from the Mexican border to Canada via the western mountains of California, Oregon and Washington states. Designated 2 October 1968.

Continental Divide Trail – 3,100 miles (4,990 km) along the Continental Divide from Mexico to Canada. Designated 10 November 1978.

North Country Trail – 3,246 miles (5,193 km) from Eastern New York State to the Lewis and Clark Trail in North Dakota. Designated 4 March 1980.

National Historic Trails

Lewis and Clark Trail – 3,700 miles (5,920 km) from Wood River, Illinois, to the mouth of the Columbia River in Oregon. Designated 10 November 1978.

Oregon Trail – 2,000 miles (3,200 km) from Independence, Missouri, to near Portland, Oregan. Designated 10 November 1978.

Mormon Pioneer Trail – 1,300 miles (2,080 km) from Nauvoo, Illinois, to Salt Lake City, Utah. Designated 10 November 1978.

Iditarod Trail – 2,037 miles (3,255 km) from Seward to Nome in Alaska. Designated 10 November 1978.

Proposed Trails

Desert Trail – 2,200 miles (3,520 km) from Canada to Mexico via Idaho, Oregon, Nevada, California and Arizona.

Florida Trail – 1,300 miles (2,080 km) through Florida from Blackwater River State Park to Everglades National Park.

Ice Age Trail – 1,000 miles (1,600 km) across Wisconsin from Potowatomi State Park to Interstate Park.

Natchez Trace – 694 miles (1,114 km) from Nashville, Tennessee, to Natchez, Mississippi.

Santa Fe Trail – 780 miles (1,248 km) from Independence, Missouri, to Santa Fe, New Mexico.

Potomac Heritage Trail – 874 miles (1,319 km) from the mouth of the Potomac River to its sources in Pennsylvania and West Virginia.

Pacific Northwest Trail – 1,200 miles (1,920 km) from the Continental Divide in Glacier National Park, Montana, to the Pacific Ocean at Cape Alava, Washington.

Hiking and conservation organisations in America

Appalachian Mountain Club, 5 Joy Street, Boston, Massachusetts 02108

American Hiking Society, 18600 SW 157th Ave, Miami, Florida 33187

California Wilderness Coalition, PO Box 429, Davis, California 95616

Friends of the Earth, 124 Spear Street, San Francisco, California 94105
The Mountaineers, 719 Pike Street, Seattle, Washington 98101
National Parks and Conservation Association, 1701 18th St, NW, Washington, DC 20009
Sierra Club, 530 Bush Street, San Francisco, California 94108
The Wilderness Society, 1901 Pennsylvania Avenue, Washington, DC 20006

CHAPTER 11

Marathon walking

The British have a tradition of long-distance walking which goes back hundreds of years. In the last century, for example, there was the Lakeland poet, William Wordsworth. More recently there has been Dr Barbara Moore, who achieved fame with her walk from Land's End to John o' Groats in the 1960s. She went on to walk across America from coast to coast, a distance of about 2,800 miles (4,500 km). John Hillaby, the President of the Backpacker's Club, has completed four major walks detailed in his books – *Journey Through Britain, Journey Through Europe, Journey to the Jade Sea* and *Journey Back Home*. Hamish Brown has also walked from Land's End to John o' Groats, as described in *Hamish's Groats End Walk*, and has climbed all the Scottish Munros in a single walk. Sebastian Snow has walked from Tierra del Fuego to the Panama Canal, the entire length of South America, as recorded in his book, *Rucksack Man*. George Meegan has gone one better, or should I say further, by walking from Tierra del Fuego to Alaska, which, at 19,000 miles (30,500 km), is believed to be the longest walk in history – although it took him seven years to complete.

My own achievements belong to the same tradition but represent a new departure. For a start, no one else has walked so far while carrying so much weight: over 40,000 miles (63,000 km) on major walks in the last ten years, with 45–60 lb (20–27 kg) on my back. Whereas George Meegan averaged less than 3,000 miles (4,800 km) a year on his seven-year walk, I would expect to cover the same distance in three years, and have in fact been averaging 4,000–5,000 miles (6,500–8,000 km) a year for more than seven years. And no one has done a major walk for six months, year after year. This is now the pattern of my life. How long it will remain so, I cannot say, but I neither want nor intend to let it lapse: if I did, I might not manage to complete the Pennine Way when I'm a hundred!

Marathon walking is by no means confined to the British, or to the young. The American David Kunst was the first person to walk around the world, completing the journey in 1974 after covering 14,500 miles (23,330 km) in four years. And numerous elderly people have been known to complete long walks. Plennie Wingo, when aged eighty-one, walked from Santa Monica in California to San Francisco, a distance of 452 miles (727 km) which he covered in eighty-five days; a slow pace, you may think, but he walked backwards! This was the forty-fifth anniversary of his 8,000 mile (12,870 km) walk from Santa Monica to Istanbul, which he also did backwards.

Perhaps the most outstanding walker of all was the American, Edward Payson Weston. His achievements are remarkable: he was the first man to walk 500 miles (800 km) in six days; in 1879 he walked 2,000 miles (3,200 km) in 1,000 hours; he walked 550 miles (885 km) in 141 hours and 56 minutes; on his seventy-first birthday he set off to walk 4,400 miles (7,080 km) from New York to San Francisco, and completed the journey in 105 days; and he died aged ninety!

So you can see, at the age of forty, I have only just begun!

While I hope that many major walks lie ahead of me, I do not think that my approach to walking is likely to change much, and I would like now to explain how I plan, prepare for and carry out long walks of 1,000 miles (say, 1,500 km) or more. Some of this will already be familiar from my accounts of individual walks in earlier chapters, but as so much depends on planning and preparation, I think it is worth devoting attention to these preliminary matters before describing the way I set about marathon walking, day by day.

Planning

Planning is the key to success. Not only does it make the walk more manageable, it is also psychologically helpful. Without a plan, time will be lost; with a plan, you have a goal, something to strive for.

Ever since my British coast walk I have planned my major walks in the same way. First, I decide when to start, which means taking into account the prevailing weather conditions. Thus on the coast walk, which I knew would take less than a year but would involve walking in winter months, I decided to head clockwise from London and cover the south-west peninsula first because that, statistically, is the mildest place in Britain during winter. (As it happened, I encountered freak conditions there which were far from mild.) In the case of the tour of Mont Blanc, timing is governed by the fact that normally the passes are free of snow only for about a month from mid-August. Again, on the Appalachian Trail in the U.S.A., the mountains will be snow-bound until April, so you cannot start much before then.

Usually I plan my walks on the basis of heading from south to north, partly for psychological reasons – for me walking northwards is uphill and challenging, whereas walking southwards is downhill and easy – but also because the sun is never in your eyes, and the map, whose top is always north, is much easier to read.

Once I have decided the overall plan of the walk and where to start from, I study all the relevant 1:50,000 series Ordnance Survey maps. When my route includes a long-distance footpath, I will obtain a copy of the appropriate guidebook, if one is available. By looking at the maps I can see where all the rights of way are, and can begin planning the route in detail. I generally link the rights of way together, using roads where necessary. I begin preparing a daily schedule, reckoning on distances of about 25 miles (40 km) per day. I have learnt from experience that 25 miles (40 km) on the map works out as 27–28 miles (43–45 km) on the ground, so, in order to calculate the distance as accurately as possible, I use a map measurer in my planning. I take no one's advice or seek any, because each walk should be 'a voyage of discovery'. I never pay any attention to the contour lines: it is immaterial just how much ascending and descending there is on the 25 mile (40 km) stretch.

If I can, I will have the schedule completely worked out a year before setting off on the walk. I like to do this because long-distance walking, as I practice it, means not only being physically fit, but also being mentally attuned to the task; and one way of preparing oneself mentally is to have everything pre-arranged several months in advance.

Preparation

With the route planning finalised, I now begin my preparation – sorting out the equipment I need, testing it to find which item is the most suitable, breaking in new boots, deciding what food to take, and beginning a training programme. At the start of the walk I am physically fit and reasonably prepared for the rigours ahead.

The equipment varies from walk to walk. There are two major factors in deciding what to take: the climatic conditions and the distance. For my walk up the Pacific Crest Trail, I carried an ice-axe, rope and crampons. Walking through deserts with these must have appeared odd, but the next day I could be 9,000 ft (2,750 m) up in snow-clad mountains. The length of a walk also dictates what equipment is needed. For a 2,000 mile (3,200 km) walk in summer months the equipment can be light, whereas on my British coastal walk of 7,000 miles (11,250 km) I needed three pairs of boots, and four sleeping bags for the different seasons. I wore out thirty-three pairs of thick woollen socks but only used two shirts!

Boots are the most important single item, and I always get a new pair for each walk. During the 1970s I wore Scarpa boots, which have never let me down; in the 1980s I have tried American and French boots. Boots of top quality need lengthy breaking in: walking 500 miles (800 km) in them before they become fully comfortable. But then they last. From experience I have found that they will cover a good 2,500–3,000 miles (4,000–4,800 km) before needing to be re-soled.

Rucksacks do not need breaking in, but I still like to make my choice well in advance. This is so that I can use the rucksack and adjust it to make sure that it fits right. I tend to go for the largest sack (95–100 litre capacity).

The sleeping bag I use depends greatly on the temperature range. Most of my walks lately have begun in cold conditions and ended in high summer. I have therefore chosen a sleeping bag that is both warm and has a full-length zip. As the weather warms up, I can undo the zip and use the sleeping bag like an eiderdown.

My choice of tent varies from walk to walk, my main criterion being that it should be large enough inside for myself as well as my rucksack. I generally use the tent for a few weekends before a major walk, in order to learn its secrets.

For cooking I have used a variety of stoves. Most recently, on the Pacific Crest Trail, and on my British marathons, I cooked with propane gas, using a stove such as the Primus Grasshopper or the Camping Gaz Globetrotter.

Finally, I select the food I am going to take with me, which must be not only tasty and satisfying but also light to carry. I test out different varieties at home or on a weekend walk, but in the main I have been using dehydrated food from Raven's Regal range. I then work out the quantities, bearing in mind that when I eventually reach civilisation again I will enjoy a massive meal.

When I have assembled all the equipment, I usually do a complete dress rehearsal two weeks before the start of my walk, in order to check that everything is exactly as I want it.

For more detailed lists of the equipment I have used on individual major walks, see pp. 104, 121, 139–40, and 144–5. And for my views on clothing, see pp. 8–16 in Chapter 2.

Physical training

While I am choosing my equipment, testing it, and breaking in my boots, I begin a full-scale training programme. Even between walks I try to keep reasonably fit by cycling and walking when I can. But with the approach of a major walk, I start training seriously about three months before setting off.

If the walk is scheduled to start in late May, I will usually do a 200 mile (320 km) walk at Easter, such as Wainwright's Coast-to-Coast Path or the Pennine Way, in order to improve my fitness and become used to carrying a 50–60 lb (22–27 kg) load on my back. Every weekend after that I carry a heavy rucksack. Then, about two weeks before departure, as part of my dress rehearsal, I will do a 100 mile (160 km) walk, such as my own Peakland Way, carrying everything that I will be taking. Only then will I feel both mentally prepared and physically ready for the journey ahead. The last three years have seen a change in my preparation. Being home for six months only, I have to do a year's work in that time. Having walked so much in Britain over the years, I tend to look elsewhere for less familiar places to explore. And to train I seek real mountains, of which there are none better than the Himalayas.

One important reason for covering such distances before a marathon walk is to harden your feet. Many people advocate rubbing methylated spirits all over your feet for about three weeks in order to harden the skin, but having tried this most diligently on several occasions, I have come to the conclusion that it does not help. I am convinced that the only way to prepare your feet is to wear your boots as much as possible before your walk.

If your boots are not fully broken in, you will get blisters; and blisters are one of the principal reasons why people give up on a walk. Suddenly carrying heavier weights than you are accustomed to can also cause blisters. Little blisters on the toes can be dealt with quite easily: all you need do is sterilise a needle or pin with a match and burst them. I do not put plasters on them, but let the air get to them and dry them out. Nor do I put on antiseptic cream, because this softens the skin when you want it to harden. On my first major walk (Hebridean Journey), I counted twenty-four blisters on my feet after seven days' walking! I just carried on, and ten days later had no blisters, just hard feet.

Large blisters on the heel are more of a problem, and you have to be careful, lest they turn septic. If a blister appears, do not burst it; cover the area extensively with padded foam, moleskin, or 'Second Skin'. Do not use a small plaster because this will help to spread the blister. You should stop early, walk around barefoot and let the air get to it. If it becomes very large, you have no option but to stop, burst it and let it dry out. On the Pacific Crest Trail I experienced the worst blister I have ever had – 2 in (50 mm) in diameter. It was brought on by the softening effect on my feet of the excessive heat as I crossed a desert, and I was forced to stop. I managed to squeeze the fluid out after seventeen pricks with a needle, walking around barefoot the next day, and then continued on my way, covering shorter distances for several days. I had no more blisters after that.

Even though you will get blisters when breaking in new boots, to use anything other than a boot is folly. Training shoes are of no use and can cause considerable damage to the achilles tendon. Wellingtons, although they keep your feet dry, do not protect or support them. I know to my cost that you cannot afford to neglect your feet. As our feet are one of the most important parts of our body, it is worth understanding a little about them.

Feet

Moira O'Brien, writing in *Medisport*, started her article on 'Aching Feet' by saying: 'The most neglected parts of the body are the feet. Only when they are painful and cause us problems do we pay any attention to them.' It is a statement I wholeheartedly endorse. As I have mentioned, I have had foot problems such as blisters and stress fractures from walking too much. Although we depend on our feet to get us around, we do in many ways abuse them and take them for granted.

The foot is one of the most complicated parts of the body. Apart from numerous ligaments and muscles, there are twenty-six different bones. Seven make up the ankle, and there are five metatarsals. Set at a right-angle to the body, the foot is narrower and thicker at the heel than at the toes. When placed squarely on the ground, the extremities and the ball of the foot touch the surface. The middle portion is an arch, and it not only propels you along but also counteracts the shock and pressure it would receive if it were flat.

The foot has two major functions: 1 it must support the weight of the body when standing; 2 it must act as a lever to propel the body forwards when walking. The main arch of the foot – between the heel and the base of the toes – is known as the medial longitudinal arch. This arch cannot be pressed flat, for the ligaments are too strong. When walking, the arch is like a semi-elliptic spring. In the walking motion the foot is almost in a rolling sequence of events. First the heel touches the ground, then the ball of the feet and finally the toes, by which time the heel is up in the air. To give some idea of just how much punishment the foot has to take: when walking, a third of the body weight is carried through the head of the first metatarsal.

Stress fractures

During my walk around the coastline of Britain in 1978 I suffered my first stress fractures: since then I have had two others. The fracture took place in the third metatarsal of my right foot: it is often referred to as a March Fracture, because many soldiers have suffered similarly. On that walk I carried 60 lb (27 kg) of equipment and averaged 28 miles (45 km) per day. In 37 days I had walked 1,028 miles (1,654 km), in 75 days 2,003 miles (3,223 km), and in 113 days 3,004 miles (4,833 km). It was around the 3,000-mile (4,827 km) mark that I began to experience trouble with my right foot. I had simply pushed the body too far and it was complaining! It was not until 300 miles (480 km) later that I had the foot X-rayed and learnt that a bone had snapped, simply through use, like metal fatigue.

Until someone had pushed themselves so far, no one knew just how much a human foot can stand. Had I carried on I would have done permanent damage. Instead, I heeded the specialist's advice, spent a month in plaster, and had very little exercise. In fact my right leg began withering away as the muscles, through inactivity, shrank. When the plaster came off, the difference between the legs was noticeable. The foot was X-rayed again, and the bone was found to have healed fully. The specialist advised that I now spend a couple of weeks walking around the garden to begin getting fit again and accustomed to walking. I found this very hard and, against his advice, I climbed several mountains over 2,000 ft (600 m) within twenty-four hours of being out of plaster.

I resumed my coast walk after only eight days out of plaster, against the advice of everyone. Although I would not admit it at the time, I was limping for the next six weeks and struggled to do 20 miles (32 km) in one day. In fact it was not until three months out of plaster that I managed for the first time to walk 30 miles (48 km) in one day. After that I became fitter and fitter, and was in fact walking better than I had ever walked before. I reached London four and a half months later, after walking 3,700 miles (5,950 km) without a rest day at an average of about 25 miles (40 km) per day overall. However, in the final two weeks of the walk, I became very tired. For the first time on a walk I lost weight and, instead of being around 11 stone (70 kg), I weighed 9½ stones (60 kg): a sign that I had pushed the body again beyond the limit and was now eating up my muscle tissue. In those final two weeks I was again suffering pain in both feet and legs. Four days from London my legs hurt very badly and I wondered whether I would make it.

This is one of the problems of a lone walker, for it is very hard to know just how far one should push oneself. Being alone, you tend just to keep going, unaware of the distances you are covering day after day. On the Appalachian Trail in America I regularly walked over 30 miles (48 km) a day, but did not suffer any foot problems. However, on my walk up the Pacific Crest Trail, I did suffer on two occasions. In both instances I had walked too far. After walking 1,600 miles (2,575 km) through California, I was determined to reach Ashland in Oregon. I pressed on, and in fifty hours (two and a half days) had walked over 90 miles (145 km). I had to stop for two days to let my feet return to normal, as they were badly swollen.

Just how far you can push yourself without suffering foot problems is not easy to answer. It very much depends on your footwear, and how much weight you are carrying, and the number of miles walked each day. Marathon runners who run 200 miles or more a week (say, 320 km) usually suffer stress fractures. I was walking at least 200 miles (320 km) a week on the coast walk. It would appear that the human foot can withstand no more than 200 miles (320 km) per week over a long period when carrying a heavy load. Someone carrying 40 lb (18 kg) of equipment and averaging 20 miles (32 km) a day can walk almost indefinitely and not suffer any foot problems, whereas someone like myself carrying 60 lb (27 kg) and walking 30 miles (48 km) a day will have problems. Weight is very important when related to human performance. Perhaps also the weight of the person's body would add strain if one is very heavy.

I am often asked: do I get cramp or aching muscles? I don't, and I believe the reason lies in my approach to walking. During the day I keep up a steady pace. Uphill I proceed at a slow pace, and when descending I relax and walk a little quicker. However, the real secret is at the end of the day. When I reach my destination, I immediately put up my tent and lie down, resting my legs. For the next twelve hours I do not get up. This allows time for my legs and feet to recover and become ready to walk 25

miles (40 km) or more the next day. Without that kind of rest I am sure
that I would soon become tired.

A day on a major walk

I will now attempt to describe what I go through on a day's walk of more
than 25 miles (40 km) while I am on a marathon.

In Britain I normally get up around 7 a.m., or rather lie in my sleeping
bag and prepare breakfast, usually a bowl of muesli and a mug of hot
sweet tea. By 7.30 a.m. I am up and packing the rucksack, taking my tent
down last. Around 8 a.m. I am on my way. In America where the daylight
hours are different – they have no long summer daylight hours – I
usually begin walking at 6 a.m.

The previous night I will have studied my route for the day, so that I
can make my start with a sense of purpose and waste no time in deciding
on my goal for the day's walk. As I stride along at a steady 3 miles (5 km)
per hour I always have my map in my hand, folded open at the correct
area. This is so that I can constantly check that I am walking in the right
direction and can quickly decide what to do upon reaching a road or fork
in the path. I have my compass handy too if I am in the mountains and
walking in mist.

As I walk I am never conscious of ticking off the miles or kilometres.
This is part of my psychology. What matters to me is where I want to be
at the end of the day. How far away my target is or how many mountains I
have to cross are of no concern to me. I forget all about that and strive
towards my destination. This way I find that I enjoy the walk more and
remain eager to see what lies ahead. While walking I keep a careful
watch on where I am putting my feet. The last thing I want on a major
walk is to trip up and twist an ankle. However, I don't keep my eyes glued
to the path beneath me. I have learnt, through experience, to read a path
ahead, rather like driving a car, and to prepare myself automatically for
the protruding rock, the bend in the path or the overhanging branch. At
the same time I am also looking out for wild flowers, birds in the bushes
and trees, and animals in the undergrowth. I frequently stop and watch a
bird through binoculars, or photograph flowers with a telephoto lens.

I break many of the accepted methods of walking. I do not stop during
the day, nor do I have a five-minute break every hour. I just keep going,
maintaining a steady pace. I carry no water and do not drink any. This is
no hardship for me. I have found through experience that once I start to
drink I simply want more and more. By about 10.30 a.m. I am eating my

first bar of chocolate. During the first couple of weeks of the walk I eat two or three bars a day. After a month I am eating four or five, and six weeks out on a walk I have reached my peak and am eating eight a day. I generally keep a few bars at the top of an outside pocket on the rucksack. I stop and slip the rucksack off and take a couple out: one to eat immediately and the other to eat an hour later.

At lunchtime I may rest for five minutes without the rucksack while I scrutinise the map. I will also eat a couple more bars of chocolate. I then walk for a good two hours before eating another bar at around 3.30 p.m. That is usually my last chocolate for the day, although if I am going to be walking until 8.00 p.m. I may nibble another bar in the late afternoon. By 2.00 p.m. I have walked 20 miles (32 km) and begin to ease off slightly. I normally work on the rule '20 miles (32 km) by 2.00 p.m.'; sometimes, '12 miles (19 km) by 12 noon'.

At around 5.00 p.m. I am beginning to look for somewhere to camp, assuming, of course, that I am close to the end of the day's walk. If there is a farm nearby I will ask permission to stop, and, touch wood, I have never yet been refused. I always camp near to water as I simply refuse to carry it. I erect the tent first before stowing the equipment inside and unrolling the sleeping bag. I don't sit outside but prefer to get my boots and socks off and let the air get to my feet. I lie down in the tent on my sleeping bag. This is important, for it relaxes my muscles which, after 30 miles (48 km) of walking, may be a little sore. A rest enables them to recover and allows me to set off again the next morning fresh and ready to walk the same distance again. As I lie down I cook the evening meal in front of me, while making notes of the day's walk, and check through the route for the morrow. My meal is generally a bowl of soup, a main course and a tin of fruit, followed by a mug of tea and half a packet of biscuits. I usually put on weight, and very seldom lose it! After the meal I lie in the tent with my head on my upright boots, reading a book. When it is time to go to sleep I lay the boots flat, heels together, forming my pillow. I generally fall asleep instantly.

It must be hard for an outsider to appreciate the mental strain I go through while on a major walk. Sometimes I find it necessary to withdraw into myself and combat the strain and loneliness of the walk. At other times I am exuberant about the walk and the scenery. When I meet people en route, I try to be pleasant and answer their questions; sometimes I just say hello and press on. As a rule I don't stay too long, for after being alone for so long I can easily start forming a 'relationship' on meeting a fellow human, which can disturb my mental approach. When I start feeling 'attached' I know it is time to move on. This does not mean I am a loner – far from it: it is simply my method of safeguarding myself against normal human pressures. I believe I am very sociable, and when I get back from a walk I like to share what I have done by writing and lecturing about it. However, while on the walk, I prefer walking alone – 'for he who travels alone travels fastest'.

Just as I like to have a goal in front of me before setting off on each day's walk, so I like to plan ahead from one major walk to the next. Indeed my major walks have themselves been a preparation for other much longer walks. Before starting off round the coast of Britain, I had successfully completed six walks of 1,000 miles (1,600 km) or more. Only on the last one did I feel ready to attempt the whole coast route. I am approaching my American walks in the same way. The Appalachian Trail served as my introduction to walking in America, in preparation for the Pacific Crest Trail.

What of the future, you may ask? Having walked so much, isn't it time to put my boots up? The simple answer is 'No'; I thirst for more and harder walks in other countries. As I write this, the next four years are basically planned with a 3,500 mile (5,600 km) walk along the Continental Divide in America, a 4,500 mile (7,250 km) walk across America from coast to coast (which I intend to complete in six months, unlike Peter Jenkins, author of *A Walk Across America* and *Walk West*, who took three years!) , a round-the-world walk, and a walk in South America.

Whilst the above may seem enough, I am forever gathering material for other ideas. In the last month, guides to and books on Australia, Tasmania and New Zealand have arrived. A major Himalayan walk is slowly taking shape, another in Africa is gathering momentum. I have not forgotten Britain, for I know there is one other walk still to be done and my route is basically planned. I don't lack ideas, just time.

The last ten years of walking have seen an idea develop into a way of life. I have no intention of retiring, and will continue my pursuit of 2,000 mile (3,200 km) walks in various parts of the world for many years to come.

CHAPTER 12

Merrill's Law

I said at the beginning of this book that there are no rules to long-distance walking, nor are there. But during the course of my major marathons I have evolved several rules of my own. Some of them may appear to be harsh, and to require too great a degree of dedication, but they have served me well over many thousands of miles, and I feel that I can recommend them. Here they are, in no particular order:

Always walk alone. Only you yourself know your capabilities. To go with someone whose pace is slower or faster than yours makes the walk more tiring. Five miles (8 km) is the furthest you should go with another person. A companion distracts your concentration and interferes with your enjoyment of the scenery; half the time you do not take in what you are seeing, whereas on your own you can absorb the countryside in all its aspects. Your companion can also upset you psychologically if he is ill or perhaps disgruntled with the bad weather.

Settle for shorts. Shorts give you freedom of movement, and I wear them all the time, whatever the conditions. I usually wear the same pair throughout a marathon, although I carry a spare one. They do not get washed, except in rain or if I swim. Likewise, I generally wear just one shirt, which also remains unwashed. And socks I prefer to wear until they are worn through – usually after about three weeks, when I throw them away.

Break in your boots. Boots are the most important single item of equipment. Before setting off on a major marathon, you should have walked at least 500 miles (800 km) in them. Until then they are not fully broken in.

Turn a blind eye to blisters. Simply ignore them. Let time do the healing. Fresh air in the evenings will help to dry them, so do not cover them with plasters or soften the skin with antiseptic cream. If they become very bad, you may have to walk barefoot for a while. On no account allow them to stop you from completing the walk.

Carry no water. Weight is an important factor in marathon walking, and I have never yet carried a container of water. Always camp near a stream, river or habitation where you can obtain water.

Do not drink during the day. This may seem odd advice, and to go against the accepted practice of normal living; but once I have breakfasted I do not drink again until the evening – which often means walking for twelve hours over a distance of 30 miles (48 km) or more without a drink. If the weather is very hot, I might have a pint of milk or an ice-cream during the afternoon; otherwise my only sustenance is chocolate – six or eight bars a day. Once you have had a drink during the day, you only want more and more.

Do not stop and rest. From the time I set off in the morning until I camp in the evening, I do not rest, not even for lunch. It is better to stay on your feet and keep your muscles active; resting causes your muscles to stiffen up and makes it hard to get going again. If I do pause, I seldom take my rucksack off, and prefer to lean against a wall with the rucksack resting on top of it, thus taking the weight off my shoulders.

Limit your conversations with people you meet. Half an hour's chat is enough! Longer than that and you may find yourself wanting to stop walking for the day. One has to keep one's objective in mind, otherwise it is easy to be distracted.

Use your evenings to recover. At the end of the day's walk, after installing myself in my tent, I remain lying down until the next morning. This is essential for one's legs. After twelve hours' rest, one's tiredness has gone, and one's vitality has been restored. Thanks to this rule, I have never had stiff limbs in the morning.

Do not take a rest day. I walk seven days a week for several months on end. It is better to have an easy day, covering only 20 miles (32 km) instead of the usual 30 (48 km), than to put your feet up altogether. Nothing is gained during a day off, and you are liable to relax mentally and lose your concentration.

Stick to your schedule. A schedule is the key to success, and it must be adhered to. It gives you a sense of purpose and a means of driving yourself on. It helps you to programme your mind, and saves you from having to think what to do next. Without a schedule, I doubt whether I would complete the walk.

Disregard bad weather. There's nothing you can do about it, so make the most of the cold, wet days as well as the idyllic, sunny ones. Often I am soaked day after day. If this happens, just carry on and ignore it, and your morale will stay high.

Do not let illness get you down. Generally if I become ill during a major walk, I try to keep going, albeit slowly. Again, I find this helpful to morale, whereas stopping and waiting to get better is bad psychologically.

Do not accept lifts. One is often offered a lift when walking on a road. I never accept the offer because to do so would ruin the purpose of the walk: if I did take one the walk would be over. I always walk facing the oncoming traffic.

Develop the three D's: drive, dedication and determination. These are the ingredients which make successful marathon walking. One must be single-minded.

Have faith. During a major walk, I do not worry that accidents may happen or tragedies occur. I do not even inform other people of my day's route or expected time of arrival. I go into the countryside and mountains for total freedom. I pray often during a walk, and have several times had deeply moving moments. At the end I always pray, and say a big 'thank you'.

The Countryside Commission

The Countryside Commission

John Dower House, Crescent Place, Cheltenham, Gloucester, GL50 3RA

In August, 1968, the Countryside Act became law. As a result, the National Parks Commission was replaced by the Countryside Commission. The National ParksCommission had been responsible for the National Parks, and the other areas were almost neglected. To remedy the situation the Countryside Commission was brought into being, with much greater powers.

The Commission is an independent statutory body with a very broad scope. It keeps a close eye on the countryside in all regions of England and Wales, especially with regard to the conservation of beauty. It helps to provide and improve facilities for enjoyment of the countryside, and helps organise access to open country. Not only is it involved with the National Parks but also with designating the Areas of Outstanding Natural Beauty, creating Heritage Coasts and the official Long-Distance Footpaths, Country Parks and picnic sites. The Commission co-ordinates the work of private bodies, and the goodwill of farmers, and helps to advise so that the scenery remains for the enjoyment of generations to come.

The Commission helps to finance local authorities, public bodies or individuals whose project merits in its view a furtherance of the aims of the Countryside and National Parks Acts. It also helps towards the running costs of the Information Centres in the National Parks.

In England and Wales today there are 9,066 sq miles (13,600 sq km) of National Parks – one tenth of the total area; 1,685 miles (2,528 km) of official long-distance footpaths; 9,652 sq miles (14,478 sq km) of designated Areas of Outstanding Natural Beauty; and 722 miles (1,084 km) of defined heritage coasts.

Countryside Commission for Scotland

Battleby, Redgorton, Perth, PH1 3EW

The Commission was established under the Countryside (Scotland) Act of 1967 and has five main aims: Protection, Recreational Provision, Conservation Education, Research and Development, and Review. Until the setting-up of the Commission there was no way of establishing statutory long-distance footpaths in Scotland. Under the 1967 Act the Commission was given 'responsibility to prepare and submit reports to the Secretary of State for Scotland on the development of routes where it thinks the public should be enabled to make extensive cross-country journeys in Scotland, away from public roads. Once long-distance routes are approved, the Secretary of State is able to reimburse the cost to local authorities of developing and maintaining them.' Three footpaths have now been approved, with the West Highland Way now open.

Areas of Outstanding Natural Beauty in Britain

The benefits of designation to rural communities have been clearly defined by the Countryside Commission. Status as an 'Area of Outstanding Natural Beauty'

'– makes it less likely that the government or public agencies will propose major new intensive developments such as reservoirs, roads or power stations

– strengthens the hand of the planning authority in rejecting proposals for new urban development which would be out of character, and strengthens their hand in obtaining high standards of design

– makes it more likely that funds will be found (e.g. from local authorities and the Countryside Commission) for conservation measures, including management agreements and tree planting

– encourages the appointment of ranger services which help farmers to solve problems caused by the number of visitors

– increases the chances that owners may gain fiscal relief from capital transfer tax.'

Areas of Outstanding Natural Beauty designated by the Countryside Commission in chronological order as established (England and Wales). Approximate area in sq miles/sq kilometres.

Gower 73/189	Surrey Hills 160/414
Quantock Hills 38/99	Cannock Chase 26/68
Lleyn Peninsula 60/155	Shropshire Hills 300/777
Northumberland Coast 50/129	Dorset 400/1,036

Malvern Hills 40/104
Cornwall 369/957
North Devon 66/171
South Devon 128/332
East Hampshire 151/391
East Devon 103/267
Isle of Wight 73/189
Chichester Harbour 29/75
Forest of Bowland 310/803
Solway Coast 41/107
Chilterns 309/800
Sussex Downs 379/981
Cotswolds 582/1,507
Anglesey 83/215

South Hampshire Coast 30/78
Norfolk Coast 174/450
Kent Downs 326/845
Suffolk Coast and Heaths 151/391
Dedham Vale 28/72
Wye Valley 125/325
North Wessex Downs 671/1,738
Mendip Hills 78/202
Arnside and Silverdale 29/75
Lincolnshire Wolds 216/560
Isles of Scilly 6/16
High Weald 560/1,450
Cranborne Chase and West Wiltshire
    Downs 371/960

Heritage Coasts

Heritage Coasts (March 1983) defined by the Countryside Commission in chronological order as established (England and Wales).
Approximate length in miles/kilometres.

North Northumberland 57/92
Sussex 8/13
Gower 34/55
Glamorgan 14/22
North Anglesey 18/29
Holyhead Mountain 8/13
Aberffraw Bay 5/8
Great Orme 4/7
Lleyn 55/88
Tennyson 21/33
Hamstead 7/11
South Pembrokeshire 41/66
Marloes and Dale 27/43
St Bride's Bay 5/8
St David's Peninsula 51/82
Dinas Head 11/18
St Dogmaels and Moylgrove 14/22
Isles of Scilly 40/64
North Norfolk 39/63
South Foreland 4/7
Dover–Folkestone 4/7
Hartland (Cornwall) 5/8
Widemouth–Pentire Head 31/50

West Penwith 34/54
Lizard 16/26
Looe–Gribbin Head 24/38
Mevagissey–Amsterdam Point 14/23
Rame Head 4/7
Trevose Head 2.5/4
St Agnes Head 6/9
Portreath–Godrevy 6/10
Suffolk 35/56
North Yorkshire and Cleveland 34/55
Purbeck 32/51
Flamborough Head 12/19
Ceredigion Coast 21/34

Proposed new coasts
Spurn Head
Chesil Beach
Lyme Bay
Scabbacombe Head
South Devon
Hartland (Devon)
Exmoor
St Bee's Head

Long-distance footpaths

Long-distance routes designated by the Countryside Commission are 'official' in the sense that the Commission makes grants-in-aid for 100 per cent of the upkeep of the paths. And, secondly, all public rights of way along these routes have been secured.

Official long-distance footpaths (March 1983) designated by the Countryside Commission (England and Wales).
Approximate length in miles/kilometres.

Pennine Way 250/402

Cleveland Way 93/150

Pembrokeshire Coast Path 180/290

Offa's Dyke Path 168/270

South Downs Way 80/129

South-West Peninsula Coast Path:

   North Cornwall 135/217

   South Cornwall 133/214

   South Devon 93/150

   Somerset and North Devon 82/132

   Dorset 72/116

Ridgeway 85/137

North Downs Way 141/227

Wolds Way 79/127

In Scotland

West Highland Way

Proposed new routes

Peddars Way and

Norfolk Coast Path

Recreational footpaths

The following is a selection of footpaths throughout England and Wales which the Countryside Commission has helped to improve and promote. These 'recreational paths' are closer to towns and transport and do not have the access to 'wilderness' that is a characteristic of the official long-distance routes. All are waymarked, but vary considerably in length from 7 to 140 miles (11 to 225 km) long. Guidebooks/booklets on these routes (containing maps) are available from H.M.S.O. The Countryside Commission publishes a detailed booklet listing 72 recreational paths.

Approximate lengths in miles/kilometres.

The Dales Way 81/130

The Ebor Way, North Yorkshire 70/112

The Calderdale Way, West Yorkshire 50/80

Colne Valley Circular Walk, West Yorkshire 15/24

Viking Way, Lincolnshire 140/225

Wirral Way* 12/19

Gritstone Trail, Cheshire 17/27

The Sandstone Trail, Cheshire 30/49
High Peak Trail, Peak District* 17/28
Tissington Trail, Peak District* 13/21
The Staffordshire Way 32/51
Jubilee Way, Leicestershire 16/25
Glyndwr's Way, Powys 121/195
Wye Valley Walk, Powys 36/58
The Knightley Way, Northamptonshire 12/19
The Grafton Way, Northamptonshire 12/20
The North Buckinghamshire Way 30/48
The Cotswold Way 100/161
The Essex Way 50/80
The Forest Way, Essex 20/32
The Oxfordshire Way 60/96
Lower Wye Valley Walk, Gwent 34/55
Usk Valley, Gwent 22/36
The Avon Walkway* 13/21
The Forest Way, East Sussex* 10/15.5

Isle of Wight
Bembridge Trail 15/24
Coastal Path 60/97
Hamstead Trail 8/13
Nunwell Trail 10/16
Shepherds Trail 10/16
Stenbury Trail 10/16
Tennyson Trail 15/24
Worsley Trail 15/24

*open to horseriders and cyclists as well as walkers.

Unofficial long-distance footpaths in England and Wales

Over the last few years there has been an incredible upsurge of interest in and development of long-distance walking routes. The following is a selection of walks in England and Wales, of 30 miles (48 km) or more. Most have a guidebook detailing the route.

Southern England

Bristol Countryway – 81 miles (129 km) from Slimbridge Wild Fowl Trust to Weston-super-Mare.
Laurence Main, *A Bristol Countryway* (Thornhill Press)
Essex Way – 65 miles (104 km) from Epping Station to Dedham Village.
The Essex Way (The East Anglia Tourist Board)
Harcamlow Way – 140 miles (224 km) Circular from Harlow.
Fred Matthews, *The Harcamlow Way* (Conservators of Epping Forest)
Inkpen Way – 62 miles (99 km) from the A339 near Basingstoke to Salisbury.
Ian Ward, *The Inkpen Way* (Thornhill Press)
Isle of Wight Coastal Path – 60 miles (96 km) Encircles Island.
Guidebooks from Isle of Wight County Council
King Alfred's Way – 108 miles (173 km) from HMS *Victory*, Portsmouth to Christchurch, Oxford.
Laurence Main, *King Alfred's Way* (Thornhill Press)
London Countryway – 205 miles (328 km) Circular from Box Hill Stepping Stones.
Keith Chesterton, *The London Countryway* (Constable)
North Buckinghamshire Way – 30 miles (48 km) from Chequers Knapp to Wolverton.
The North Buckinghamshire Way (The Ramblers' Association National Office, see p. 179)
Oxfordshire Way – 65 miles (104 km) from Bourton-on-the-Water to Henley-on-Thames.
Alison Kemp, *The Oxfordshire Way* (Oxfordshire Branch of the Council for the Preservation of Rural England)
Oxon Trek – 63 miles (101 km) Circular from Bladon.
Laurence Main, *The Oxon Trek* (Thornhill Press)
Saxon Shore Way – 140 miles (224 km) from Gravesend to Rye.
Information from Kent Rights of Way Council

Somerset Way – 108 miles (173 km) from Minehead Station to Bath Abbey.
Laurence Main, *A Somerset Way* (Thornhill Press)
South Wessex Way – 117 miles (187 km) from Petersfield to Sandbanks, Poole Harbour.
Laurence Main, *A South Wessex Way* (Thornhill Press)
St Peter's Way – 45 miles (72 km) from Chipping Ongar to St Peter's Chapel, Bradwell-on-Sea.
Fred Matthews & Harry Bitten, *The St Peter's Way* (Conservators of Epping Forest)
Sussex Border Path – 150 miles (240 km) from Emsworth Station to Rye.
Aeneas Mackintosh & Ben Perkins, *The Sussex Border Path*
Thames Walk – 156 miles (250 km) from Putney Bridge, London, to Thames Head, Gloucester.
The Thames Walk (by and from Southern Area Ramblers' Association)
Thames Valley Heritage Walk – 107 miles (171 km) from Thames Valley to Woodstock.
Miles Jebb, *The Thames Valley Heritage Walk* (Constable)
Thamesdown Trail – 54 miles (86 km) Circular from Cricklade.
Laurence Main, *The Thamesdown Trail* (First published in 1978 by author; reprinted 1980 by Thornhill Press)
Three Forests Way – 60 miles (96 km) Circular from Loughton.
Fred Matthews & Harry Bitten, *The Three Forests Way* (Conservators of Epping Forest)
Two Moors Way – 103 miles (165 km) from Ivybridge to Lynmouth.
Helen Rowett, *Two Moors Way* (The Ramblers' Association National Office)
Wessex Way – 103 miles (165 km) from Overton Hill to Swanage.
Alan Proctor *The Wessex Way* (Thornhill Press)
Wiltshire Way – 162 miles (259 km) Circular from Salisbury Cathedral.
Laurence Main, *A Wiltshire Way* (Thornhill Press)
Vanguard Way – 63 miles (101 km) from East Croydon Station to Exceat Bridge, Cuckmere.
The Vanguard Way (Vanguard Rambling Club)

Midlands and East Anglia

Cal-Der-Went Walk – 30 miles (48 km) from Horbury Bridge, Wakefield, to the A57 at the Ladybower Reservoir.
Geoffrey Carr, *The Cal-Der-Went Walk* (Dalesman Publishing Co. Ltd)
Cotswold Way – 100 miles (160 km) from Bath to Chipping Campden.
Mark Richards, *Cotswold Way* (Thornhill Press)
R. G. Sale, *A Guide to the Cotswold Way* (Constable)
Derbyshire Gritstone Way – 56 miles (100 km) from Derby Cathedral to Edale.

Gritstone Trail Walker's Guide (by and from Cheshire County Council)
Limey Way – 40 miles (64 km) from Castleton to Thorpe.
John N. Merrill, *The Limey Way* (First published by Dalesman Publishing Co. Ltd; reprinted 1983 by JNM Publications)
Navigation Way – 100 miles (160 km) from Birmingham to Chasewater.
Peter Groves, *The Navigation Way* (Tetradon Publications Ltd)
Peakland Way – 100 miles (160 km) Circular from Ashbourne.
John N. Merrill, *The Peakland Way* (First published by Dalesman Publishing Co. Ltd; reprinted 1983 by JNM Publications)
The Trail-Blazer Challenge Walk – 25 miles (40 km) Circular from Bakewell.
John N. Merrill, *The Trail-Blazer Challenge Walk* (JNM Publications)
Peddars Way – 50 miles (80 km) from Holme-next-the-Sea to Knettishall Heath Country Park (to be part of the Norfolk Way – 87 miles (139 km) – and including the coast from Cromer to Hunstanton).
Bruce Robinson, *The Peddars Way* (Weathercock Press Ltd)
Sandstone Trail – 32 miles (51 km) from Beacon Hill, Frodsham, to Grindley Brook.
Sandstone Trail (by and from Cheshire County Council)
Staffordshire Way – 90 miles (135 km) from Mow Cop to Kinver Edge.
The Staffordshire Way (by and from Staffordshire County Council)
Viking Way – 112 miles (179 km) from Barton-on-Humber to Oakham.
Viking Way (information by and from Lincs. and South Humberside Ramblers' Association)
West Midland Way – 162 miles (259 km) Circular from Meriden.
Eric Jones and Ron Leek, *A Guide to the West Midland Way* (Constable)

Northern England

Allerdale Ramble – 55 miles (88 km) from Seathwaite to Skinburness.
Harry Appleyard, *The Allerdale Ramble* (from Allerdale District Council)
Bolton Boundary Walk – 50 miles (80 km) Circular from Affetside Cross.
Michael Cresswell, *Bolton Boundary Way* (from Town Hall, Bolton)
Bounds of Ainstry – 44 miles (70 km) Circular from Tadcaster.
Beating the Bounds of the Ainstry (by and from West Riding Area Ramblers' Association)
Calderdale Way – 50 miles (80 km) Circular from Clay House, Greetland.
The Calderdale Way (Calderdale Way Association, from West Yorks. County Council)
Cleveland Way Missing Link – 50 miles (80 km) from Scarborough to Helmsley.
Malcolm Boyes, *A Guide to the Cleveland Way and Missing Link* (Constable)
Crosses Walk – 53 miles (85 km) Over the North York moors.
Malcolm Boyes, *The Crosses Walk* (Dalesman, 1979)

Coast to Coast Walk – 190 miles (306 km) from St Bee's Head to Robin Hood's Bay.
A. Wainwright, *A Coast to Coast Walk* (Westmorland Gazette)
Cumbria Way – 70 miles (112 km) from Ulverton to Carlisle.
John Trevelyan, *The Cumbria Way* (Dalesman Publishing Co. Ltd)
Dales Way – 81 miles (131 km) from Ilkley to Bowness on Lake Windermere.
Colin Speakman, *The Dales Way* (Dalesman Publishing Co. Ltd)
Derwent Way – 90 miles (144 km) from Barmby-on-the-Marsh to Lilla Howe on the North Yorkshire Moors.
Richard C. Kenchington, *The Derwent Way* (Dalesman Publishing Co. Ltd)
Ebor Way – 70 miles (112 km) from Helmsley to Ilkley.
J. K. E. Piggin, *The Ebor Way* (Dalesman Publishing Co. Ltd)
Eden Way – 55 miles (88 km) from Coltar Riggs near Hawes to Wetherall.
Geoffrey Berry, *Across the Northern Hills* (Westmorland Gazette)
Hadrian's Wall – 75 miles (120 km) from Wallsend to Bowness on Solway.
Hull Countryway – 48 miles (77 km) Circular from Hull.
Alan Killick, *The Hull Countryway* (Lockington Publishing Co.)
Leeds to the sea – 44 miles (70 km) Leeds to Kilburn (a further 46 miles, 73 km on the Cleveland Way to Saltburn-by-the-Sea).
A Walk from Leeds to the Sea (by and from West Riding Area Ramblers' Association)
Lyke Wake Walk – 40 miles (64 km) from Osmotherley to Ravenscar.
Bill Cowley, *Lyke Wake Walk* (Dalesman Publishing Co. Ltd)
Minster Way – 51 miles (82 km) from Beverley to York Minister.
Ray Willis, *The Minster Way* (Lockington Publishing Co.)
Reivers Way – 150 miles (240 km) from Corbridge to Alnmouth.
H. O. Wade, *The Reivers Way* (Frank Graham)
Rosedale Circuit – 30 miles (48 km) Circular from Rosedale Abbey.
Information available from the Rambling Club Secretary, Blackburn Welfare Society, Brough, E. Yorks.
Ryedale Round – 165 miles (264 km) Circular from York Minster.
Walking Round Ryedale with Ken Piggin (Lockington Publishing Co.)
Teesdale Watershed Walk – 49 miles (78 km) Circular from Middleton in Teesdale.
Gene Robinson, *Feats for Feet. Two Long-Distance Routes in the Pennines* (Teesdale Mercury Ltd)
Wear Valley Way – 46 miles (74 km) from Killhope Wheel Picnic Area to Wellington Picnic Site.
White Rose Walk – 40 miles (64 km) from near Newton-under-Roseberry to Kilburn White Horse.
Geoffrey White, *The White Rose Walk* (Dalesman Publishing Co. Ltd)
Yoredale Way – 100 miles (160 km) from York Minster to Kirkby Stephen.
Yorkshire Dales Centurion Walk – 100 miles (160 km) Circular from Horton-in-Ribblesdale.

Jonathan Ginesi, *Official Guide Book to the Yorkshire Dales Centurion Walk* (John Siddall (Printers) Ltd)

Wales

Glyndwr's Way – 120 miles (192 km) Knighton to Welshpool.
Glyndwrs Way (Leaflets from Powys County Council)
Offa's Dyke to the sea – 80 miles (128 km) from Kington to Aberystwyth.
From Offa's Dyke to the Sea through picturesque Mid-Wales (by and from C. D. Ehrenzeller)
Wye Valley Walk – 36 miles (57 km) from Hay-on-Wye to Rhayader.
Wye Valley Walk – Llwybr Bro Gwy (by and from Powys County Council)

Competitive and challenge walks in Britain

Competitive walks

The word 'competitive' is used guardedly in this section, as all the following walks can be done whenever one wants to and at whatever pace. Basically they are walks where there is some kind of challenge detailed by the originator or author. Generally one is out to complete the walk in under a certain period of time, such as the Lyke Wake Walk in under a day – 24 hours. However, competitive spirit does come into this section as people try to beat the record time for the walk or attempt to do a 'first' such as the first winter crossing. For many of the walks there are badges and certificates available for those successfully walking the route within the time limit. Many of the walks make a pleasant weekend (2-day) trip. The following is a general list of some of the walks in this category:

Bilsdale Circuit – 30 miles (48 km) Circular from Newgate Bank car park, north of Helmsley in North York Moors. Complete within 12 hours.

Cal-Der-Went Walk – 30 miles (48 km) From the River Calder in West Yorkshire to the River Derwent in North Derbyshire. Complete within 12 hours.

Cheviot Hills 2,000 ft Summits Walk – 20 miles (32 km) Circular from Langleeford near Wooler. Involves crossing the six summits over 2,000 ft (610 m). Complete within 12 hours.

Depth of Surrey – 38 miles (61 km) A walk across Surrey from the Star & Garter at Colnbrook in the north to Haslemere Station in the south. Complete within 24 hours.

Haworth Hobble – 33 miles (53 km) Circular from Haworth Church. Involves 4,000 ft (1,220 m) of ascent over the rugged South Pennines. Complete within 12 hours.

Limey Way – 40 miles (64 km) From Castleton through twenty limestone dales of the Peak District to Thorpe. Complete within 24 hours.

Lyke Wake Walk – 40 miles (64 km) Across the North York Moors, from Osmotherley to Ravenscar. Complete within 24 hours.

Six Shropshire Summits Walk – 36 miles (58 km) From Corndon, Powys to Horseditch Cottages near Titterstone Clee. Complete within 18 hours.

Derwent Watershed Walk – 40 miles (64 km) Circular walk from Yorkshire Bridge Inn near Bamford, Derbyshire. A walk that encircles Kinder and Bleaklow. Complete within 24 hours.

Surrey Hills Walk – 50 miles (80 km) Across Surrey from the Hampshire border at Frensham to the Kent border at the 'Old Ship', Tatsfield. Complete within 24 hours.

Swale Watershed Walk – 60 miles (97 km) Circular walk from Richmond. Complete within 48 hours.

Three Peaks of Yorkshire Walk – 24 miles (39 km) Circular from Horton to Ribblesdale. 5,000 ft (1,525 m) of ascent over Pen-y-ghent, Whernside and Ingleborough. Complete within 12 hours.

West Pennines Circuit – 35 miles (56 km) Circular walk from Darwen taking in the three towers of Darwen, Rivington and Holcombe. Complete within 12 hours.

The Trail-Blazer Challenge Walk – 25 miles (40 km) Circular from Bakewell around Central Region of the Peak District. Originated and devised by John Merrill.

The three most arduous walks are:–

The Bob Graham Round – starts from Keswick. Although a popular fell run in under 24 hours gains admission to the Bob Graham Club, the circuit can be walked in under 48 hours. The circuit is named after Bob Graham, who in the 1930s traversed 42 peaks in the Lake District within 24 hours. His original circuit has since been expanded to include other mountains.

The Three Peaks – 420 miles (676 km) From Fort William via Ben Nevis, Scafell Pike and Snowdon to Caernarvon. The fastest time so far is by Ann Sayer in 1979: 7 days and 31 minutes.

Land's End to John o' Groats – 874 miles (1,406 km) No time limit, but it has now been walked in 14 days. There is no set route; the direct way is 874 miles using roads. To use long-distance footpaths, such as I used in 1977 (see pp. 83–5), the mileage was 1,608 miles (2,587 km).

Challenge walks

Throughout the spring and summer a whole range of Challenge Walks are held annually. They are usually organised by the Long-Distance Walkers' Association, the Ramblers' Association, Youth Hostels' Association, the Y.M.C.A., and by the Scouts. The walks range from 20–100 miles (32–161 km) long. There are also the annual 'Karrimor Marathon' and the 'Ultimate Challenge'.

Outdoor organisations in Britain and Eire

The Backpackers' Club

Eric Gurney, National Organising Secretary, 20 St Michael's Road, Tilehurst, Reading, Berkshire, RG3 4RP.

Founded to look after the interests of 'lightweight' walkers and campers: 'backpacking', an American word, is believed to be Britain's fastest-growing outdoor activity. The club is unusual in that it does not have a constitution or committees. The charter of the club is the 'Ten rules of the Countryside Code'. Every member is encouraged to get involved. The membership is now in excess of 2,000, and is offered the following facilities:

1. Discount facilities from equipment and clothing retailers in various parts of the country.

2. *Farm Pitch Directory*: for exclusive use of members, detailing places to camp, mostly at farms, well off the beaten track.

3. Comprehensive equipment and advisory service on all aspects of backpacking: advice on what equipment to buy if a beginner, walking routes, campsites, food and clothing.

4. Insurance: a camping equipment and personal effects insurance scheme.

5. *Backchat*: club magazine produced every two months.

6. Forest Scheme: arranging exclusive camps in Forestry Commission forests. Pitches already in Thetford Forest, Norfolk.

7. Weekends: weekend meets are arranged most weekends in different parts of the country between September and June – detailed in *Backchat*.

8. County Co-ordinator: local co-ordinator who keeps in touch with members in his county.

9. Badge: each member receives a membership card and cloth badge. The A.G.M. is held in May each year.

The Camping Club of Great Britain and Ireland Ltd

11 Lower Grosvenor Place, London, SW1W 0EY

Founded in 1901, the club is the oldest camping club in the world. Membership of the club offers considerable benefits, organises meets and rallies throughout Britain, overseas tours for members (the club is a founder member of the I.F.C.C. – International Federation of Camping and Caravanning), and a programme of activities for the youth membership. Members can also use the club's chain of sites, many for club members only, and are sent a guide listing 2,000 sites and a monthly magazine: *Camping and Caravanning*.

The Council for the Protection of Rural England (C.P.R.E.)

4 Hobart Place, London, SW1W OHY

The Council's slogan – 'fights to save your countryside' – is a very modest statement, considering the extensive and dedicated work the Council has done since their foundation in 1926. Today there are more than 30,000 members. The vital work of C.P.R.E. is performed by its branches. They fight their own battles, but ask help from head office when needed. They are very active at local level, concerning themselves with public inquiries, checking the planning applications, contributing to county structure plans, and looking after listed buildings under threat.

There are similar organisations in Wales and Scotland.

The Countrywide Holidays Association (C.H.A.)

Birch Heys, Cromwell Range, Manchester, M14 6HU

The Co-operative Holidays Association, as it was called then, was founded in 1893 and is the oldest organisation in the Outdoor Activity holiday field.

Today the C.H.A. has 24 large guesthouses (accommodation for 50–85 guests), mostly operating throughout the year. All are situated in good walking areas, such as near Hope in the Peak District, Fowey in Cornwall, Borrowdale in the Lake District and at Onich in Scotland. A very comprehensive range of holidays is arranged using these centres, and also overseas centres: 'Adventure Tours'. At three guesthouses – Filey, Eskdale and Westward Ho! – children from the age of a few months are given their first walking holiday. This also enables the older children to do a more strenuous walk while the other parent takes the younger child on an easier walk.

Forestry Commission

231 Corstorphine Road, Edinburgh, EH12 7AT

The Forestry Commission was established in 1919 and is responsible for over 3,000,000 acres of land throughout Britain.

Of particular interest to the walker is the Commission's work under the objective – 'To provide recreational facilities'. In recent years there has been an 'opening up' of forest areas, with facilities for day visitors, in the form of car parks, forest walks, picnic areas and viewpoints. Although the forest roads are meant solely for foot use, in some forests 'forest drives' have been created. There are many camping and caravan sites on forest land and cabins providing self-catering holidays (one week or more). The first Forest Park was established in Argyll in 1935 and today there are about 450,000 acres covered in Forest Parks, which includes 145,000 acres in the Border Forest Park.

There are waymarked footpaths and information boards in many of the forests, and literature on the natural history of a forest can be obtained from a Visitor Centre. Four general maps – North England, South England, Wales and Scotland, show walking routes throughout Britain and are available from the Forestry Commission.

The Holiday Fellowship Ltd

142 Great North Way, London, NW4 1EG

The Holiday Fellowship is one of the oldest and leading youth holiday organisations in the country and was founded in 1913. Spread throughout Britain are seven youth guesthouses and twenty-three adult guesthouses for schoolchildren and other parties. They also organise trips to several centres abroad. Holiday fellowship is a member of SAGTA (School and Group Travel Association).

From several centres in Britain, used as bases, long-distance footpaths are walked. These include the South-West Way Coastal Path, the Cotswold Way, the Cleveland Way and the South Downs Way. Holidays are also arranged from centres graded into eight grades: grade eight (the lowest) involves walking under 5 miles (8 km) along level paths and lanes; grade one (top grade) involves ascents over 2,000 ft (610 m), rock scrambling with exposure and rough walking.

Long-distance Walkers' Association

Hon. Membership Secretary: E. Bishop, 4 Mayfield Road, Tunbridge Wells, Kent

This Association was formed in 1972, to further the interests of those who enjoy long-distance walking.

The Association rules that a long walk is more than 20 miles (32 km). They organise many activities and hold an annual marathon of 100 miles (161 km), somewhere in Britain, such as the Tanners Marathon or the Downsman Hundred.

There are several local groups throughout the country, and members receive the Association's publication, *Strider*, which is produced at least three times a year.

Mountain Bothies Association

Membership Secretary: Richard Butrym, Tigh Beag, Macleod Homes, North Connel, Oban, Argyll, Scotland

Founded in 1965, the Association has the following aim:

'To maintain simple unlocked shelters in remote country for the use of walkers, climbers and other outdoor enthusiasts who love the wild and lonely places.'

There are now more than forty bothies, mostly in Scotland.

The Bothy Code is as follows:

1. Whenever possible, seek owner's permission to use a bothy, particularly if proposing to take a group of six or more, or to use it as a base over a period. Note that all use of bothies is at own risk.

2. Do not stray from recognised routes during stalking and game shooting seasons (mainly mid-August to mid-October).

3. Leave bothies cleaner, tidier and in better condition as a result of your visit.

4. Burn all rubbish you can; take all tins and glass away with you.

5. Lay in a supply of fuel and kindling for the next user (don't cut live wood).
6. If you leave unused food, date perishables and leave safe from vermin.
7. Do not burn, deface or damage any part of the structure.
8. Guard against risk of fire and ensure that the fire is out before leaving.
9. Secure windows and doors on departure. (Swinging doors are a trap to animals who get in and cannot get out.)
10. Safeguard the water supply. Do not use the neighbourhood of the bothy as a toilet.
11. Protect and preserve animal and plant life.
12. Respect the countryside, its occupants and the country way of life.
13. Reports on the state of bothies maintained by the Association will be welcomed by the Maintenance Organiser or the General Secretary.

The National Trust
42 Queen Anne's Gate, London, SW1H 9AS

Founded in 1895, the National Trust is a charity, 'to ensure that places of historic interest and natural beauty are held permanently for the benefit of this and future generations'. The first property was 4½ acres (2 hectares) of cliffland overlooking the Barmouth estuary in North Wales. In 1907 the Trust was incorporated by an Act of Parliament which gave it its mandate, 'to promote the permanent preservation for the benefit of the nation of land and buildings of beauty or historic interest'. One unique provision of the Act gave the Trust the power to declare its property 'inalienable'. This means that no property could be sold or given away unless by the will of Parliament. Apart from the many houses (more than 160) that the Trust own, they are the third largest landowner in Britain with 412,000 acres (166,728 hectares) of land, and covenants over a further 74,000 acres (about 30,000 hectares). Some of their land includes parts of the Peak District National Park, the Lake District, Snowdonia, the Brecon Beacons, and more than 400 miles (650 km) of coastline.

Throughout England and Wales there are National Trust Centres run voluntarily by National Trust members. Meetings are arranged on a wide range of subjects relating to the property of the National Trust.

Members who subscribe to the Trust receive an annual list of properties open to the public, and other literature; through their subscriptions they support the work of the Trust. Members are admitted free to Trust properties normally open to the public in England, Wales, Northern Ireland and Scotland–a reciprocal arrangement exists for members of the National Trust for Scotland.

The National Trust for Scotland
5 Charlotte Square, Edinburgh EH2 4DU

The Trust owns some 90 properties and 90,000 acres (36,422 hectares). It was formed in 1931, and has preserved many of Scotland's finest examples of historic and scenic treasures, including the islands of Canna, Fair Isle, Iona and St Kilda.

The Nature Conservancy Council
London address: 19/20 Belgrave Square, London, SW1X 8PY
The Council was established in 1973 by Act of Parliament and is the official body responsible for 'the conservation of flora, fauna and geological and physiographical features throughout Great Britain'. The Council has more than 135 National Nature Reserves which cover approximately 300,000 acres (121,410 hectares) altogether. The Council own some of them while others are leased or are under a nature reserve agreement, such as St Kilda, which is the property of the National Trust for Scotland but leased to N.C.C. The public are allowed into the majority of reserves, but to sensitive areas by permit only.

The Ramblers' Association
1/5 Wandsworth Road, London, SW8 2LJ
The premier national body and an organisation that perhaps all walkers should support. The R.A. is a voluntary organisation with charitable status. There are now more than 31,000 individual members and over 400 affiliated organisations. The aims of the R.A. are summed up as follows:
'to encourage rambling and mountaineering, to foster a greater knowledge, love and care of the countryside and to work for the preservation of natural beauty, the protection of footpaths and the provision of access to open country'.

To meet these aims the Association has a considerable list to its credit. We have in Britain 120,000 miles (over 193,000 km) of public footpaths and bridleways. To safeguard these a network of R.A. footpath inspectors keep an avid watch. During the 1930s and 1940s there was considerable activity concerning mass trespasses on wild and remote private moorland (see Howard Hill's book *Freedom to Roam*) to gain access and right to walk in this open country. The R.A. fought hard, and in 1949 the National Parks and Access to Countryside Act came into force and empowered county councils to make agreements with landowners. Today more than 60,000 acres (24,300 hectares) in the Peak District are subject to agreements and the land is 'open country'. Sadly, in much of the other moorland areas of Britain, no agreements exist.
There are numerous benefits of membership, and these are some:

1. There are about 160 local groups who individually run regular walks and check any footpath violation.

2. The R.A. magazine, *Rucksack*, is published three times a year.

3. Each member receives a copy of *Bed, Breakfast and Bus Guide*, which details more than 2,000 places where hikers are welcome.

4. 'Footpath Worker', a bulletin reporting all aspects of footpaths.

5. Press bulletin, which contains details of extracts from newspapers about footpaths, countryside and forests.

6. The R.A. also has a considerable range of publications on the individual long-distance footpaths, the law of footpaths and bridleways and guidelines for sponsored walks in the countryside.

Youth Hostels' Association – England and Wales

National Office: Trevelyan House, 8 St Stephen's Hill, St Albans, Herts
From humble beginnings in 1909 the movement has spread throughout the world. The Association in England and Wales, which began in 1930, now has 269 hostels, from special purpose-built buildings, to halls, farms, castles, and shepherd's huts. The area is broken down into eleven regions:

Border and Dales 19 hostels
30 Balliol Square, Durham, DH1 3QH
Lakeland 29 hostels
Eleray, Windermere, Cumbria, LA23 1AW
Yorkshire 26 hostels
96 Main Street, Bingley, W. Yorkshire, BD16 2JH
Peak 24 hostels
Crompton Chambers, 55 Dale Road, Matlock, Derbyshire, DE4 3LT
North Wales & Isle of Man 22 hostels
Secretary, Merseyside YH Ltd, 40 Hamilton Square, Birkenhead, Merseyside, L41 5BA
South Wales 32 hostels
131 Woodville Road, Cardiff, CF2 4DZ
Midland 19 hostels
116 Birmingham Road, Lichfield, Staffs., WS14 9BW
Eastern 25 hostels
East Bay House, East Bay, Colchester, Essex, CO1 2UE
London 5 hostels
58 Streatham High Road, London, SW16 1DA
Southern 31 hostels
58 Streatham High Road, London, SW16 1DA
South-West 38 hostels
Belmont Place, Devonport Road, Stoke, Plymouth, PL3 4DW

Y.H.A. publish a quarterly newspaper, *Hostelling News*, have regional shops and run adventure holidays.

Scottish Youth Hostels' Association

National Office: 7 Glebe Crescent, Stirling, FK8 2JA
In Scotland there are approximately 80 hostels, and the Association is divided into five regions:

Aberdeen
11 Ashvale Place, Aberdeen, AB1 6QD
Dundee
86 Bell Street, Dundee, DD1 1JG
Edinburgh
161 Warrender Park Road, Edinburgh, EH9 1EQ

Glasgow
12 Renfield Street, Glasgow, G2 5AL
South-West
Craigweil House, Craigweil Road, Ayr, KA7 2XJ

The S.Y.H.A. organise 'Breakaway Holidays' in all manner of outdoor activities in different Scottish localities. They also produce a quarterly magazine, *The Scottish Hosteller* and an annual Handbook which gives the accommodation details of every Hostel.

Youth Hostels' Association of Northern Ireland (Y.H.A.N.I.)
56 Bradbury Place, Belfast, BT7 1RU
There are thirteen hostels situated on the Antrim Coast, in the mountains, and in rural settings. The majority are on or close to the 450 mile (725 km) Ulster Way.

Mourne Wall Walk – 22 miles (35 km)
The Y.H.A.N.I. annually organise this tough walk, held on the first Sunday in June. The route follows the wall over twelve summits and involves ascending 10,000 ft (3,048 m). About 2,000 people attempt the walk and about half that number reach the finishing line. The successful receive a badge and certificate.

Irish Youth Hostels' Association *(AN OIGE)*
29 Mountjoy Square, Dublin
The I.Y.H.A. has 52 hostels throughout the country, with 9 in the Wicklow mountains and 13 in the Cork/Kerry area. Three are on islands – Cape Clear, Valentia and Aran in Donegal. The Association produces a hostel map for the whole of Ireland and a series of guides to walks from hostels and area guides.

If I may add a personal note here, I would say that hostelling is one of the finest ways to appreciate Ireland, and to have a holiday that you will never forget. In 1974 I walked up the whole length of the west coast of Ireland from Cape Clear to Malin Head (see pp. 90–92), staying in about 15 hostels en route. The scenery on the west coast and on the offshore islands is second to none.

Mountain rescue

The Mountain Rescue Committee

The Hon. Secretary, Mountain Rescue Committee, 18 Tarnside Fold, Simmondley, Glossop, Derbyshire, SK13 9ND

The Committee dates back to 1933 when the Joint Stretcher Committee was formed by the Rucksack Club and the Fell and Rock Climbing Club, to suggest a suitable type of stretcher for use in Britain. During the Thirties the Committee grew, with many organisations joining. With the increase of mountain activity after World War II, the Committee changed its name in 1946 to the Mountain Rescue Committee. In 1949 the then Ministry of Health accepted responsibility for much of the equipment needed through the National Health Service. to the Rescue Posts. Many items are still not provided by the N.H.S. and are provided by the Committee, and in 1950 it became a Charitable Trust. A separate Committee was formed for Scotland in 1964.

The Committee's report for 1982 provides the following information about the help given to walkers and climbers by mountain rescue teams:

'During 1982 Mountain Rescue Teams in England and Wales attended 350 incidents, assisting a total of 524 people, of which 42 were fatalities.

112 searches were carried out for 251 people lost or benighted. Of these only 38 were injured . . .

Of the 12 incidents involving winter hill walkers who slipped on snow/ice it is distressing to note that 10 of the incidents were probably caused by lack of crampons. Several of the injured suffered severe head injuries (2 fatal).

The Helvellyn Edges once again took their toll, highlighting that in certain winter conditions, hill walking takes on all the seriousness of snow/ice climbing, and demands appropriate techniques and equipment.

Those who slipped tended to do so on the descent, when the modern short ice axes offer little security to rubber-soled walkers on hard snow . . .'

The report also mentions the fact that of the 75 slips incurred during fell walking, 14 involved smooth-soled footwear. And it lists various factors which led to the exhaustion or collapse of walkers/climbers: 'Journey too demanding/load too heavy/lack of food/lack of fitness and training/poor navigation/poor planning/lack of adequate clothing and equipment/set off too late with no torch, etc.

Further information as to the nature of the accidents, the main causes, and the areas where accidents took place, may be found in the report.

Immediate action in case of an accident

1. Make sure the airway of the injured person is clear.
2. Stop any bleeding by pressure with handkerchief or first aid dressing, etc.
3. Make the injured person as comfortable as you can; keep him dry, insulate him from the ground, moving him the least you have to in the process (especially if there is risk of damage to the spine), make him warm (extra clothing, survival bag).
4. Note state of consciousness; if unconscious, secure him to the rock with a belay to prevent a further fall.
5. Try to attract help by shouting, whistle blasts, torch flashing; use the distress signal: 6 shouts or whistle blasts, repeated at one-minute intervals.
6. Send for help from a telephone. Dial 999, ask for Police or a Rescue Post, whichever is the quicker. The message should be written and must give the exact location (grid reference), time of accident, nature of injuries.

FURTHER READING
Safety on Mountains, Sports Council
Mountain Rescue, R.A.F. Training Handbook
Hamish MacInnes, *International Mountain Rescue Book*
Jane Renouf and Stewart Hulse *First Aid for the Hill Walker and Climber* (Penguin, 1978; reissued by Cicerone Press 1983)
Mountain and Cave Rescue Handbook, Mountain Rescue Committee

Country Code

A guide issued by The Countryside Commission

Enjoy the countryside and respect its life and work   Set a good example and help to preserve good relations with those who live and work in the countryside.

Guard against all risk of fire   Plantations, woodlands and heaths are highly inflammable: every year acres burn because of casually dropped matches, cigarette ends or pipe ash.

Fasten all gates   Even if you find gates open, fasten them behind you. A gate left open invites animals to wander, a danger to themselves, to crops and to traffic.

Keep your dogs under close control   Farmers have good reason to regard visiting dogs as pests; in the country a civilised town dog can become a savage. Keep your dog on a lead wherever there is livestock about, also on country roads.

Keep to public paths across farmland   Crops can be ruined by people's feet. Grass is a valuable crop, flattened hay and corn is very difficult to harvest.

Use gates and stiles to cross fences, hedges and walls   Repairs are costly for the farmer, so keep to recognised routes.

Leave livestock, crops and machinery alone

Take your litter home   All litter is unsightly and some is dangerous as well. Take litter home for disposal; in the country it costs a lot to collect it.

Help to keep all water clean   Your chosen walk may well cross a catchment area for the water supply of millions. Do not pollute streams, ponds, and other water sources, including cattle troughs.

Protect wildlife, plants and trees   Wildlife is best observed, not abused. To capture, injure or kill wild animals and birds, pick or uproot flowers, make carvings on tree trunks, deface rocks and so on, is to destroy man's natural heritage. Help to protect plants, birds and animals by leaving them alone.

Take special care on country roads   Country roads have special dangers: blind corners, high banks and hedges, slow-moving tractors, and farm machinery. Children, animals or birds are specially at risk. Motorists should reduce speed and take extra care. Walkers should keep to the right, facing oncoming traffic.

Make no unnecessary noise   Do not spoil other people's enjoyment of peaceful surroundings or disturb livestock and wildlife.

Bibliography

General books on walking

Great Britain

Melvin Bell, *Britain's National Parks* (David & Charles, 1975)

G. R. Birch, *Backpacking Equipment* (Blandford Press, 1978)

Alan and Barbara Blatchford, *The Long Distance Walker's Handbook* (Greenway, 1980)

Derrick Booth, *Backpacking in Britain* (The Oxford Illustrated Press, 1974)

– *Lett's Guide: The Backpacker's Handbook* (Charles Letts, 2nd edn, 1979)

Frank Duerden, *Rambling Complete* (Kaye and Ward, 1978)

Charlie Emett and Mike Hutton, *Walks through Northern England* (David & Charles, 1982)

Peter Gilman, *Fitness on Foot* (The Sunday Times, 1978)

Rob Hunter, *The Spur Book of Walking* (Spurbooks Ltd, 1978)

Peter Lumley, *The Spur Book of Hill Trekking* (Spurbooks Ltd, 1977)

– *Teach Yourself Books – Backpacking* (Hodder, 1974)

John Mann, *Walk – It Could Change Your Life – Handbook* (Paddington Press, 1979)

Michael Marriott, *The Footpaths of Britain* (Queen Anne Press, 1981)

T. G. Miller, *Long Distance Paths of England and Wales* (David & Charles, 1977)

Roy Milward and Adrian Robinson, *Upland Britain* (David & Charles, 1980)

Adam Nicolson, *The National Trust Book of Long Walks* (Weidenfeld & Nicolson, 1981)

Penguin Footpath Guides – see Westacott

Don Robinson, *Backpacking* (EP Publishing Ltd, East Ardsley, Wakefield, West Yorkshire 1981)

David Sharpe, *Ramblers' Ways* (David & Charles, 1980)

Roger Smith, *Weekend Walking* (Oxford Illustrated Press, Yeovil, 1982)

Roland Smith, *Wildest Britain: A Visitors' Guide to the National Parks* (Blandford Press, 1983)

Kate Spencer and Peter Lumley (eds.), *Backpacker's Guide–an annual* (The Kate Spencer Agency)

Hugh D. Westacott, *The Penguin Footpath Guides: The Brecon Beacons National Park; Dartmoor for Walkers and Riders; The Devon South Coast Path; The Dorset Coast Path; The North Downs Way; The Ridgeway Path; The Somerset and North Devon Coast Path.*

– *The Walker's Handbook* (Penguin, 1978; 2nd enlarged edn, 1980)

David Wickers and Art Bederson, *Britain at Your Feet* (Kogan Page, 1980)
Peter Williams, *Hill Walking* (Pelham Books, 1979)
Ken Wilson and Richard Gilbert, *Big Walks* (Diadem Books, 1980)
– *Classic Walks* (Diadem Books, 1982)

Wales
W. A. Poucher, *Wales* (Constable, 1981)
– *The Welsh Peaks* (Constable, 1979)
Richard Sale, *A Cambrian Way*. A 260-mile footpath from Cardiff to Conway.
  (Constable, 1983)

Scotland
David and Kathleen MacInnes, *Walking Through Scotland* (David & Charles,
  1981)
  Published in collaboration with the Ramblers' Association
D. G. Moir, *Scottish Hill Tracks: Old Highways and Drove Roads* (2 vols,
  Bartholomew, 1975)
W. H. Murray, *The Companion Guide to the West Highlands of Scotland* (Collins,
  new edn 1977)
W. A. Poucher, *The Highlands of Scotland* (Constable, 1983)
– *The Scottish Peaks* (Constable, 5th edn 1979)
Books published by the Scottish Mountaineering Trust, Edinburgh:
J. C. Donaldson and H. M. Brown (eds), *Munro's Tables* (rev. edn 1981)
W. H. Murray, *The Scottish Highlands* (1976)
  and eight associated district guides

Ireland
Joss Lynam (ed.), *The Irish Peaks* (Constable, 1982)
– (ed.), *Irish Walk Guides*, six regional guides (Gill & Macmillan, Dublin)
H. Mulholland, *Guide to Eire's 3,000-Foot Mountains* (Mulholland, Wirral, rev.
  edn 1981)
Claud W. Wall, *Mountaineering in Ireland* (Mountaineering Clubs of Ireland,
  new edn 1976)

Europe
David Brett, *High Level* (Gollancz, 1983). Across the Alps, from France to
  Switzerland, using local buses.
Craig Evans, *On Foot Through Europe* (Quill, New York, 1982). There are
  seven volumes in all, each with a different sub-title, beginning *A Trail Guide
  to*, as follows: *Europe's Long-distance Footpaths*; *West Germany*; *Austria,
  Switzerland and Liechtenstein*; *the British Isles*; *Scandinavia*; *Spain & Portugal*;
  France & The Benelux.
John Hillaby, *Journey through Europe* (Granada, 1974)
Arthur Howcroft and Richard Sale, *A Walker's Guide to Europe* (Wildwood
  House, 1983).

Jonathan Hurdle, *Alpine Pass Route* (Dark Peak Ltd, 1983). A 15-day walk across the Swiss Alps from near Liechtenstein to Montreux.
Rob Hunter, *Walking in France* (Oxford Illustrated Press, 1982; Hamlyn Paperbacks, 1983).
Adam Nicolson, *The elf book of Long Walks in France* (Weidenfeld, 1983).
W. A. Poucher, *The Alps* (Constable, 1983).
W. E. Reifsnyder, *Hut Hopping in the Alps* (Sierra Club, 1973).
K. Reynolds, *Walks and Climbs in the Pyrenees* (Cicerone Press, 1978).
E. Roberts, *High Level Route* (West Col, 1973). This is the Alpine route, not the Pyrenean.
Brian Spencer, *Walking in the Alps* (Moorland Publishing, 1983).
L. Spring and H. Edward, *100 Hikes in the Alps* (Cordee, 1979).
S. Styles, *Backpacking in the Alps and Pyrenees* (Gollancz, 1976).
G. Vernon, *Pyrenees High Level Route* (West Col, 1981). The same author has written other guidebooks: *Pyrenees West*, *Pyrenees East* and *Pyrenees-Andorra-Cerdagne*, all published by West Col.
Youth Hostels' Association, *Guide to Europe* (London, 1982).

The Himalayas
Stan Armington, *Trekking in the Himalayas* (Lonely Planet Publications, PO Box 88, South Yarra, Victoria 3141, Australia, 1979).
T. Iozawa, *Trekking in the Himalayas* (Yama-Kei, Tokyo, 1980).
Hugh Swift, *Trekker's Guide to the Himalayas and Karakoram* (Hodder, 1982).

North America
Hilary and George Bradt, *Backpacking in North America: The Great Outdoors* (Bradt Enterprises, Chalfont St Peter, Buckinghamshire and Boston, Massachusetts, 1979).
Colin Fletcher, *The Man Who Walked Through Time* (Vintage Books, 1967).
– *The Thousand Mile Summer* (North Books, 1964)
John Hart, *Walking Softly in the Wilderness*. The Sierra Club Guide to Backpacking (Sierra Club Books, 1977)
Peter Jenkins, *A Walk Across America* (Fawcett Crest Books, 1979)
– *Walk West* (Fawcett Crest Books, 1983).
Francis Parkman, *The Oregon Trail* (New American Library, 1981; Penguin, ed. David Levin, 1983). (This is history, not walking.)
Eric Ryback, *The High Adventure of Eric Ryback* (Bantam Books Inc, 1971)
– *The Ultimate Journey* (Chronicle Books, 1973).

Major marathons
Hamish Brown *Hamish's Mountain Walk* [Scotland] (Gollancz, 1978).
– *Hamish's Groats End Walk* (Gollancz, 1981).
John Hillaby, *Journey through Britain* (Granada, 1970).
– *Journey to the Jade Sea* (Granada, 1973).
– *Journey through Europe* (Granada, 1974).

– *Journey through Love* (Granada, 1983).
John Merrill, *Turn Right at Land's End* (Oxford Illustrated Press, 1979).
– *From Arran to Orkney* (Spurbooks, 1980).
– *Emerald Coast Walk* (Walking Boots Ltd, 1982).
Sebastian Snow, *The Rucksack Man* (Sphere Books, 1977).

Magazines

Backchat (6 issues a year) Eric Gurney, Backpackers' Club, 20 St Michael's Road, Tilehurst, Reading, Berkshire, RG3 4RP

Camping and Caravanning (monthly) Camping Club of Gt Britain & Ireland Ltd, 11 Lower Grosvenor Place, London, SW1W 0EY

Camping Magazine (monthly) Link House Magazines Ltd, Link House, Dingwall Avenue, Croydon, CR9 2TA

Climber and Rambler (monthly) Holmes McDougall Ltd, 10–12 York Street, Glasgow, G2 8LG

Drive and Trail (6 issues a year) Automobile Association, Fanum House, Basingstoke, Hants, RG21 2EA

Footloose (monthly) Footloose Ltd, 26 Commercial Buildings, Dunston, Gateshead, NE11 9AA

Guiding (monthly) The Girl Guides' Association, 17–19 Buckingham Palace Road, London SW1W 0PT
(Also publishers of *Today's Guide* and *The Brownie*)

The Great Outdoors (monthly) Holmes McDougall Ltd, 10–12 York Street, Glasgow, G2 8LG

High (monthly) Dark Peak Ltd, 336 Abbey Lane, Sheffield, S8 0BY

Hostelling News (quarterly) Youth Hostels' Association, Trevelyan House, 8 St Stephen's Hill, St Albans, Herts, AL1 2DY

Mountain (6 issues a year) Mountain Magazine Ltd, c/o PO Box 184, Sheffield, S11 9DL

Practical Camper (monthly) Haymarket Publishing, 38–42 Hampton Road, Teddington, Middlesex, TW11 0JE

Rucksack (3 issues a year) The Ramblers' Association, 1–5 Wandsworth Road, London, SW8 2LJ

Scouting (monthly) The Scout Association, Baden-Powell House, Queen's Gate, London, SW7 5JS

Strider (3 issues a year) The Long-Distance Walkers' Association, 11 Thorn Bank, Guildford, Surrey

The Traveller (quarterly) Wexas International Ltd, 45 Brompton Road, London, SW3 1DE

Index

Africa, 158
Alpine Clubs, 105, 112–13
Alps, xi, 4, 75, 95, 96–109, 111–14, 141
America, x, 4, 15, 17, 20, 21, 32, 131–47, 148–9, 155, 158, 187
America, coast-to-coast walks, 131, 148, 149, 158
American hiking and conservation organisations, 146–7
American maps, 138, 140
Amicola Falls National Park, Georgia, 136–7
Anglesey, Isle of, 61
Annapurna, trek around, 4, 117, 121–6, 127
Appalachian Trail, U.S.A., 4, 17, 21, 131–40, 145, 149, 158
Appalachian Trail Conference, 136, 140
Ardennes, 105, 111
Areas of Outstanding Natural Beauty in Britain, 7, 30, 163, 164–5
Arran, Isle of, 3, 72, 73, 80
Australia, 158
Austria, 4, 94, 104–6, 111–14
Austrian Alpine Club, 105, 112–14

Backpackers' Club, 148, 175, 188
Baxter State National Park, Maine, 139
Belgium, 106–7
Ben Nevis, Scotland, 24, 72, 73, 78, 174
Bergans, equipment manufacturers, 80
Berghaus of Newcastle, clothing and equipment manufacturers, 12, 104, 121, 140, 144
Black Mountains, Wales, 58, 61, 62, 69
Black's of Greenock, equipment manufacturers, 104, 121, 140, 144–5
blisters, 40, 81, 141, 152–3, 159
boots, walking, 8–10, 40, 104, 108, 121, 140, 144, 151, 152–3, 159
Brecon Beacons, Wales, 26, 32–3, 58, 61, 69, 178
Brett, David, xi
Britain, x, 5–7, 30–89, 111, 131, 136,

148–54, 154–5, 156, 158, 163–82, 185
British coast walk, my, 3, 4, 30, 52, 76, 83, 85, 140, 149, 150, 154–5, 158
Brown, Hamish, 75, 148, 187
Brown, Joe, 34

Cairngorms, Scotland, 25, 75, 79, 83–4
Cambrian Way, Wales, 61
Camping Club of Great Britain and Ireland, 175, 188
Canada, 4, 131, 140–41, 144
Cascade Trail, Oregon, 141
Central Highlands, Scotland, 73–4
Centurion Walk, Yorkshire Dales, 36, 172
challenge walks, 30, 35, 36, 42, 47, 48, 62, 173–4
Cheviot Hills, 38, 41, 173
Clarke, Clinton, 141
Cleveland Way, North York Moors, 32, 37, 40, 42–4, 59, 166, 174; see also 'Missing Link'
cliff walking, 38, 42–3, 59, 61, 66–7, 82, 86
clothing, 2, 10–16, 18, 104, 121, 142, 159
coast walk, my British, see British coast walk
coastal walking, 30, 54–9, 61, 63–5, 74, 90–92
Commons, Open Spaces and Footpaths Preservation Society, 33
compass reading, 27–8
competitive walks in Britain, 30, 173–4
Connemara, Ireland, 86, 91
Constance, Lake, Switzerland, 111, 112
Continental Divide Trail, U.S.A., 131, 145, 158
cooking, 21, 104, 122, 129, 139–40, 145, 151
Corsica, 94, 109–11, 112
Cotswold Way, 32, 48–50, 58, 84, 167, 169, 174
Council for the Protection of Rural England, 176

Country Code, 33, 175, 184
Country Parks, 31, 163
Countryside Commission, 25, 33, 44, 163–7
Countryside Commission for Scotland, 164
Countryside Holidays Association, 176
Crane, Richard and Adrian, xi
Cuillin Hills, Skye, 25, 72, 75, 80

Dales Way, 36, 59, 166, 171
Dartmoor, 24, 32–3, 38–9, 58
Denmark, 111, 112
Derbyshire boundary walk, my, 3, 30, 31
Derwent Watershed Walk, 34, 45, 174
Dingle peninsula, Ireland, 86, 87
direction, walking, 40, 66, 149–50
distance, measuring, 28, 97, 150
Donegal, Ireland, 86, 91–2, 181
Dorset Coast Path, 54–6, 166
Dower, John, 33
Drake, Anthony, 49

East of England Heritage Walk, 3, 30–31, 68–71
Eire, 86–92, 181, 186
Emerald Coast Walk, my, 3, 90–92, 181
England, 24, 30–60, 64, 68–71, 83–5, 86, 163–80
E-paths, 93, 94, 104–10, 111–12; see also
    Grande Randonnée routes;
    long-distance footpaths in Europe
equipment, 6, 8, 14, 16–22, 40, 104, 121, 150–51
equipment lists, 18, 104, 139–40, 144–5
Eskdale Outward Bound School, 2
Europe, x, xi, 93–116, 129, 186
European maps, 94, 104
European Ramblers' Association, 93, 111
European Trek, my, xi, 4, 10, 14, 22, 93, 94, 106–9, 129
Everest base camp, trek to, 4, 117–23, 127, 141
Exmoor, 24, 32–3, 38, 39, 58

feet, 154–5
food, x, 18, 22, 29, 51, 104, 110, 122–3, 125, 129, 145, 151, 157, 160
Forestry Commission, 33, 175, 176
France, 93, 106–9, 111, 112, 114
From Arran to Orkney, 3, 82

Germany, West, 111, 112, 116

Giffard Pinchot National Forest, Washington, 143
glacier walking, 2, 93
Glen Coe (Glencoe), Scotland, 24, 72, 73, 77–8
Glyders Way, Wales, 61
Gore-Tex clothing, 12–14, 16, 104
Gore-Tex equipment, 9, 14, 104, 140
Graham, Bob, 35, 174
Grande Randonnée routes, 93, 94, 102–12
Great Smoky National Park, Carolina, 134, 138
Guinness Book of Records, The, 60

Hadrian's Wall, Northumberland, 38, 41, 59, 171
Hebridean Journey, my, 3, 71, 79–81, 92, 152
Helambu, Nepal, 4, 117, 126–30
Heritage Coasts, in Britain, 7, 30, 163, 165
High Peak Trail, Peak District, 34, 48, 167
High Sierras, California, 142, 144
Hillary, Sir Edmund, 120
Hillaby, John, 148, 186–7
Himalayan Rescue Association, 118
Himalayas, x, 4, 107, 117–30, 141, 152, 158, 187
Holiday Fellowship, The, 177
Holland, 94, 106

Icknield Way, 50
Ireland, 3, 83, 86–92, 181, 186
Irish Youth Hostels Association, 181
island walking, 61, 75, 79–83
Italy, 111, 112, 116

Jenkins, Peter, 158
John Muir Trail, California, 141
Jotunheimen, Norway, 2, 93, 115
Jura Mountains, 106–7, 111, 114

Karrimor, equipment manufacturers, 17, 174
Kerry, Ring of, 86, 92, 181
Kinder, mass trespass on, 33, 34
Kunst, David, 148

Lake District, 2, 21, 24–5, 32–3, 35–6, 59, 113, 139, 176, 178
Land's End to John o'Groats walk, 4, 30, 55, 68–71, 72, 83–5, 148, 174

Langtang, Nepal, 4, 117, 126–30
Lassen Volcanic National Park,
    California, 142
Limey Way, Peak District, 34, 46, 47–8,
    170, 173
Loch Lomond, Scotland, 4, 24, 73, 75,
    76–7
long-distance footpaths (in Britain),
    official, 4, 7, 39–45, 50–57, 58, 61,
    63–7, 68–71, 72, 76–9, 83, 86, 150,
    163–4, 166, 177
long-distance footpaths (in Britain),
    unofficial, 4, 7, 30, 45–50, 58, 61,
    83, 86, 168–72, 177
long-distance footpaths in Europe, 93,
    94–116; see also E-paths; Grande
    Randonnée routes
long-distance trails in America, 131–40,
    141–4, 145–6
Long-Distance Walkers' Association,
    174, 177, 188
Lowe, equipment manufacturers, 17
Luxembourg, 106–7, 111
Lyke Wake Walk, North York Moors, 37,
    42, 47, 171, 173

Mackaye, Benton, 131
Maiden's Way, 41
magazines, British, 188
Malvern Hills, 32
Manning Park, Canada, 144
map reading, 27–8
map retailers in England, 29
maps, see American maps; European
    maps; Forestry Commission;
    Ordnance Survey maps
marathon walking, x–xi, 4, 148–58,
    159–61, 177, 187
marathon walks, my, x, xi, 148–58
    in America, xi, 4, 21, 131–45, 149–51,
        153, 155, 158
    in Britain, 3–4, 30–32, 49, 55, 58–60,
        72, 79–85, 92, 140, 149, 150–52,
        154–5, 158
    in Eire, 3, 90–92, 181
    in Europe, 4, 10, 14, 22, 93, 104–9
    route-planning, 3, 105, 136, 149–50,
        158
    preparation, 85, 137, 149, 150–51
    training, 68, 83, 129, 137, 140–41,
        152–3
Marble Mountain Wilderness, California,
    142

Marston-to-Edale walk, 34
Mediterranean Sea, 93, 107, 108, 111,
    112
Meegan, George, 148
Merrill, Sheila, 4–5, 76
Mexico, 4, 131, 140–41, 144
'Missing Link' (Cleveland Way), 37, 170
Moher, cliffs of, 86, 91
Monsal Trail, Peak District, 34
Mont Blanc, Tour of, 94–101, 104, 141,
    149
Moore, Dr Barbara, 83, 148
Mountain Bothies Association, Scotland,
    177–8
mountain rescue, 182–3
mountain walking, 7, 64, 69, 72–81, 85,
    90–92, 93–116, 117–30, 131–40,
    141–4, 150, 156
Mourne, Mountains of, 89, 181
Munros, Irish, 86, 87, 92
Munros, Scottish, 72, 75, 148

Naismith, W., 28
National Historic Trails of America, 146
National Park walk, my, see Parkland
    Journey
National Parks: in America, 32, 134–9,
    142–4, 145; in England and Wales,
    7, 24, 25–6, 30, 32–9, 61–3, 68–71,
    163; in Europe, 110, 115
National Scenic Trails of America, 141,
    145–6
National Sports Council of Eire
    (COSPOIR), 89, 92
National Trust, The: Eire, 92; England
    and Wales, 30–31, 33, 178;
    Northern Ireland, 89; Scotland, 178,
    179
Nature Conservancy Council, 33, 179
Nepal, 117–30, 141; see also Annapurna;
    Everest; Helambu; Himalayas;
    Langtang
New Forest, 24–5
New Zealand, 120–158
Norfolk Broads, 33
North Cascades National Park,
    Washington, 143
North Cornwall Coast Path, 54–5, 56–7,
    83, 166
North Downs Way, 52–3, 166
North York Moors, 24, 26, 32–3, 37, 42,
    47, 59
Northern Highlands, Scotland, 74, 83–4

Northern Isles Journey, my, 81–3
Northumberland National Park, 32–3,
 37–8, 41
Norway, 2, 93, 115–16
Noyce, Wilfrid, 126

Oats Cross Dartmoor Walk, 39
O'Brien, Moira, 153
Offa's Dyke Path, Wales, 58, 61, 62,
 66–7, 83–4, 166
Olympic Peninsula, Oregon, 143
Ordnance Survey, The, 23–4, 87
Ordnance Survey maps, 23–7, 87, 89,
 152
  Landranger Series, 24–5, 37, 39, 42,
   44, 45, 48, 50, 52–3, 55, 63, 66, 79,
   81, 150
  National Series, 24, 80
  Outdoor Leisure Maps, 25–6, 34–7,
   45, 61
  Pathfinder Series, 26
  Tourist Maps, 24, 38, 45, 61
Orkney Islands, 3, 72, 75, 81–3, 85, 140

pace, walking, x, xi, 5, 28–9, 85, 105, 137,
 141, 148, 154–5, 156–7
Pacific Crest Trail, U.S.A., 4, 131,
 137–8, 140–45, 150, 153, 155, 158
pack weight, x, xi, 5, 19, 28, 85, 124, 144,
 148, 154–5
Paps of Jura, 72, 74–5, 97
Parkland Journey, my, 3, 30, 32, 49,
 58–60, 68–71
Peak District, Derbyshire, 1, 21, 24, 25,
 30–31, 32–3, 34–5, 36, 39, 45–8,
 59, 85, 176, 178
Peak District High Level Route, 34, 45–6
Peakland Way, 4, 34, 36, 45–7, 59, 83,
 152, 170
Pembrokeshire Coast National Park, 33,
 58, 63
Pembrokeshire Coast Path, 4, 5, 32,
 58–9, 61, 63–5, 166
Pennine Way, 1, 4, 8, 17, 30, 31, 32,
 37–8, 39–42, 45, 46, 48, 59, 83–4,
 134, 148, 152, 166
Pentland Hills, Scotland, 74
Pilgrims' Way, 52–3
Pyrenees, xi, 4, 95, 104, 108–9, 111–12

Ramblers' Association, 30, 39, 44, 49,
 174, 179, 188; see also European
 Ramblers' Association

Rannoch Moor, Scotland, 76–7
Raven's Regal foods, 104, 145
recreational paths, 30, 166–7
ridge walking, 30, 50–52, 53–4, 72, 75,
 139
Ridgeway, The, 50–52, 166
rights of way, public, in England and
 Wales, 25, 30, 31, 44, 47, 150
Rivers' Way, 48
Rohan, clothing manufacturers, 11, 104
route-planning, 23–9, 149–50; see also
 marathon walks, my
Royal Society for the Protection of Birds,
 33
rucksacks, 16–17, 18–19, 104, 121, 144,
 151

St Kilda, island of, 75, 80, 179
Sandstone Trail, Cheshire, 84, 167, 170
Scotland, 5, 21, 24, 30, 37, 40, 41, 70–71,
 72–85, 86, 164, 176, 178–9,
 180–81; see also Countryside
 Commission for Scotland; Munros,
 Scottish; National Trust for Scotland
Scottish Isles, 74–5, 79–83
Scottish Youth Hostels Association,
 180–81
Scout Association, 174, 188
Seattle Mountaineers Club, 143–4, 147
Shenandoah National Park, Virginia, 134,
 138
Shetland Islands, 3, 72, 75, 81–3, 140
Skyline Trail, Washington, 141
sleeping bags, 20, 121, 140, 145, 151
Snow, Sebastian, 148, 188
Snowdon Horseshoe Walk, Wales, 62
Snowdonia, Wales, 24–6, 32–3, 59,
 61–2, 139, 178
Somerset and North Devon Coast Path,
 55, 57, 58, 83, 166
South Cornwall Coast Path, 54–5, 56,
 166
South Devon Coast Path, 54–5, 166
South Downs, 33
South Downs Way, 53–4, 166, 174
South-West Peninsula Coast Path, 38,
 54–7, 166, 174
Southern Ireland, see Eire
Southern Upland Way, Scotland, 79
Southern Uplands, Scotland, 73
Spain, 93, 104, 110–11, 116
Speyside Way, Scotland, 74, 79
Sports Council for Northern Ireland, 89

Stephenson, Tom, 39
Surrey Hills, 53, 174
Sweden, 21, 115
Swiss Alpine Club, 113, 114
Switzerland, 94, 105, 108, 111–12, 114

Tasmania, 158
tents, 14, 19–20, 104, 121, 140, 151
Three Peaks of Yorkshire challenge walk,
    36, 174
Three Sisters Wilderness, Oregon, 143
Tissington Trail, Peak District, 34, 46,
    167
Torridon mountains, 75
Trail-Blazer Challenge Walk,
    Derbyshire, 48, 170, 174
trails, American, 131–44, 145–6
trails, English, 34–5, 166–7
trekking, see Himalayas
triangulation pillars, 26–7
Trossachs, The, Scotland, 24, 73, 76
Two Moors Way, Devon, 38, 39, 58, 169
Turn Right at Land's End, 3, 85

Ulster Way, Northern Ireland, 87, 88–9
United States of America, see America

Vosges mountains, 111

Wainright's Coast to Coast Walk, 35,
    36–7, 152, 171
Wales, 21, 24, 30, 32, 58–9, 61–70,

83–5, 113, 163–70, 172, 178, 180,
    186
walking 'my way', x–xii, 3–7, 28–9, 40,
    58, 82, 148, 149–53, 154–8,
    159–61; see also direction; distance;
    food; pace; pack weight
water, 51–2, 121, 124, 142, 156, 159–60
West Highland Way, Scotland, 72, 73,
    76–8, 164
Western Highlands, Scotland, 73
Weston, Edward Payson, 149
Whillans, Don, 34
White Mountains, New Hampshire, 134,
    135
White Rose Walk, Yorkshire, 37, 171
Wicklow Mountains, Ireland, 87, 89, 181
Wicklow Way, Ireland, 89
Wiltshire Downs, 50–51
Wingo, Plennie, 149
Wolds Way, Yorkshire, 43, 44–5, 60, 166
Wordsworth, William, 32, 148

Y.M.C.A., 174
Yorkshire Dales, 1–2, 25, 32–3, 36,
    40–41, 59, 172
Yosemite National Park, California, 32,
    141
youth hostels, 32, 40, 43, 44, 86, 105
Youth Hostels' Association, England and
    Wales, 29, 174, 180, 188
Youth Hostels' Association, Northern
    Ireland, 181
Yugoslavia, 112